Constructing the past

This book is published as part of the joint publishing agreement established in 1977 between the Fondation de la Maison des Sciences de l'Homme and the Press Syndicate of the University of Cambridge. Titles published under the arrangement may appear in any European language or, in the case of volumes of collected essays, in several languages.

New books will appear either as individual titles or in one of the series which the Maison des Sciences de l'Homme and the Cambridge University Press have jointly agreed to publish. All books published jointly by the Maison des Sciences de l'Homme and the Cambridge University Press will be distributed by the Press throughout the world.

Cet ouvrage est publié dans le cadre de l'accord de co-édition passé en 1977 entre la Fondation de la Maison des Sciences de l'Homme et le Press Syndicate de l'Université de Cambridge. Toutes les langues européennes sont admises pour les titres couverts par cet accord, et les ouvrages collectifs peuvent paraître en plusieurs langues.

Les ouvrages paraissent soit isolément, soit dans l'une des séries que la Maison des Sciences de l'Homme et Cambridge University Press ont convenu de publier ensemble. La distribution dans le monde entier des titres ainsi publiés conjointement par les deux établissements est assurée par Cambridge University Press.

Constructing the past

Essays in historical methodology

Edited by

JACQUES LE GOFF

and

PIERRE NORA

with an introduction by COLIN LUCAS
Fellow of Balliol College, Oxford

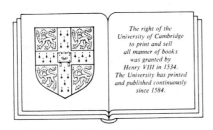

*The right of the
University of Cambridge
to print and sell
all manner of books
was granted by
Henry VIII in 1534.
The University has printed
and published continuously
since 1584.*

CAMBRIDGE UNIVERSITY PRESS

Cambridge
London   New York   New Rochelle   Melbourne   Sydney

EDITIONS DE LA MAISON DES SCIENCES DE
L'HOMME

Paris

Published by the Press Syndicate of the University of Cambridge
The Pitt Building, Trumpington Street, Cambridge CB2 1RP
32 East 57th Street, New York, NY 10022, USA
10 Stamford Road, Oakleigh, Melbourne 3166, Australia
and Editions de la Maison des Sciences de l'Homme
54 Boulevard Raspail, 75270 Paris Cedex 06

Originally published in French as *Faire de l'histoire*
by Gallimard 1974
and © Editions Gallimard 1974
First published in English by Editions de la Maison des Sciences de l'Homme
and Cambridge University Press 1985 as *Constructing the past*
English translation © Maison des Sciences de l'Homme and Cambridge
University Press 1985

Printed in Great Britain at the University Press, Cambridge

British Library cataloguing in publication data

Constructing the past: essays in historical
methodology.
1. Historiography – France
I. Le Goff, Jacques   II. Nora Pierre   III. Faire
de l'histoire *English*
907'.2044   D13.5.F7

Library of Congress cataloguing in publication data

Faire de l'historie. English. Selections.
Constructing the past.
Translation from the French of ten essays from Faire de l'histoire, 1974.
Includes index.
1. History – Methodology – Addresses, essays,
lectures. I. Le Goff, Jacques, 1924–   . II. Nora,
Pierre. III. Title.
D16.F32513 1985   907'.2   85-7696

ISBN 0 521 25976 2
ISBN 2 7351 0100 2 (France only)

Contents

Introduction

COLIN LUCAS

The essays presented in this volume are selected from a larger collection published in 1974 under the title *Faire de l'histoire*. The original editors (Jacques Le Goff and Pierre Nora) employed a territorial image to describe the state of historiography at the time: 'nowadays, the domain of history is without limits and its expansion proceeds along lines or zones of penetration which leave between them areas which are either exhausted or still undeveloped'. The purpose of the collection was, they felt, to illustrate and to promote a 'new type of history'.

Even in the early 1970s, let alone in the 1980s, the so-called 'new history' was not the exclusive preserve of French historians. In particular, the 'new economic history' and cliometrics developed predominantly in the United States and, though represented in France, especially by Jean Marckiewicz, were not really part of the mainstream of historiographical renewal there. Moreover, a decade after this collection was originally published, the methodology and subject matter which it discussed and demonstrated had entered the habits of mind of historians generally. Indeed, some leading English historians at least could now say that there was really nothing much new about new history: its extension of subject matter and methodology was just a manifestation of the dynamic process of historiography which, over a period of time, extended the diversity of subject matter and the assumptions of its vision of the past.[1] Of course, these commentators were in part only applying to new history one of its own most fecund perceptions – that the short-term development only finds significance when placed within a more enduring system or structure.

One point, however, remains true whatever the subsequent general diffusion of a 'new type of history' and whatever individual precursors may be discovered among earlier historians in different countries. It is that the impetus for renewal came principally from France and that a distinctive approach to the writing of history could for some decades be classed as characteristically French, even if many (and many academically prominent) French historians did not practise it and even if individual historians in other countries displayed

1

analogous attitudes. In 1972, the *Journal of Modern History* could still give the title 'History with a French Accent' to a number devoted to the work of Fernand Braudel, the principal contemporary exponent of this approach. Some brief remarks about this French context will therefore help to understand the essays in this collection.

It is tempting to regard the new historiography developing in France as a school, whose progress may be analysed in the dialectical terms of a conflict with the academic establishment culminating in a victory in the early 1970s. Certainly, the movement began with Lucien Febvre and Marc Bloch (although the preoccupations of Henri Berr foreshadowed and then ran parallel to theirs) and with the foundation of their journal *Annales* in 1929. Certainly, it has been in the pages of *Annales* and around its editors that the movement has debated and crystallised ever since. In their own writings and in the pages of their journal, Febvre and Bloch set out to develop a type of history in deliberate and explicit opposition to that found in the writings of professors such as Lavisse, Seignobos and Langlois and in the articles in journals such as the *Revue historique*. Under the pen of Febvre at least, the opposition was one of fiery polemic, and his conception of the movement was well rendered by the title he gave to a collection of his essays – *Combats pour l'histoire*. If the intensity of the combat was partly an expression of Febvre's temperament, it also belonged to a more general intellectual confrontation during the 1930s in which, as H. Stuart Hughes put it, 'the customary warfare among ideological schools mounted to an unprecedented shrillness, as rival intellectual clans threatened to devour each other whole'.[2]

This division was reflected in the institutional careers of the protagonists. Although Bloch became professor at the Sorbonne, it was in the unprestigious chair of economic history. Febvre never gained a Sorbonne chair although he was elected to the Collège de France on the second attempt. However, neither Bloch nor Berr ever made it to the Collège. Fernand Braudel (Bloch and Febvre's successor as the mentor of the new history) had a characteristically non-establishment career in the 1930s – *professeur de lycée* in Algeria, lecturer at São Paulo University, and finally member of the Ecole Pratique des Hautes Etudes. Elected to the Collège de France in 1949, he was never connected with the Sorbonne except as a student.

Febvre, Braudel and their disciples have tended to make a great deal of this pattern. Yet, its importance derived principally from the subtle pecking orders in French academe and the perceived paramountcy of the Sorbonne (at least until 1968) with its elections prepared by ritual visits by candidates to electors. After all, there was no mean prestige attached to the Collège de France. In 1946 the Sorbonne awarded the doctorate without demur to Braudel's highly innovative thesis on the Mediterranean. Moreover, although Braudel did not have a university career, Febvre and Bloch were both professors at Strasbourg after the First World War, and it was here that they received considerable intellectual stimulus from men such as the sociologist Maurice Halbwachs. In fact, it was after the Second World War that the separation between university and new historians became more entrenched with the creation in 1947 of the Sixth Section of the Ecole Pratique des Hautes Etudes, devoted to interdisciplinary studies in the social sciences.

Nonetheless, this background was significant. For five decades it gave the movement an intense self-awareness and a group identity in which personal contacts reinforced a collective ethos around the persons of Febvre, Bloch and Braudel and around the *Annales* journal. It was this which doubtless drove the process of innovation on further and gave it a more distinct individuality than it might otherwise have achieved. Yet, although this nexus has undoubtedly been the heart of the development of a new historiography in France, it is doubtful whether one should call it a school, *l'école des Annales* as it has been termed. Certainly, it is not an image that would have appealed to Febvre or Bloch. Indeed, the great diversity of the *Annales*, not to say its eclecticism, rather negates so determinate a description. Furthermore, after 1945, the history associated with the *Annales* and the Sixth Section was also being developed in other more orthodox institutions, even the Sorbonne. Georges Lefebvre and Roland Mousnier serve as examples. Similarly, Marxist historians (whose premises were not shared by Febvre and Bloch) also participated in the growing complexity of historical study espoused by this group of scholars: Pierre Vilar's essay in this collection is some echo of this.

Ultimately, it was above all a mode of thought that was initiated by Febvre and Bloch, a mode of thought that was shared by their followers and that was progressively diffused among other scholars not properly speaking of their circle. It was a basic assumption about the nature and process of history; it was an attitude to what constituted the proper object of a historian's attentions; it was a vision of the relationship between the study of man in his historical dimension and the other human sciences (and in some situations by extension the natural sciences).

Combats pour l'histoire – this did indeed begin as a battle waged to wrest possession of history away from the Sorbonne by redefining the subject, a battle to occupy the territory of history by delineating anew its extent and to reconstruct history by discovering its solid foundations. Febvre and Bloch denounced the history written by the Sorbonne as *histoire événementielle*, a term of condemnation in their vocabulary. They set out to evict the 'event' from history. It is easy to be misled by this terminology, especially in translation when it is rendered, for example, as 'narrative'. Certainly, as far as Bloch and Febvre themselves were concerned, event both in the sense of action confined in time and space and also chronology remained present in their writings. What they meant by the term was what the Sorbonne historians wrote, that is to say the history of the high politics and diplomatic relations of nation-states. For Bloch and Febvre, such history was merely the relation of a

sequence of heterogeneous happenings without claim to represent in themselves a meaningful sequence, let alone to be the prime movers in the
development of civilisations in the past. In its place, they sought after a whole
history of human experience.

In opposition to this *histoire événementielle* they set out to construct a more
complete history, what Febvre termed *une histoire vraie* or *une histoire à part
entière*. In part, this was the logical outcome of the realisation that history was
not 'value free' and that historical facts were in reality constructs. They
rejected the view that each historical moment possessed a unique individuality
whose meaning could be made manifest through study of the written document
without reference to general concepts and without more than cursory insertion
into its most immediate context. They understood that the human experience
was the composite result of the interaction of many phenomena, many of which
were either autonomous or only partially subject to human volition. They
inherited from Durkheim the view that the individual could only be meaning-
fully comprehended within his social context. They believed that this external
context could be observed, analysed and understood by the same kind of logic
as that employed by natural science.[3] In this they distanced themselves from
the early twentieth-century idea of the historian's empathetic understanding of
his subject based on the reading of the document and on reflection about his
own human experience. This *histoire à part entière* was therefore a history that
sought a synthesis of all the material, physical and mental forces that had
shaped the life of man in past societies. Bloch and Febvre sought to create a
historical discipline that would bring together geography, economics, sociology, psychology, anthropology, philology, and any other relevant human or
natural science in order to produce a total picture of past societies, a picture
that would relate all the forces at work into an interacting hierarchy.

This was the great innovation. On the one hand, history ceased to be the
story of the elites and became that of the mass of men hitherto deemed by
professional historians to be without history (and one can understand why
annalistes have always traced their lineage to Michelet); on the other, the
proper object of a historian's attentions was extended to cover a whole range of
phenomena from material structures through to the secret and the
unconscious. Inevitably, the historian's focus was shifted from the individual to
the collective, from political to social history, from description to analysis,
from monocausal to multidimensional explanation. Bloch and Febvre opened
the door to all that had previously been perceived either to be without history
or to be unhistorical, extending thereby the historian's legitimate sources well
beyond the conventional document to the widest range of written and unwrit-
ten evidence. Through that door pressed two generations of imaginative and
enterprising historians who, by 1974, had transformed both the subject matter
and the methodology of history.

There were perhaps three dominant characteristics in the development given by the second and third generation scholars to the directions mapped out by Febvre and Bloch – the interdisciplinary approach in conjunction with social sciences; quantification; the search for global history.

From the very beginning, cross-fertilisation with the social sciences had been central to the process of renewal in the minds of Febvre and Bloch. It remained so for their successors. Braudel, for example, referred to 'a community of human sciences' and saw the relationship between history and the social sciences as 'an exchange of services'.[4] It is a measure of the distance travelled since 1929 that what appeared then as strikingly, if not dangerously, novel should now be a commonplace assumption. Of course, that relationship has been far from easy over the last fifty years, as Lawrence Stone has pointed out.[5] Yet, the opening to social science brought two profound reorientations to French historiography. The first, and the more obvious, was simply the diversification of the objects of study through the validation, definition, and conceptual and methodological approach provided by the social sciences. The second, and more important, was the effect that the contact had upon the perception of the process of writing history. The new historians set out to make history take its place among the social sciences, to turn history into a *science humaine*. Even though *science* should here be understood only as organised knowledge, the word does imply that knowledge should be organised according to criteria derived ultimately from the hard sciences. In particular, this meant the application of the principle that microphenomena are indeterminate whereas macrophenomena are determinate. As a consequence, the individual 'fact' or 'event' only achieves significance when it can be inserted into some more general sequence of comparable 'facts' or 'events'. Thus, for instance, a particular epidemic or famine must be placed in the context of the sequence of diseases or famines which form the system to which it belongs; in turn, its impact can only be understood (in anything other than a trivial sense) by reference to the sequences of births, marriages and deaths that constitute the demographic system.

Although this was less true of Febvre and Bloch themselves, the fundamental assumption of the developing new history after 1945 was, therefore, that the past must be conceived of in terms of structures and systems and that the historian must seek not merely to identify these systems but to relate them in a hierarchy. Structure in this context does not simply mean social structure, although clearly social formation is to be considered as a system, but more importantly the enduring physical, material and eventually mental structures within whose boundaries human individual and collective behaviour is confined. The quality of endurance possessed by structures means that they must be studied over the long duration (*longue durée*). History must be understood as the composite result of a bundle of systems or structures, each of which has its own internal coherence that the historian must seek out and demonstrate.

The diachronic character of systems in respect of each other and the disparity of endurance between different structures (for example, between physical geography and social formation) resulted in the perception that historical time is divided by and large into three. Long duration reveals the enduring character of phenomena – say, geography or climate or disease or patterns of production and exchange. The medium term, called conjuncture (*conjoncture*), reveals rhythms and modifications in the system, which might be movements akin to sea tides or else indicators of more profound change – say, alternating periods of activity/inactivity of volcanoes or declining/rising mean temperature levels or prevalence/recession of certain diseases or economic cycles. In practice, the student of this historiography may feel some uncertainty about long duration and conjuncture. Different historians appear to envisage rather different time-spans from each other. Thus, Braudel defines long duration as almost motionless history (as, for instance, in physical geography) and conjuncture as the history of slow rhythms perhaps over centuries; others, such as Le Roy Ladurie, seem to employ long duration for the characteristics of, for example, an economic system or a social formation enduring over several centuries, whereas conjuncture is applied to quicker, medium-term rhythms. Perhaps, rather than worry about how short is long and how quick is slow, it is as well to conceive of four divisions of time with the almost immobile history constituting one apart.

However, there is no such uncertainty about the short term. This refers to the event – say, Krakatoa or the 1768 hurricane at Havana or the Black Death or the Wall Street Crash. The event has never been absent from French new history, whatever its protagonists and critics may have said. Nonetheless, it is true to say that the short term is the element of historical time that has given this type of historiography the most trouble. In 1966, Braudel made a significant addition to his original formulation that events are mere surface agitation, flashing lights in history 'hardly lit before the night reclaims them'. Nonetheless, he now continued, 'every event, however brief, is certainly a testimony, it lights up some corner of the landscape of history or even sometimes its profounder levels'.[6] By this definition, therefore, events are to be seen as windows through which one may perceive, however darkly, some of the strands in the bundle of systems and see them in the process of interaction.

Nevertheless, however one divides time duration and articulates the relationship between the basic durations, it is essential to remember that these historians do not conceive of a single, linear time nor of one single development which is identifiable link by chronological link. Rather, since history is a composite of different systems each with its own characteristic rhythm (and each to be considered in terms of long duration, conjuncture and event), history becomes a composite of different times moving at different speeds. In this sense, the issue of three or four time durations is a slightly false problem since the same time-span in terms of years is more or less long according to the system to which it refers. Above all, however, in this historiography history is in essence a diachronic assemblage.

The other two characteristics of the development of French new history (quantification and global history) follow from these propositions. The desire for organised knowledge and the preoccupation with long duration inescapably led to the search for measurable information. In part, perhaps, this was a pursuit of the historian's old dream of value-free knowledge. More importantly, there could be no identification of systems without the quantification which demonstrates the repetition upon which systems are based. It is quantification which, in this approach to history, provides the surest distinction between the significant and the random or trivial. The collection of elements susceptible of quantitative or serial treatment increasingly became the principal research activity of the majority of new French historians in the two decades after the Second World War. The centrality of quantification to this historiography is expressed by the fact that François Furet's essay comes first in this translated collection. The main beneficiaries have been economic history (discussed here by Pierre Chaunu) and historical demography (represented here by André Burguière), the former entirely renewed and the latter an entirely new discipline.

One must not overemphasise the pervasiveness of quantification in the 1950s and 1960s. Historians such as Jacques Le Goff and Robert Mandrou were beginning to explore the history of culture and collective mentality in a manner unaffected by it. Even among its devotees, the better historians were never enslaved by it: Emmanuel Le Roy Ladurie's seminal thesis on the Languedoc, for example, sought explanatory inspiration from psychology and anthropology as well. However, the need to measure all that is measurable does usually inform the treatment of the domains entered by the new historians (as evidenced here by Roger Chartier and Daniel Roche), even if Pierre Chaunu would not command unanimity for his claim here that serial history can be applied to the whole system of civilisation.

Nonetheless, Chaunu's assertion that 'a global history of the systems of civilisation is gradually emerging' does reflect the ambition of this historiography from Febvre and Bloch onwards. 'Global' history or 'total' history (although in practice this latter term is more used by Marxist historians in this context) is not so much a world history, though that would presumably be the ultimate goal. Rather, it is the ambition to write a history that puts together all the separate systems in order to display the 'system of systems' which would correspond to Febvre's call for *une histoire vraie*. It is of course an ambition difficult to realise. The actual hierarchy of systems can be matter for considerable debate (to many, Chaunu's claim in the essay printed here that economic history is 'the unifying human science of our time' would seem special pleading); the diachrony inherent in the gathering of the separate systems makes it difficult to render the simultaneous diversity/diverse simultaneity that is the hallmark of this perception of the past. Indeed, Fernand Braudel's *La Méditerranée et le monde méditerranéen à l'époque de Philippe II* (first published in 1949) has been the only real attempt to write such history. With its tripartite division of the subject matter into long duration, conjuncture, and event (the last, subordinate part containing the political history), the book is a monument to what the premisses of the new historiography might lead to in the construction of the history of past societies. At the same time, it also reveals some of the vital ambiguities in this methodology, especially by the apparent arbitrariness of its emphases among the themes within each part and by the difficulty in keeping the diversity of material under control.

The third generation of scholars (I take Braudel to be the second generation) has been more limited in its ambition and more successful. Its work has been limited only in the sense of a retreat in practice from the kind of global approach attempted by Braudel. The benefit was a much sharper definition of structure and a much more compelling analysis of the relationship between long duration and conjuncture. It is in this context that, for example, Pierre Goubert's study of the Beauvaisis and Emmanuel Le Roy Ladurie's study of the peasantry of the Languedoc have had their seminal influence. It has been arguably a more profound influence on the definition of the historical problematic and on the conduct of research than that of Braudel, whose influence was more to have assumed the mantle of Febvre as mentor, stimulator, propagandist and conscience of the new historiography. Moreover, as the third generation shaded into the fourth generation in the 1970s, the focus of interest shifted away from the 'system of systems' towards definable problems in history (*histoire-problème*). It can be argued that *histoire-problème* and *histoire-globale* are incompatible, even if the former may eventually lead cumulatively back to the latter. This shift was accompanied by the decline of economics and sociology as the inspiring social sciences and the rise of the influence of social anthropology. This development is reflected in this collection of essays. It is expressed (in the original French edition) by the editors' introductory definition of historical understanding as proceeding by zones of penetration. It is reflected here in the contents – the first five essays represent in some sense the earlier preoccupations and the acquired, well-colonised lands of new history by 1974; the second five essays reflect the newer preoccupation with the arcane, rarely directly stated and often unconscious world of *mentalités*, the world of belief, symbol, and cultural patterns.

The essays translated here represent, then, the point which the new French historiography had reached by 1974. At this time, this historiography had in fact reached a moment of sea change. Already in 1972, Hugh Trevor-Roper was noting that it was undergoing a process of 'almost bureaucratic consolidation'.[7] By then, it had to all intents and purposes overwhelmed what it had previously seen as the opposition and it was itself fast becoming the established orthodoxy in research and in the teaching of history in faculties and schools.

This development was finally consolidated in January 1975 when the Sixth Section acquired the right to award higher degrees. However, it was a victory accompanied by unease. 'Is this triumph a good thing?', questioned Braudel in 1976.[8] Of course, in part, as Braudel said, this unease derived from the fear that such a victory could undermine the vigour of a movement that had owed much of its dynamism to its combative posture. Yet, this malaise went much deeper, as both Braudel, and Le Goff and Nora (the editors of the original French edition) understood.

Many criticisms of greater or lesser merit had been levelled against the new French historiography. However, two seem to reveal the heart of the dilemma felt in the early 1970s. The first was the argument that too often this history involved an obsession with all that was quantifiable and the dismissal of all that was not. Two consequences appeared to flow from this. The one was that, since statistical series tend to emphasise repetition and the unchanging character of structures, historical change was liable to be ignored or go unexplained – and change, by common consensus, is what the study of history is principally about. The other was that, taken to its logical conclusion, this process turned the historian into a mere gatherer of statistical data. There was some ground for this criticism. After all, Le Roy Ladurie once wrote that historians would become programmers (although he did not say that they would only be that) and he also propounded the thesis of 'immobile history'.[9] The same sort of premiss is displayed by Burguière in his essay in this collection when he suggests that 'quantitative history has been able to entertain the hope that it may one day measure the unmeasurable, that it may . . . gain access to the basis of human behaviour, to motivations which remained unexpressed'.

In fact, of course, Le Roy Ladurie himself demonstrated with *Montaillou* the hypothetical nature of his other pronouncements. At the same time, the development of the social anthropological influence was instrumental in bringing the role of quantification into perspective during the 1970s and earlier 1980s. Nonetheless, in 1974, it was an awareness of this element of malaise that lay behind Le Goff and Nora's injunction in their introduction to the essays that history 'must also define itself as the science of change, of transformation'. The same awareness informed François Furet's discussion (in the essay translated here) of precisely what can and cannot be attained by quantification. Indeed, back in 1959, Furet had put his name to the statement that 'from a scientific point of view, the only social history is quantitative history'.[10] The subsequent development of his interests (to which this essay is an interesting, strategic testimony) through political and cultural history towards epistemology and ideology reflects the evolving awareness of the mainstream in this historiography after the 1960s.

The second criticism had to do with the ambiguity of the relationship between social science and history. This was indeed a crucial problem since that relationship stood at the heart of the new historiography. At the end of the

1950s, Braudel had perceived that the objectives had modified: 'With Marc Bloch and Lucien Febvre, History wanted to conquer and organise the domain of all the Sciences of Man to its own benefit, or at least to enrich its own problematic and renew its techniques through the booty of its incursions into that domain. Today, the problem is to participate fully in the necessary reunion of the Sciences of Man.'[11] The problem was what history had to do to qualify as a fully fledged member of the human sciences. It was in this context that Le Roy Ladurie made his remark in 1968 about historians becoming programmers, for he saw in the computer the means of maintaining French historians as the 'avant-garde'.

However, as many social sciences affirmed their paradigms and asserted the exclusive validity of their models, they tended either to see history as merely a testing bed or else to dismiss it entirely.[12] Historians were in some sense confronted by a demand for loyalty or at least for accreditation by the social sciences from which they sought to learn. In some cases, historians reacted by simply taking over the models appropriate in other disciplines; in more cases, historians acquired the language and symbols of their social science referent at a time when the social sciences were often developing autonomous and internalised discourses. Historians aiming to practise history as a *science humaine* were caught between social science and history in that double jeopardy of scholarly rigour where the models and assumptions of the one were applied in the fundamentally different circumstances of the other. As a result, what one may term the characteristic 'personality' of history and of the historian tended to disappear in a blurring of the frontier between the disciplines. What had begun, with Febvre and Bloch, as an attempt to lift history out of compartmentalised study and to stress the pluridimensionality of history now seemed in danger of falling back into a new and more hermetic compartmentalisation.

It was this issue that preoccupied Braudel, Le Goff and Nora in the mid-1970s. Braudel had already seen the danger in 1956 when he warned his colleagues that their task was, in the spirit of Febvre and Bloch, to work towards a 'new humanism'.[13] It was a theme taken up by Le Goff and Nora in their introduction to this 1974 collection. There was more than a hint of historiographical crisis in what they had to say. History was undergoing 'the aggression of social sciences'; 'the field which it used to occupy alone as the systematic explanation of society in its time dimension has been invaded by other sciences with ill-defined boundaries which threaten to absorb and dissolve it' (a striking inversion of Braudel's earlier image of what Bloch and Febvre's history had been about). The task of the new historians was, in their view, to combat the danger of history becoming something other than history. Braudel, too, in 1976, evoked the danger, personalising it around Michel Foucault whom he saw as epitomising the absorption and dissolution of history by another discipline – in this case, philosophy. His message was much the same: history has a distinctive personality as a discipline and it must be affirmed by historians. 'Confronting the philosophers', he wrote, 'who declaim loudly, perhaps even too loudly, today's historians, it seems to me, are afraid to utter their own tongue, the language of an old craft that must be formed close down to the earth. New methods allow better employment of the tools, but the tools are the old tools.'[14]

Eleven years on, the essays in this translation can still be read with great profit. They can be read on two levels. First, they are all statements about and exercises in those 'zones of penetration' through which French historiography renewed the study of the past. Second, the collection can now be read as a document itself, illustrating the point reached by that new historiography when it finally imposed itself in France and was in the process of extending its influence elsewhere. The collection illustrates both its strengths, its continued progress in diversifying the objects of study, and also some of its dilemmas and unease.

NOTES

1 *Times Higher Education Supplement*, 4 November 1983.
2 H. Stuart Hughes, *The Obstructed Path* (New York, 1969), p. 15.
3 See G. G. Iggers, *New Directions in European Historiography* (Middletown, 1975), pp. 43–79.
4 Foreword to T. Stoianovich, *French Historical Method* (Ithaca, 1976), p. 12.
5 L. Stone, *The Past and the Present* (London, 1981), pp. 3–44.
6 F. Braudel, *La Méditerranée et le monde méditerranéen à l'époque de Philippe II* (1st edition, Paris, 1949), p. 721 and *ibid.* (2nd edition, Paris, 1966), II, 223. His other definitions of time are based on the first edition, p. xiii.
7 H. R. Trevor-Roper, 'Fernand Braudel, the *Annales*, and the Mediterranean', *Journal of Modern History*, XLIV (1972), p. 472.
8 Foreword to Stoianovich, p. 16.
9 E. Le Roy Ladurie, *Le Territoire de l'historien* (Paris, 1973), p. 14 (originally published in 1968), and 'L'histoire immobile', *Annales ESC*, XXIX (1974), pp. 673–92.
10 F. Furet and A. Daumard, 'Méthodes de l'histoire sociale', *Annales ESC*, XIV (1959), p. 676.
11 F. Braudel, 'Les *Annales* ont trente ans', *Annales ESC*, XIV (1959), p. 1.
12 See Stone, *op. cit.*
13 F. Braudel, 'Lucien Febvre et l'histoire', *Annales ESC*, XII (1956), p. 182.
14 Foreword to Stoianovich, p. 16.

1. Quantitative methods in history[1]

FRANÇOIS FURET

Quantitative history is fashionable today both in Europe and in the United States. The last half century has seen rapid growth in the use of quantitative sources and of counting and quantifying methods in historical research. But, like all terms which are in fashion, 'quantitative history' has ended up taking on such a wide range of senses that it can mean almost anything. From the critical use of simple counting procedures undertaken by the political arithmeticians of the seventeenth century, right through to the systematic use of mathematical models in the reconstruction of the past, quantitative history refers to many things under the same label. It may mean a type of source, or a type of procedure, but in all cases, in one way or another, explicitly or not, it implies a particular way of conceptualising the past. Moving from the general to the particular, and trying to define the specificity of historical knowledge in relation to the social sciences in general, we can distinguish three sets of problems relating to quantitative history.

1. The first set of problems concerns methods of processing quantitative historical data: the construction of different data groups, the geographical units by which such groups are defined, the thresholds separating subgroups within the groups, methods of calculating correlations between two different series of data, the value of different types of statistical analysis applied to different kinds of data, the interpretation of statistical relations, etc.

Such problems relate to the technology of research in the social sciences. They can certainly also raise methodological questions: not only because no technique is 'neutral', but also, and more specifically, because any statistical procedure necessarily poses the question of whether and to what extent historical or sociological knowledge is compatible with, or exhausted by, a mathematical conceptualisation based on probabilities. But neither the technical discussion nor the theoretical debate are specific to history: they concern the whole of the social sciences, and quantitative history is in this respect no different from what is today referred to as empirical sociology, which can be considered as simply a contemporary version of quantitative history.

2. The term 'quantitative history' also refers, at least in France, to the

project and the work of certain economic historians.[2] Here the concern is to make history into a kind of retrospective econometrics,[3] using the model of present-day national accounting to fill in, for previous centuries, all the columns of a kind of imaginary table of economic input and output. Believers in this econometric history plead for systematic and total use of quantification: in their eyes it is the indispensable condition for the elimination of any arbitrary element in the choice of data, and the condition for the use of mathematical models in the processing of those data, starting from the concept of general equilibrium as it has been imported into economic history from political economy.

True quantitative history would thus, according to this view, be the result of a twofold reduction of history: firstly, a reduction, provisional but perhaps permanent, of its field of analysis to the economic field; and, secondly, the reduction of its descriptive and interpretative system to the one which has been developed by the most rigorously constituted of present-day social sciences – political economy. One could, moreover, suggest the same analysis in relation to demography and demographic history: a conceptually constituted science furnishes data and tools to a particular historical discipline, which in this way becomes as it were a by-product of the parent discipline, simply transposing to the study of the past its questions and its concepts.

Of course, the data must exist for the past as they do for the present; or, if not actually exist, then at the very least be subject to precise elaboration, reconstruction or extrapolation. This imperative in fact sets a first limit to the total quantification of historical data: such quantification, supposing that it is even possible before the nineteenth century, certainly cannot go back further than the period of statistical or proto-statistical listing which coincides with the centralisation of the great European monarchic states. History did not begin with Petty or Vauban.

Furthermore, there is no reason why the historian should accept, even on a temporary basis, the reduction of his field of research to economics or demography. Two possibilities seem open to history. The first one is that it is reduced to the study of a predetermined and limited sector of the past, within which mathematical models established by certain of the social sciences as testing procedures are then applied. In this case we end up with contemporary political economy, which seems to me to be the only social science having at its disposal such models; and then history is reduced to nothing more than an additional bank of data. The second possibility is to take the discipline of history in its widest possible sense, that is to say in its conceptual indetermination with all its multiplicity of levels of analysis, and from that point to devote oneself to the description of these levels and to the task of establishing simple statistical links between them, starting with hypotheses which, whether they are original or imported, are nothing more than the intuitions of the historian.

3. This is why, even if one chooses to add the epithet 'quantitative' to

history, one cannot escape the specific goal of historical research: the study of time, of the diachronic dimension of phenomena. Now, in this respect the most general and at the same time the most elementary ambition of quantitative history is to set out historical reality in temporal series of homogeneous and comparable units, and in that way to measure the evolution of that reality at given intervals, usually annual. This fundamental logical operation is definitive of what Pierre Chaunu has called serial history:[4] and it is a necessary, although not a sufficient, condition of strictly quantitative history as we have defined it above. For serial history has the decisive advantage from a scientific point of view of replacing the ineffable 'events' of positivist history with the regular repetition of data selected and constructed because of their comparable nature. But this does not imply that the serial method claims to be an exhaustive description of the corpus of documents adopted, nor does it imply that this is a global system of interpretation or a mathematical formulation since, on the contrary, the distribution of historical reality into series presents the historian with materials broken up into different levels, into different subsystems, and he is then free to establish or not to establish connections between these levels.

Thus defined, quantitative history and serial history can be seen to be at the same time linked and different. But they share a common ground which is their foundation: the replacement of events by series, that is to say the construction of historical data on the basis of probabilist analysis. To the classic question, 'What is a historical fact?', they both reply in a radically new way which transforms the historian's conception of the object of analysis – time. I would like to advance a few ideas concerning the scope of this internal revolution.

I should add, in order to avoid any misunderstanding, that this article has no normative claims: serial history has in the last ten or twenty years shown itself to be one of the most fruitful lines of development of historical knowledge; it also has the immense advantage of providing this very old discipline of history with a rigour and an efficiency greater than those offered by qualitative methodology. But that does not alter the fact that serial history is, by its very nature, incapable of treating and even of approaching important areas of historical reality. This may be for purely circumstantial reasons like the irremediable absence of data, or for more fundamental reasons concerning the irreducibly qualitative nature of the phenomenon studied: but it is the reason why, for example, historians of antiquity, who work on data covering very large periods of time, or specialists in intellectual biography, who concentrate precisely on that which is unique and incomparable in the creative process, are less often tempted by the charms of serial history than, let us say, historians of agrarian structures in modern Europe.

In this respect another and perhaps more fundamental problem should be raised. Without a doubt serial history brings with it precise methods for measuring change, but to what extent does it allow the historian to conceptualise profound mutations in history? By its very nature a series is made up of identical units: that is the condition of their comparability. The long-term temporal variation of these units often points to a cyclical pattern, and seems to suggest a system of change within stability: there is an underlying equilibrium. But when the temporal variation of one or several series reveals a tendency towards indefinite cumulative growth, then the breaking up of this tendency into relatively small units (in yearly or ten-yearly divisions, for example) tends to obscure the definition of the threshold beyond which we can say that the very structure of time and of rhythms of change is transformed. This leads to formidable problems of dating and periodisation. Furthermore, it is quite possible that the decisive historical mutation will not be recorded by any series which relates internally to a particular system, precisely because it results either from some innovation which goes totally unrecorded by the counting procedures of the time, or from some external factor which throws the age-old equilibrium of the system into imbalance: these methodological problems are at the heart of the current discussion of the problem of industrial take-off.[5] In other words, if it can be said that no methodology is innocent, then serial history, because it privileges the long term and the equilibrium of systems, seems to me to put a kind of premium on stability: this is a good corrective to the identification between history and change which we have inherited from the nineteenth century, and to that extent it is an extremely important stage in the constitution of history as a science; but the fact remains that we must also perceive the method's presuppositions and limits.

But the question of the limits of serial history, which cannot adequately be dealt with within this article, must not serve as an excuse for intellectual laziness or traditionalism. If, today, history everywhere is leaving behind the storytelling model in order to confront problems, this is in large part due to changes in the elements of the puzzle from which it reconstitutes images of the past. Historical reality presents a completely new countenance to today's historian. History has come to a greater awareness of its own presuppositions. We have probably not yet exhausted all the benefits of this new departure.

The historian's sources

Since quantitative history supposes the existence and the development of long series of homogeneous and comparable data, the first problem to arise in a new form concerns the historian's sources. Generally speaking, European archives were built up and classified in the nineteenth century according to procedures and criteria reflecting the ideological and methodological preoccupations of history at that particular time. On the one hand, national values tend to predominate and there is therefore an emphasis on political and administrative sources. But a further consequence is that documents are kept and classified according to a narrow vision of what research should be: an archive is constituted for the study of events rather than for the study of long-term developments. It must be established and criticised for its own sake, and not as an element in a series. It refers to something outside itself: the historical 'fact' which naive positivism falsely sees as the reality to which the document is in some sense a testimony. In this sense, a historical document is a unique, discrete, particular moment within a global evolution which either remains temporally indeterminate or is divided up into centuries, reigns, ministries. In short, an archive is the memory of nations, in the same way that, within an individual life, the letters which we keep testify to the choices which our memory has made.

In quantitative history, on the other hand, data do not refer outwards to some ill-defined external sequence of 'facts'; rather, their coherence is guaranteed by internal criteria. A fact ceases to be an event chosen to illustrate the significant moments within a historical evolution whose meaning has already been decided, and becomes a phenomenon chosen and perhaps even constructed because it is repetitive and therefore comparable over time. This means that the very conception of an archivist's work is radically transformed at a time when the technical possibilities opened up by the electronic processing of information are more and more numerous. This meeting of a methodological and a technical revolution – which, one might add, are not unrelated – allows us to envisage the building-up of new archives kept on computer and based not only on new systems of classification, but above all on a conception of documentary criticism quite different from that which was developed by the nineteenth century. The document, the *datum*, no longer exist in their own right but in relation to the series which precedes and follows them. The objective element is no longer their relation to some indefinable external reality, but their relative value. In this way the old problem of the criticism of a historical document is immediately transformed. 'External' criticism is no longer based on comparison with contemporary texts of another nature, but on compatibility with a text of the same nature occupying a different position in the temporal series. 'Internal' criticism is at the same time considerably simplified in that many of the operations involved in the checking of data can now be left to a computer.

The coherence of the data is first established at the point where the data are collected from primary sources: a minimal ordering of the document ensures that over long periods of time and for each time unit, the same data are to be found in the same logical order. In this respect, the use of a computer by the historian is not only an immense practical step forward in terms of the time which is gained (especially when the data, as in the Couturier method,[6] are collected and recorded verbally with a tape recorder); the use of the computer is also an extremely useful theoretical constraint, since the ordering of a documentary series which is to be put on to computer forces the historian from the very beginning to give up epistemological naivety, to construct the object of research, to think about hypotheses, in short to move from the implicit to the explicit. The second, internal, stage in the criticism of the documents consists of testing the compatibility of the data with the preceding and following data, in other words the elimination of errors: in this sense the second stage is a consequence of the first, and can furthermore be automated to a significant extent, through programmed testing procedures.

Quite understandably, in its early days serial history began by using those historical series which most easily lent themselves to this kind of work. In other words economic, fiscal or demographic documents. The revolution brought about by the computer in the collection and processing of data has progressively increased the possibilities for the exploration of these numerical series. Today such exploration encompasses any kind of historical data which can be reduced to some form of computerised language: not only fiscal rolls or market price lists, but also a relatively homogeneous series of literary texts such as the cartularies of the Middle Ages or the *cahiers* of the Estates General in *ancien régime* France.

The first task of serial history, the very condition of its development, is, then, clear: it must first constitute the material which it is to analyse. Classical historiography was constructed from archives which had been built up and were treated according to critical rules inherited from Benedictine scholars of the eighteenth century and the German historians of the nineteenth. Today's serial historiography must reconstitute its archives as a result of the twofold methodological and technical revolution which has transformed the methods and the rules of the discipline.

But at this point a new problem arises. The revolution of which we have spoken reveals the extent to which historical sources lead a precarious existence, their conservation due to chance, and their partial or total destruction being entirely possible. In this respect, I am far from sure that history is as different as is sometimes claimed from the other human sciences, which have a more clearly defined object. History is in fact characterised by the extraordinary, indeed almost boundless elasticity of its sources. A shift in the curiosity of the researcher is sufficient for enormous dormant documentary areas to be discovered: no nineteenth-century historian, for example, thought to study the parish registers which today, especially in France and in England, are one of our most reliable sources of knowledge about pre-industrial society.

Furthermore, sources which have already been used in the past may be redirected towards other ends if the researcher invests them with new meaning: descriptions of price variations can lead to sociological or political analyses, at which point we pass from the work of D'Avenel to that of Labrousse. Demographic series, studied for example for information concerning growth in the use of contraception by married couples, can be instructive in relation to problems of mentality or of religious practice.[7] If the signatures on notarial deeds are subjected to counting procedures, these sources can yield statistics concerning literacy. If biographies are systematically compared with respect to common criteria, and with a given hypothesis in mind, they can constitute documentary series which put one of the oldest kinds of historical storytelling to a completely new use.

History, hitherto, has been almost exclusively based on the written traces of human existence. It seems probable that the oral interview, which is such a fruitful source of data for empirical sociology, is of little use for the historian, except for the contemporary period. But, on the other hand, there exists a wealth of non-written sources which are still to be listed and systematically described. The rural habitat, the organisation of agricultural land, religious and profane iconography, the organisation of the pre-industrial urban space, the interior furnishing of houses: one could build up an interminable list of all the features of civilisation which, once listed and carefully classified, would allow historians to constitute new chronological series and would provide a completely new set of materials corresponding to the conceptual broadening which is currently taking place within the discipline. For it is not the sources which define the questions asked by a discipline, but the questions which determine the sources.

It would of course be a mistake to push such an argument too far. If one looks for a moment at the demands which certain contemporary social sciences place upon documentation, it becomes clear that history is faced with certain irreparable gaps: it is difficult to imagine replacement sources, or indeed extrapolations, which would furnish statistics for an input–output analysis of the French economy under Henri IV, not to mention more remote periods. But the real significance of this observation is that, conceptually, history cannot be reduced to political economy. In fact, the problem of sources for the historian is not so much a problem of absolute gaps as one of incomplete series: not only because of the difficulties of interpolation or extrapolation, but also as a result of the chronological illusions which these difficulties are liable to foster.

I will take the classic example of popular rebellions in France at the beginning of the seventeenth century. As a result of the abundance of administrative sources on this subject from the first half of the seventeenth century, this period is better known than any other between the end of the Middle Ages and 1789 as far as peasant uprisings are concerned. As chance would have it, a large proportion of these archives (the Séguier collection) finally found its way to Leningrad, and, as a result, Soviet historians have put forward a Marxist interpretation of the French *ancien régime* which has provoked much debate and, as a result, has given still more prominence to these archives. But there is a problem which logically precedes the debate about the interpretation of the archives, a problem concerning the hypothesis which is implicit to both interpretations: the notion that at this particular time, that is to say when the absolutist state is coming into being and levels of taxation are probably therefore increasing rapidly, a particular concentration of peasant rebellions, in itself a classic aspect of French history, takes place. Such a chronological concentration can only be established with certainty if a long homogeneous series is examined, and differences with earlier and later periods are noted. It so happens that such a series cannot be constituted, and this for various reasons. Firstly, because no single homogeneous source concerning such rebellions exists over a long period of time: and there is every reason to believe that the survival of an exceptionally rich collection concerning this area, like the Séguier collection in Leningrad, consisting entirely of the papers of one family and therefore subject to the chance of men's lives and careers, falsifies our chronological perception of the phenomenon. Secondly, peasant rebellions are an aspect of history which does not provide us with direct historical sources, in that peasants are illiterate and therefore strangers to the world of the written word. Today, we may have access to such rebellions through administrative or judicial archives; but for this very reason, as Charles Tilly has noted, any rebellion which escapes repression also escapes history, and the relative richness of our sources over a given period may be more a reflection of institutional changes (a strengthening of repression, for instance) or purely individual changes (the particular vigilance of a given administrator, for example) than a reflection of the incidence of the phenomenon which is being studied. The different frequencies of peasant rebellion under Henri II and Louis XIII may well reflect the progress of monarchic centralisation more than anything else.

The handling of serial sources, then, forces the historian to think very carefully about the effect which the conditions under which these sources were organised may have on their quantitative use. In this respect, I shall distinguish three sets of sources, in order of increasing complexity in the constitution of series:

1. Sources which by their very nature are numerical, which are brought together as such, and are used by the historian to answer questions directly related to their original field of investigation. Examples of this category might be French parish registers for the demographic historian, nineteenth-century French prefectorial surveys of industrial or agricultural statistics for the economic historian, or data concerning American presidential elections for the specialist in socio-political history. Such sources sometimes have to be standardised, when, for instance, there is variation in the geographical breakdown or changes in criteria of classification; it is also possible, when there are gaps in the sequence of documents, to extrapolate certain elements. But in each case these operations are carried out with a minimum of uncertainty.

2. Sources which, like the first set, are structurally numerical, but which are used by the historian in a substitutive way in order to answer questions which are totally foreign to their original field of investigation. Examples here might be the analysis of sexual behaviour from parish registers, the study of economic growth from price series, or the analysis of the socio-professional evolution of a

population group from a fiscal series. The historian's task here is more difficult, and in two ways: firstly, he must be all the more meticulous in the formulation of questions, because the original documentary material was not constructed to answer those questions and, therefore, the problem of the material's relevance to the questions will constantly arise. Secondly, the historian will more often than not be forced to reorganise the material completely to make it usable, which inevitably lays the results open to question.

3. Sources which are not structurally numerical, but which the historian wishes to use quantitatively by a process of double substitution: the sources must, firstly, be made to provide unequivocal answers to the historian's questions; but it must also be possible to reorganise the sources into series, in other words into comparable chronological units, and this necessitates a standardisation which is obviously even more complex than in the previous case. Data of this type – and, the further back one goes into the past, the more such data are in a majority – can be subdivided again into two categories: firstly, non-numerical sources, which are nevertheless serial and therefore easily quantifiable, like, for instance, notarial marriage contracts in modern Europe, which can serve the historian as indicators of endogamy, social mobility, income, literacy levels, etc. Secondly, strictly qualitative sources, which are therefore not of a serial nature or at the very least are particularly difficult to serialise and standardise, like, for example, the administrative and judicial sources which were mentioned earlier, or iconographic remnants of long lost religions.

It remains true that in all these cases today's historian must give up methodological naivety and think about the conditions under which historical knowledge is established. The computer makes him free to do this by liberating him from the task which hitherto occupied the major part of his time: the collection of data on file cards. But the computer at the same time forces him to undertake preliminary work on the organisation of series of data and on their meaning in relation to what he is looking for. Like all the social sciences, but perhaps a little later than the rest of them, history today is moving from the implicit to the explicit. The coding of data supposes that they are defined; this definition in its turn implies a certain number of choices and hypotheses which must be thought out consciously because they must be compatible with the logic of a computer program.

For this reason, the mask of some kind of historical objectivity hidden in the 'facts' and discovered at the same time as them, has been removed for ever; the historian can no longer avoid being aware that he has constructed his 'facts', and that the objectivity of his research depends not only on using correct procedures for the elaboration and processing of these 'facts', but also on their relevance to his research hypotheses.

Serial history, therefore, is not only, nor indeed predominantly, a transformation of historical materials. It is a revolution in historiographical consciousness.

The historian's 'facts'

The effect of systematic analysis of chronological series of homogeneous data is in fact to transform the historian's conception and representation of time, which is the specific object of historical knowledge.

1. 'Event-based' history is not to be defined by the predominant importance attached to facts of a political order; neither is it constituted simply by the fact of recounting certain events selected on a temporal axis; such a conception of history is above all founded on the idea that these events are unique and cannot be integrated into any kind of statistical distribution, and that this unique event is the primary material of history. That is why the two most marked features of this kind of history – contradictory features moreover – are its insistence upon the short term and its finalist ideology; since the event, this sudden irruption of the irreplaceably new into the chain of time, cannot be compared with any antecedent, the only way of integrating it into history is to give it a teleological meaning: it has no past but it can have a future. And since history has evolved since the nineteenth century as a way of internalising and conceptualising the notion of progress, the 'event' serves more often than not to indicate the coming of some political or philosophical state: the republic, liberty, democracy, reason. This ideological consciousness on the part of the historian can take more refined forms: it can for instance bring together a whole accumulation of knowledge about a given period, forming unifying historical patterns less directly linked to political choices or sets of values (like for instance the 'spirit of an age', 'the vision of the world'). But this consciousness nevertheless reflects in the last analysis the same compensatory mechanism: in order to be intelligible, the event needs to be situated within a global history defined independently of it. Whence the classical conception of historical time as a series of discontinuities described in the continuous mode – a story.

Serial history, on the other hand, describes continuities in the discontinuous mode: it is history as problem rather than history as story. Since, by its very nature, it distinguishes the different levels of historical reality, it must by definition destroy any pre-established conception of a 'global' history: for it questions the very postulate of a supposedly homogeneous and identical evolution of all the elements within a society. The analysis of series of data can only be meaningful if it is conducted over the long term, so that short and cyclical variations can be distinguished from long-term trends; the series reveals a temporal dimension different from the mysterious and unpredictable thrust of the event, a dimension which is now measurable, comparable, and differential in two senses, depending on whether one examines it within one series or whether one compares one series with another.

In this way, serial history has fractured the old hermetic empire of classical historiography by means of two distinct but related operations. The analytical deconstruction of reality into levels of description has opened history up to concepts and methods imported from the more specific social sciences such as political economy, which has probably been the driving force behind this historical renewal. Secondly, the quantitative analysis of the different speeds of change within these levels has, finally, made time, which is the dimension of human activity most essential to history's very existence, into a scientifically measurable object.

2. If the hypothesis-making activities of the historian have, as a result of this, been displaced from the level of the philosophy of history to that of a series of specific but homogeneous data, then the hypotheses which are formulated more often than not gain in explicitness and formulability. On the other hand, the result is also an atomisation of historical reality into such distinct fragments that the classical claim of history to be able to grasp reality in a global way has been called into question. Should this claim then be abandoned?

My reply is that such a claim should probably be kept as the far horizon of history but that, in order to progress, we should abandon it as a starting-point for research, for fear of returning to the teleological illusion described earlier. Contemporary historiography is moving forward because it limits its object, defines its hypotheses, and constitutes and describes its sources as carefully as possible. That is not to say that it should limit itself to the microscopic analysis of one single chronological series; it can bring several such series together and at that point offer interpretations of a system, or a sub-system. But the global analysis of the 'system of systems' is today probably beyond its means.

I shall take as an example demographic and economic history, which are the most advanced sectors of contemporary French (and probably international) historiography. The last twenty years in France have seen a large number of demographic and economic studies of the 'modern' period, which is therefore relatively well known from this point of view.[8] Having begun with the analysis of market price lists and the reconstitution of prices, French history then proceeded to compare these series with the evolution of the population studied in demographic series. This led progressively to the development of the concept of an 'economic *ancien régime*', an economic system based upon the predominance of cereal production vulnerable to the caprices of the weather, and, secondly, upon the periodical purging of the system by cyclical crises, indicated by sudden price increases and equally sudden drops in the population curve.

Subsequently, however, the price series, to which can be attributed ambiguous and varied meanings, were complemented by a series of indicators better adapted to the study of the volume of production, and by the use of series bearing on the development of supply and demand, themselves in turn crucial in the evolution of prices. On the production side, we should mention tithe sources which, since they affect the same percentage of the harvest every year, tell us nothing about the absolute volume of production, but are valuable in relative terms; we should equally mention, at a macro-economic level, the protostatistical sources collected by the administration of the *ancien régime*, which can be reorganised according to modern principles of national accounting. On the demand side, leaving aside global demographic movements, we should observe the reconstruction of the amounts of money in circulation, analysed under the following headings: communal and manorial incomes, tithes, ground rent, industrial profits, and wages.

As a result of this combination of various demographic and economic series, Le Roy Ladurie was able to extend the analysis of the old agrarian economy.[9] His work, based on a diverse and rich sample of data, especially cadastral plans, covering the whole of Languedoc from the fifteenth to the eighteenth century, studies the whole system of rural land ownership during the period. It is the history of a very long agrarian cycle, characterised both by a general equilibrium and a series of disequilibria. The general equilibrium corresponds roughly to the Malthusian model, the model which Malthus discovered and fixed for posterity at the precise moment when it was ceasing to apply, when the economy and demography of Britain were beginning to take off: the economy of ancient Languedoc is dominated in the long term by the relation between agricultural production and the number of men; society's inability to raise agricultural productivity, and the absence of an indefinite reserve of good land represent a series of structural impediments to decisive growth, in much the same way as the famous 'monetary famine' dear to the hearts of historians of prices. The monetary explanation thus loses its central role, but is integrated into a diverse and unified system of interpretation.

In the long term this structure of the ancient economy appears to function as an internal law. But despite this, the different variables within the system – number of men, development of ownership, distribution of ground rent, movement of productivity and prices, etc. – allow us to identify periods. The structure, chronologically considered, thus includes several types of combinations of series, in other words several conjunctures. What is more, the attentive examination of these successive conjunctures and of their common and different features, in fact allows us to perceive the global structure. This apparent paradox may cast light on the debate between synchronic and diachronic, which often separates anthropologists and historians, and which is currently at the very heart of developments within the social sciences. This periodic structure, in the short and middle term, which constitutes the 'event' in the economic order, does not necessarily conflict with a theory of general equilibrium. On the contrary, the empirical description of periodic structures may allow us to be clearer about the theoretical conditions of the equilibrium: its elasticity indicates its limits.

3. But the preceding example – Le Roy Ladurie's Languedoc – is a special

one to the extent that the correlation between different demographic and economic series takes place within a relatively homogeneous regional space and a clearly defined area of human activity, the agrarian economy. In reality, 'sector-based' serial history, when extended to different spaces, leads to the analysis of regional or national imbalances. And 'global' serial history (or at least that with global aspirations), even when it is restricted to a limited geographical area, is likely to lead to the analysis of temporary imbalances between the different speeds of development of various levels of human activity.

The first of these points is now commonplace, thanks to growing numbers of studies in regional economic history. The specialist in economic history is more accustomed than many to the idea of measurable gaps between nations, and between different areas influenced in different degrees by the same conjuncture, or responding differently to conjunctures separated in time. There are innumerable examples of this, and some of them raise problems which have become classic in European history: the question, to which attention has recently returned,[10] of the comparative growth rates of France and England in the eighteenth century; the opposition between the agricultural expansion of Catalonia in the eighteenth century and the decline of Castille, demonstrated by P. Vilar;[11] or the contrast, in seventeenth-century France, between the Beauvaisis of P. Goubert,[12] desperately poor, and deeply affected as early as the middle of the century by economic and demographic recession, and on the other hand, the Provence of Baehrel,[13] relatively more fortunate, or at least affected considerably later by declining growth. More generally, the date of this reversal, of this descent into the 'tragic' seventeenth century, varies widely according to region, but also according to the nature of the various economies in question. Moreover, it now appears less and less probable that there was one single conjuncture for the urban and for the rural economy.[14]

Serial economic history, then, leads us to an analysis of different conjunctures or of the same conjunctures affecting different areas at different times – a kind of geographical chronology; and secondly to the examination of the structural differences which may be indicated by chronological contradictions. In fact, cycles taking place at different times according to region or country, but fundamentally similar in their structure, simply reflect geographical variations on a similar history; whereas contradictory developments either within one geographical area (for example as between town and country), or between two areas, probably suggest different economic structures.

But history cannot simply be reduced to the description and interpretation of economic activity. History's specificity compared to the other social sciences is precisely that it is unspecific, that it aspires to an exploration of time in all its dimensions. It is, of course, easy to understand why economics has been a privileged area within quantitative history, since economic indicators are necessarily measurable, since the concepts which it has allowed historians to develop are extremely precise, and since the problematic of growth is central to modern Western conceptions of historical change. But man is not solely an economic agent. Today's world offers too many examples of cultural resistance to the general spread of the Western model of economic growth for the historian not to have to question the Victorian concept of progress (or indeed its Marxist mirror-image); history must also become interested in the political and ideological analysis of past societies.

But doing this cannot and must not mean a return to the old history based on a teleology of 'progress', extrapolating from economic development to cultural life, either by assuming some kind of 'natural' peaceful adaptation, or by the necessary mediation of revolution. These are ideological tools of the nineteenth century which are of no use today. It is not by hanging on to them that the historian will remain faithful to the 'global' character of the discipline. On the contrary, such an ambition will only be fulfilled if the historian is prepared to list and describe levels of human activity other than the objective processes of economics, but using the same methods of serial history. History must now start from the hypothesis that the nature of historical time may be different according to the level of reality or the partial historical system which is being analysed.

In practical terms, there is a very long way to go. History must establish potential indicators (quantifiable or otherwise) of what I would call 'politico-ideological' society. It must constitute its documentation, find out in what ways that documentation is representative and in what ways it can be used comparatively from one period to another. The sources are available, just as rich as in the economic and demographic areas; many series are also available, and are just as homogeneous. They concern such topics as popular literacy,[15] the sociology of education or religious feeling,[16] the consumption of ideas by elites, the explicit and latent content of political ideologies, etc. In theoretical terms, the important thing is, of course, to build up the elements of a global historical picture progressively; but a first priority must be to analyse the different rates of change and development at different levels within the historical whole. In that way the two most urgent aims of historiography today will be achieved:

1. The first of these is the revision of the traditional historical periods, which are to a large extent an ideological inheritance from the nineteenth century, and which presuppose precisely that which remains to be demonstrated: that the different elements of the historical whole, within one given period, evolve roughly in parallel. Instead of taking as one's starting-point a given periodisation, it is probably more fruitful to consider the problem from the point of view of the different elements described. The concept of the Renaissance, for example, is doubtless relevant with respect to cultural history, but far less meaningful when data concerning agricultural activity are under consideration.

2. The next question is this. Within a given period, which levels of reality are undergoing rapid development or decisive change, and which are the sectors

marked by a greater inertia, in the middle or long term? It is far from clear, for example, that the dynamics of French history, let us say since the great period of 'growth' of the eleventh and twelfth centuries, are essentially economic: it is quite possible that developments in education, culture and state intervention were more important than the growth of the national product. This is an ambitious hypothesis upon which to close, but I can perhaps add a note of humility if I say that my hypothesis will remain unverifiable until history as a whole starts to learn the methods of serial history.

NOTES

1 This article appeared, under the title 'L'histoire quantitative et la construction du fait historique', in *Annales ESC* (1971), no. 1, pp. 63–75.

2 *Histoire quantitative de l'économie française*, ed. J. Marczewski (Paris, ISEA, 1961–8). Cf. especially vol. 1, *Histoire quantitative, buts et méthodes*, by Marczewski.

3 The term is Pierre Vilar's.

4 P. Chaunu has defended and used this terminology in numerous works, most notably: 'Histoire quantitative ou histoire sérielle', *Cahiers Vilfredo Pareto* (Geneva, 1968); 'L'histoire sérielle: bilan et perspectives', an article which appeared simultaneously in the *Revue historique* (April–June 1970), and in the *Revue roumaine d'histoire* (1970), no. 3.

5 Cf. P. Deane and W. A. Cole, *British Economic Growth, 1688–1959: Trends and Structures* (Cambridge University Press, 1962); D. Landes, *Prometheus Unbound* (Cambridge University Press, 1969); F. Crouzet, 'Angleterre et France au XVIIIe siècle', *Annales ESC* (1966), no. 2.

6 M. Couturier, 'Vers une nouvelle méthode mécanographique', *Annales ESC* (1966), no. 4.

7 E. Le Roy Ladurie, 'Révolution française et contraception, dossiers languedociens', *Annales de démographie historique* (1966); and 'Révolution française et funestes secrets', *Ann. hist. Rév. fr.* (October–December 1965). Also A. Chamoux and C. Dauphin, 'La contraception avant la Révolution française: l'exemple de Châtillon-sur-Seine', *Annales ESC* (1969), no. 3.

8 The bibliography here is so vast as to discourage even an attempt to summarise it.

9 E. Le Roy Ladurie, *Les Paysans de Languedoc* (SEVPEN, 1966). My argument here is a shorter version of my article in *Social Science Information* (1968): 'Sur quelques problèmes posés par le développement de l'histoire quantitative'.

10 F. Crouzet, *op. cit.*

11 P. Vilar, *La Catalogne dans l'Espagne moderne* (SEVPEN, 1962), especially vol. 2.

12 P. Goubert, *Beauvais et le Beauvaisis de 1600 à 1730* (SEVPEN, 1960).

13 R. Baehrel, *Une croissance: la basse Provence rurale, fin du XVIe siècle–1789* (Paris, 1961).

14 D. Richet, 'Croissances et blocages en France du XVe au XVIIIe siècle', *Annales ESC* (1968), no. 4.

15 See M. Fleury, 'Les progrès de l'instruction élémentaire de Louis XIV à Napoléon III', *Population* (1957); L. Stone, 'Literacy and education in England, 1640–1900',

Past and Present (February 1968); C. Cipolla, *Literacy and Development in the West* (Penguin, 1969).

16 G. and M. Vovelle give a brilliant demonstration of how to use iconographic series for the study of religious feeling in their *Vision de la mort et de l'au-delà en Provence* (Cahier des Annales, 1970).

2. Economic history: past achievements and future prospects

PIERRE CHAUNU

Economic history is a relatively new area of a discipline which, with all its ambiguities and dangers, can be traced back almost to man's original inhabitation of cities. In recent times, as an increasing number of quite disparate areas of study have come to be included within this misconceived whole, professional historians have lost any sense of the novelty of a specifically economic history. They have tended rather to consider it an ancient and commonplace form, whereas in fact it cannot be said to have emerged much before 1890. The first tentative chapters on economics appear in the huge nineteenth-century histories of nation-states, when history was more in vogue than ever before. Four-fifths of the exposition is devoted to the State, with economics being left to the end of the book, along with society, the history of ideas and art.

Consider Lavisse's unrivalled contribution. His hesitant inclusion of raw (or almost raw) economic data, and his juxtaposition of an economic and a political event, suggest that autonomous research into economics was then beginning. Ernest Labrousse[1] has recently called our attention to the value of Emile Levasseur's writings.[2] In almost every country, the turn of the century saw the launching of huge collections of documents, and with it the publication of the first histories of prices,[3] which are simply compendia of raw data. It was Rogers's contribution[4] in England (which is still helpful today) which began the process. Wiebe,[5] in Germany, followed suit, as did the Viscount d'Avenel[6] and Zolla[7] in France. Nor should we forget Natalis de Wailly[8] and J.-J. Clamageran,[9] who tried to write economic histories of the State.

We ought not to be surprised at this archaeology of both economic and quantitative history, at this emergence of an economic supplement within an already flourishing historical tradition.[10] It is clearly linked to the changes brought about in industrial societies by the railways. National rivalries did much to encourage it, as did the development of economic thought (Pareto and the emergence of marginalist economics) and the growing awareness on the part of both liberal political economists (Juglar) and their Marxist critics, of the economic and social importance of crises. All of these tendencies had been at

28

work from the middle of the nineteenth century onwards, but no one attempted an autonomous historiography of the economic domain until the 1880s and the 1890s. It was not by chance that this first, admittedly very modest, body of critical writing emerged when it did. The great depression (1873–4 to 1900–5), in Simiand's periodisation, clearly played a part in stimulating this inquiry. We are familiar with the significance of the long-term fall in agricultural prices in societies in which the agricultural sector remained, socially if not economically, the most substantial one. For a part of the intellectual elite still lived in the country (this was the case with the Viscount d'Avenel) or received a part of their income from rent (which was affected in the long term by the tendency of agricultural revenues to fall). We are also familiar with the serious tensions accompanying the transition from the second to the third stage of industriali-sation. Intellectual concerns do not reflect these changes in any immediate or mechanical sense, and in a period in which systems of communication were neither so diverse, nor so rapid, nor so efficient as they are in our own post-industrial societies, this process was a heavily mediated one, and new developments only percolated slowly.

Many of the changes thus took a long time to come to fruition. The gloom of the end of the nineteenth century continued to weigh upon people's minds when, in material terms, it had already, five or ten or even fifteen years before, given way to the aggressive growth of the beginning of the twentieth century. It must, nevertheless, be admitted that the impetus of the 1890s, because so little credence was given to it, did not succeed in forcing economic history out of its inchoate form until the real historiographical revolution of the end of the 1920s.

Economic history, the unifying human science of our time, was born between 1929 and the beginning of the 1930s in that anguished and painful atmosphere of worldwide crisis.

I

Economic history as we know it today dates from the turning-point of 1929–33. Studies done before then are merely of documentary value, and have become a part of the history upon which we feed. Before 1929 we are dealing with an archaeology of economic history.

Did a new epoch, in terms of intellectual creation, really begin then, or is it the occasion of a cyclical and structural economic crisis which obliges us to stop at this date? Or did historians at the start of the 1970s focus their attention on the early 1930s because one generation replaced another then?[11]

The generation of historians who are now in their forties, fifties or sixties, and who hold the key research and teaching posts, began to write when under the shadow of the great economic crisis. Everyone in France is aware of the key parts played by Ernest Labrousse (born in 1895) and by Fernand Braudel (born in 1902), and of their respective intellectual empires. The major contributions to economic history in the period after the Second World War, Ernest Labrousse's *L'Esquisse du mouvement des prix et des revenus en France au XVIIIᵉ siècle*,[12] his *La Crise de l'économie française à la fin de l'Ancien Régime et au début de la Révolution*,[13] and Fernand Braudel's *The Mediterranean and the Mediterranean World in the Age of Philip II*,[14] are all books whose inspiration and conception reflect the atmosphere of the crisis of 1929.

Conversely, those who are in their forties and fifties and who hold responsible posts today are not able to remember as far back as the start of the 1930s. If we are to periodise this intellectual history, a span of fifty years seems an altogether appropriate one.[15] Moreover, in an objective sense, the mutation occurring at the end of the 1920s and at the beginning of the 1930s is clearly a crucial one for historians.

Everything points to the years 1929 and 1930. The years between 1928 and 1937 also served by and large to confirm the decisive changes in science which occurred at the beginning of the twentieth century between 1898 and 1905 (from quantum theory to the first formulation of the special theory of relativity). If the early 1930s are a particularly significant period it is because there is then both a maturation of the fundamental discoveries of the turn of the century and a phase of radical innovation. The theory of general relativity dates from the First World War, but circumstances did not favour its diffusion. Fifteen years were to pass before the appropriate conclusions could be drawn, and it could begin to be checked. The theory of relativity did not modify science deeply, but it did give rise to parallel or complementary endeavours. Thus, Louis de Broglie's wave mechanics, created in 1923, had won the day by 1929. The physics of relativity was ready, by the beginning of the 1930s, to travel beyond the world of scholarship. Langevin and Russell added a philosophical dimension to it, and the notions of relativity and of the quantum began to affect general culture also. The intellectual foundations of philosophy, which had stood firm for so long, were shaken.

Then radioactivity, the springboard for all later developments, was discovered. Lord Rutherford achieved the first induced transmutation in Cambridge in 1919. By 1933, forty or so natural radio isotopes had been discovered. Frederick and Irene Joliot-Curie discovered the valuable artificial isotopes, and by 1937, 190 had been created. Hubble, with the aid of the new Mt Wilson telescope, discovered the redshift between 1924 and 1928, thus paving the way for a new theory of an expanding universe and for a new cosmogony. He was to do as much for astronomy in the thirties as Herschel had done at the end of the eighteenth century. This new start was as little appreciated as was that of Fleming in his own field, the discovery in 1929 of *Penicillium notatum*. But who could ever have foreseen the ultimate significance of the first tentative developments of cybernetics in the thirties?

There was thus relativity and radioactivity on the one hand, and redshift, antibiotics and cybernetics on the other. In a very different domain of knowledge there was Freud, and more abstruse still, the work of the School of Bible Studies in Jerusalem. As an intellectual discipline, history cannot be considered apart from the entirety of knowledge that is produced. Nevertheless, quite obvious social and economic mediations caused it to develop further in the years 1929–39. This is an aspect of the problem that should be borne in mind.

History is the oldest of the social sciences. Narration and chronicle, such as they were practised by the great historians, from Herodotus by way of Las Casas to Michelet, have never been concerned with events alone. Society, the implication has always been, must be treated as a system. There have always been correspondences between history as written and history as lived, between the civilisation giving rise to the historiography, and the organisation of the past in historical discourse. These correspondences may be discreet, and the relationship may be so profound as to be almost imperceptible. This was the case at the end of the nineteenth century during the epoch of 'positivist', hypercritical and scientistic historiography.

The shift in historiography at the beginning of the 1930s was marked, first of all, by a growing awareness of these previously hidden correspondences. Quantitative economic history, in its original manifestation, was an attempt at an answer, without frills, to the disturbing problems of the period. The link between the human sciences and the historical revival was clearly, as it was declared to be, a response to the number one problem, the crisis. To grasp the extreme closeness of the connection one only has to read and ponder the classic multidisciplinary study which François Simiand published in this agonising period. The title of this committed work is so clear a reflection of the time that it may serve to define the programme for economic history which was established in these years: *Long-Term Economic Fluctuations and the World Crisis.*[16] The term 'world crisis' was on everyone's lips; everyone was preoccupied by it. A bibliography of some tens of thousands of titles dealing with the subject over forty years testifies to this fact.

Everything possible has been said on the subject, almost all the hypotheses have been formulated. It is worth recalling that, in the United States, the levels of production reached in 1929 were not achieved again until the turning-point of 1941–2, with their entry into the war; that in 1932 only 17 per cent of the 1929 levels of steel production was achieved, with agricultural machinery standing at 20 per cent, textiles at 70 per cent, and agricultural production at 94 per cent.[17] We should bear in mind that the crisis was almost as severe in the whole of industrialised North-West Europe, and was particularly so in Germany. It was also equally severe in those countries which were much less industrialised, and which were at best artificially shielded by the State's protectionist measures, and which enjoyed growth only by virtue of a closed economic cycle. This was the case in South America (in Brazil, for instance), where an almost nonexistent industry and an agriculture geared to the export market were as much in crisis as the American steel industry. It was also the case in the USSR, which did not in any real sense overtake the industrial growth rate of Tsarist Russia until the eve of the Second Five Year Plan (1934), and which was far from equalling 1913 rates of agricultural production.

In France, a thoroughly heterogeneous economic ensemble, but apparently a relatively sheltered one, the Monnet planning commission calculated that losses due to the non-renewal of plant between 1930 and 1939 amounted to more than all the losses occasioned by the Second World War. Finally, and most crucially, there was a really serious demographic crisis. Between 1930 and 1939, almost all the industrial countries had a net coefficient of reproduction lower than one. When the crisis was at its height, some large capitals (Vienna and Stockholm) knew rates as low as 0.4 or 0.5. This destructive attitude, in both the short and long term, towards life itself, clearly reflects a very profound disorientation. It has reappeared in as exacerbated a form in Europe since 1970. The self-regulating mechanisms began to work in the opposite direction between 1937 and 1942 and the demographic situation picked up between, roughly speaking, 1942 and 1945, and 1962 and 1964. A crisis of these dimensions, affecting all domains at once,[18] cannot be understood mon-istically, that is, by employing a single explanatory system. François Simiand had felt this to be the case, even if his system seems today to be inadequate. In fact, the crisis of the thirties is the epitome of a structural readjustment. It was the result of a number of superimposed causes, belonging to very different levels, which had a knock-on effect. The period 1929–39 marks the end of a kind of latency period: a whole series of boundaries were crossed, new technological frontiers and a new system of civilisation emerged. 1930 marks the end of a kind of growth typical of the nineteenth century, a growth which links the old, traditional appeal to space and number with a new and ever more exclusive appeal to innovation.

II

So it was that, between 1929 and 1932, modern economic history was born. A serious attempt[19] at a scientific history of prices was launched and, in a matter of years,[20] it was possible to posit long and intricate series which could be traced back a long time. Historians linked up the protostatistics of the eighteenth and early nineteenth centuries with statistics developed later in the nineteenth century, finally coming across a prestatistics which, in the Mediter-ranean countries, may easily be traced back to the fourteenth century. Some-times, as in the case of Italy, it is possible to go back as far as the thirteenth century. The collective enterprise most characteristic of this period is the journal founded by Marc Bloch and Lucien Febvre in 1929, the *Annales*. Its full title, the *Annales d'histoire économique et sociale*, is illuminating too. It was between 1929 and 1932 that François Simiand, advancing an incomplete but nevertheless coherent explanation of the crisis of 1929, perfected his theory of movements in the *longue durée*, thus superseding Kondratieff's unconvincing hypothesis regarding the connection between such movements and cycles of solar activity.[21] His theory of phases was to be remarkably influential among French historians. From 1932, François Simiand[22] had begun to account for the 1929–32 crisis in terms of a superimposition of a cyclical crisis upon a change of phase, comparing the situation in these years with those of 1873, 1817, and even hazarding the same kind of interpretation with regard to the beginning of the seventeenth and the middle of the fourteenth century.

An economic history with a systematic approach to problems of quantification was born at this time. Two essential developments occurred. First, a connection was made between a particular branch of history and a contemporary human science. For economic history is not simply a branch of history, it is also a science which is the handmaiden of political economy. It enables one to apply to the past, flexible models based upon the mathematical analysis of the quantifiable data of economic activity. Second, history has always favoured the study of movement. This partly quantitative economic history is a history of *movement*, of variation, and of the wave structure of the economy. This concern was ultimately to produce a kind of hybrid form, half-way between traditional and new historiography. After Simiand, even structural history was to become, in Ernest Labrousse's terms, a history of change and of variation.

The second crucial variation of the thirties was geographical history.[23] This new development, largely inspired by Fernand Braudel, may also be said to imply an emphasis upon continuity. Braudel, in the preface to his work on the Mediterranean,[24] gave an account of the narrow positivist version of history which, by the end of the thirties, could not help but seem exhausted. He noted its admirable techniques, but described it as little more than an impressive instrument of research[25] which served simply to update the chronicles of a State. What was most lacking in history before the thirties was a genuinely theoretical perspective. Human geography, at the time of Albert Demangeon and in the wake of Vidal de la Blache, was in a position to provide historians with a set of eminently transposable theoretical systems. The history of geohistory from 1930 to 1945 may, if we stretch a point a little, be regarded as the history of the development of one work in particular, as Braudel shifted his attention from Philip II's Mediterranean *politics* to the Mediterranean *world* at the time of Philip II. To write of the Mediterranean in this context is to write of space, of three million square kilometres of water, of two million square kilometres of earth, of four thousand years of history also, given that writing originated in the Mediterranean. To study it in this way was to uncover a shadowy sea, to recover space, authentic space, from a definition of it in terms of the State, and to consider thereby the countryside, the dialogue between man and the earth and between man and climate. By lifting the screen of the

State, it became possible to consider the age-old struggle between man and things without the *diminutio capitis* of the framework of the nation-state, with its administrative geography and its frontiers. Whilst still being defined as history, geohistory rested upon a sense of time as extremely long, as almost geological in nature.

The immobility of geohistorical time was thus in dialectical opposition to the short-term and unstable time favoured by Simiand and Labrousse. Their schools, and that of Labrousse in particular, had developed a cyclical dynamics[26] which allowed them, in advance of structuralism, to give a more refined sense of the short term than was then possible in conventional history. The geographical dimension thus laid siege to history at the very moment when space had ceased to be the crucial factor in growth, and when the last flag-waving colonial empires, the legacy of a nineteenth-century Europe whose pace was slowing down, were about to dissolve and to turn into more complex systems of dependence. The economic history of the thirties and forties thus stands at the crossroads between cyclical dynamics and the analysis of the space–time dyad.

Between 1945 and 1960, French historians were encouraged by Ernest Labrousse and Fernand Braudel to come to terms with, and so to supersede this twofold innovation. They dreamed of combining Simiand's teaching with that of geohistory. They sought to define economic totalities ranging in size from small regions[27] (the model for which was the Beauvaisis)[28] to provinces of almost national dimensions[29] such as Catalonia),[30] to provinces considered in the very long term,[31] and finally, through a kind of inquiry which presages a new and quite different form of economic history,[32] to the vast spaces that the oceans cover (the South Atlantic,[33] the Portuguese presence there,[34] the Atlantic parallelogram of the Indies Trade,[35] the Indian[36] and the Pacific[37] Oceans). Such a study of the ocean spaces[38] may well be the most obvious attempt at combining the cyclical dynamic of the Simiand–Labrousse schools with Fernand Braudel's geohistory. Macrospatial investigations of this sort lead quite naturally to structural and cyclical analyses.

Economic history necessarily began in a somewhat narrow manner, treating cycles in terms of prices alone. Since 1950, however, it has transcended this first stage. Analyses of trading patterns,[39] among other things, have replaced impossible production.[40] Impossible production was a perfect expression of the preconceptions of the first generation of economic historians who resorted to quantification. They began with the prices model and sought to define the wave structure, the cyclical dynamics of the ancient economies of the pre-State epoch. This first generation quantitative history was, however, still too marked both by the anxieties of the 1929–32 crisis[41] and by their ambition of producing a precise quantification, to be able to settle for the modest but useful substitute of a history assessed, as Fernand Braudel so successfully did, in global terms.[42]

It is certainly tempting to endorse the subsequent criticisms of the quantitativists of the Kuznets and Marczewski schools,[43] namely that first generation quantitative history may well have devoted too much of its energy to highly precise series within minority sectors, thereby disregarding the larger-scale sectors of the economy. We are now, in the closing decades of the century, witness to a third development, the emergence of what I shall here call serial history. Yet if the grandiose ambitions of contemporary historians do not seem far-fetched, it is largely thanks to the intellectual rigour of a diachronic approach to cyclical dynamics and first generation economic history, and to the confidence that successors were able to place in their results.

The research of the last ten years enables us to make a first preliminary assessment. Three laws would appear to have been established. First, we have sought to demonstrate, with particular reference to the Spanish or Hispano-American part of the Atlantic,[44] the pertinence of the quadricyclical hypothesis[45] to a very wide sector of the economy.[46] There is definitely some correlation between Kitchin, Juglar and Kondratieff cycles and the other phases. This hypothesis has been proven in a very large number of cases.[47] The first law of cyclical dynamics may therefore be formulated as follows: the wave structure of economies and societies is universal. The multicyclical hypothesis is applicable everywhere and has not been refuted. When considering the fact that, from the end of the thirteenth to the end of the eighteenth century, fluctuations may all be plotted within two almost horizontal planes, it should be borne in mind that this rectification was done subsequently. The theory of the full world,[48] the Malthusian checks borrowed from M. M. Postan,[49] researches in historical demography, and the large-scale investigation conducted by the Sixth Section of the Ecole des Hautes Etudes into what tithes[50] tell us of agricultural production, all serve to suggest that there was in the West, for the very long stretch from the thirteenth to the beginning of the nineteenth century, an almost horizontal *trend*, a slightly rising trend and not, it must be stressed, the erroneous horizontality that was too hastily alleged on the basis of minute and unrepresentative samples.[51]

The second law follows on from the first. It allows one to assert the existence of an economic cycle. As protostatistics is left behind, the many thousands of curves which are plotted, ever more systematically, upon the basis of minutely calculated series, are almost always linked by positive correlations. Typical examples of this would be the positive correlation between prices and trade within that part of the Atlantic linking Seville (i.e. Europe) and America, the positive correlation linking prices and production levels of the Iberian-dominated parts of the Atlantic and the Pacific in the sixteenth, seventeenth and eighteenth centuries, the correlations between prices/trade, population and production levels[52] which hold for all sectors.

The third law informs us that, from the thirteenth to the twentieth century, from the less to the more developed sectors, and from the non-European world to the world that emerges from old Latin Christendom, we find a tendency for amplitudes to diminish and for periods to shorten. There are no exceptions to this law. Whether outside Europe or within it, population curves, prices, indices of economic activity and production levels all serve to confirm it.

III

The nature of research in economic history has already altered. At the beginning of the 1950s, in the United States, it fell under the shadow of political economy. In Europe, however, a form of research had emerged that was both more ambitious in its aims and changed in its basic motivation, but it did not at this stage intervene in researches into cyclical dynamics. The name of Simon Kuznets stands out here. To give the reader some idea of his work, I shall simply refer to an already published debate[53] and recapitulate, in outline, its conclusion. From now on I shall reserve the term 'quantitative history' for projects of the sort pursued by Simon Kuznets and Jean Marczewski. I shall employ this term only when the results may be filtered through an accountancy matrix that is at once national, regional and macrospatial,[54] and only when quantification is global, systematic and total.

Indeed, in a technical sense this form of history is linked to the spread of the great national accounting systems through those countries which have been most industrialised and are therefore best provided with economic statistics. This is still progressing and, if we discount several relatively minor mistakes (having to do, for the most part, with protostatistics), the totalising economic history of the economists has made a real contribution to our knowledge of the past.

This line of inquiry has its limitations and dangers, however, and it seems highly likely that it, too, will soon be superseded. The truth is that it is linked to preoccupations which seem less pressing at the beginning of the seventies than they did in the fifties. This kind of quantitative history is, above all, a history of growth. The first economic history was essentially a history of cyclical dynamics. As such, it stemmed from the crisis of the 1930s. The quantitative history practised by economists was, first of all, a history of spurts, of growth and of the disparities affecting growth. Without Rostow's achievements it would be unthinkable.[55] It would also be unthinkable if there had not been decolonisation, if the Third World (situated, as it is, outside Europe and North America) had not been discovered, if the regional disparities between North and South within the Mediterranean countries had not come to light and, above all, if the famous scissors effect had not been identified. The acceleration in economic growth, the unfortunately quite temporary improvement in the demographic health of the developed countries, the renewed rise in population in industrial Europe and in North America, the demographic explosion (as it has quite arbitrarily been termed) in the Third World, have all pointed to the existence of a very ancient structure of development.

Development, before it reaches the threshold of a hypothetical maturity, is at first cumulative. The most developed sectors are the ones which tend to develop the fastest, and the distance between developed industrial countries and culturally traditional and inward-looking sectors tends therefore to increase. It is vital to emphasise the mechanisms of development, as opposed to *growth*,[56] and one must distinguish between the most general features and those specific to the form of development which acted as a motor for the English and European take-off.[57]

This second form of economic history has its own limitations and dangers. It clearly cannot be employed before the nineteenth century, for it presupposes total and circular quantification within a closed system of accounting, and is anyway restricted to privileged sectors in industrial Europe and America. The existence of an extensive protostatistics in England allowed Gregory King to venture a little further back, and Phyllis Deane and W. A. Cole[58] have used this inspired pioneering work as a basis for the only more or less successful quantitative history so far produced which starts at the end of the seventeenth century. But their quantification clearly cannot be called total, and only to a limited extent answers to Kuznets's and Marczewski's criteria.

How, on the other hand, are we to assess the contribution of the *New Economic History*?[59] It hardly deserves to be called a history at all, for it relies on a very short term, and one which does not extend very far back from the present time. It is restricted to the highly developed American sector, and there it sifts through an abundance of collections of statistics which have, for the most part, been preselected. The *New Economic History* is therefore no more than the North American section of the second form of quantitative economic history, a history suited to the age of national accounting and of models. Even in terms of the American economy itself, the *New Economic History* finds itself embarrassed as soon as it comes to the 1830s. The authors do not make any claims to incorporate the period between 1800 and 1830 into their system, for it seems to them so distant as to be a prehistory. They are more or less aware that a structural modification occurred in these years, the effect of which is to make any link between the earlier and the later periods both hazardous and doubtful. This is why, revealingly enough, they resort to theoretical models entailing hypotheses which cannot be historically verified. The most famous example of this is the patently absurd supposition that the American economy would have developed without the railroads.

The *New Economic History* also rests upon a large number of philosophical preconceptions. Its *homo oeconomicus*, although appropriate in a few exceptional cases, seems to me to be an excessively polished conception. He is so perfect that he might have been dreamed up by writers on political economy at the time of Jean-Baptiste Say. He knows neither hesitation nor conflict, and his reaction to profit (and to profit alone) is pure and instantaneous; he has no body, no sexuality, no emotions, no roots, no wit and no soul. He is invariably aware and well-informed, ready, much like one of Vaucanson's machines, to react solely to his profit. When all is said and done, we are dealing here with a transition, but to advance is clearly not necessarily to progress. If one is to avoid slipping back from the Age of Computers into the Stone Age, one must also know how to preserve the knowledge that one has acquired, a task that is becoming more difficult day by day.

There is little point in attempting global quantification if the price of this attempt is a regression, as far as the handling of statistics is concerned, to an earlier stage of historical research. This is not the main drawback, however. This would seem to me to consist in the fact that the new quantitative economic history is less able than either the cyclical dynamics or the geographical history of the 1930s to the 1950s to transcend the economic sector in the strict sense of the term.

IV

This is why the new quantitative economic history has almost immediately given rise to new developments. For some years now, we have seen the emergence of what I would be tempted to call 'a return to serial history'. We have also witnessed what I shall here term 'the intrusion of the quantitative element into the third level of historical explanation'. Structural dynamics may be traced back as far as 1890, but it enjoyed a boom period between 1930 and 1935, reaching its high point between 1950 and 1960. Globalising quantitative history emerged around 1930, took off at the beginning of the sixties, and reached its high point between 1965 and 1968. It is far from being exhausted even now [1973], for it is capable of forming a wide range of different combinations with cyclical dynamics and geohistory.

The appearance of the third generation[60] of computers has also opened up an enormous number of new possibilities. Marcel Couturier, Emmanuel Le Roy Ladurie and François Furet were among the first in France to take advantage of them. Indeed, there has been hardly a single important work in economic history since 1968 which does not involve massive use of computerised information. The new quantitative economic history was not born at the same time as the computer, but its spread was much favoured by the prestige of an instrument which so multiplies all our resources. Rather than contributing to the progress of economic history, the computer helps to transform the methods of economic history.

It is here that our conception of history changes most drastically. For economic history nowadays is not so much an object of study, but rather a state of mind, a set of methods and an approach. If we are to take risks and make experiments in writing history we should, I have argued, subsume the quantitative within the serial method. Serial history includes all the quantitative forms of history within itself, indeed it transcends them. It is capable of commenting upon the third level of historical inquiry, and it thus hints at the possibility of producing analyses which cover whole systems of civilisation.

Serial history has also had its own, quite specific concerns. Alphonse Dupront, who began by studying the Crusades, has focused attention upon the most hidden aspects of collective consciousness, studying words as well as objects, and attending to everything from the panic-stricken expressions of faith to the vocabulary of the Enlightenment. Serial history, inasmuch as it clearly reflects the anxieties and preoccupations of the present time, involves a range of different alliances with a number of the human sciences which have as yet to benefit from serial runs. These would include social anthropology and its allied disciplines, together with collective psychology. Demography, one of history's oldest allies, would also be involved.

Economic history is continually improving its techniques, and its wayward intellectual trajectory often causes it to make quite unexpected and unintended discoveries. I shall give three examples of this process here. Emmanuel Le Roy Ladurie has shown, from his *The Peasants of Languedoc*[61] to his major inquiry into the state of the army in 1826,[62] that a diachronic approach to physical anthropology is both desirable, possible and illuminating. We need, in short, to know what the basic human material in any given period is. Le Roy Ladurie[63] has also shown how a history of climatic variation is possible in both the short, the medium and the very long term.[64] The Centre for Research into Quantitative History at the University of Caen has perfected a method which I shall here call a method for serial administrative history and for a diachronic approach to cartography.[65] It allows one to put to good use a range of scattered statistical data, across the whole period of existence of traditional society, in a regional context, from the end of the thirteenth to the beginning of the nineteenth century. One is thus able to recover material which could not be used by traditional methods, and to exploit it very thoroughly. If this method was so fruitful it was because of the remarkable stability of the rural habitat from the twelfth to the nineteenth century throughout the known world. The coming of computers has enabled the full potential of this method, which was conceived in terms of a study of population across a very long term,[66] to be realised. Serial administrative history, like a diachronic approach to cartography, cannot help but remind us of the privileged role in the past of historical demography.

Indeed, it was historical demography, the first offshoot of economic history, which was originally responsible for the chain reactions of serial history.[67] For if we lack what Ernest Labrousse has in traditional terms called a divisor or, more accurately, a weighted divisor, what sort of economic history can we lay claim to? This science of the *longue durée*, the long term, has been a peculiarly French one, for France has served as a kind of laboratory for the sudden rise in average age of the industrial populations.[68] It is a science which requires long series, it is a science of long runs. For the last ten years historical demography has been the crucial sector, the most fruitful area[69] in all historical research.[70] The brilliant Fleury-Henry method belongs to history and, if we stretch a point a little, to genealogy. For what could be more historical, in the traditional sense of the term, than the hypothetical reconstruction of a family, and what could be more serial than a method which allows one to calculate the net coefficient of reproduction and of life expectancy at Colyton from the sixteenth century down to our own day?

The value of today's demographic history lies in its results, and of course its repercussions. Exhaustive investigation of bankruptcy records in the archives of the poor obviously leads to a serial religious history,[71] to a history of attitudes to the nature of life, to a history of the phenomenon of the couple, and therefore of the most basic structure of social existence, to a history of love, of life and of death.

I have tried elsewhere[72] to show how it is that serial history, which began as an economic and social history, came to tackle the third level of historical inquiry, which entails a study of the essential aspects of systems of civilisation, from affective and intellectual matters to questions of collective psychology. This branch of history has been in existence for several decades now. Alphonse Dupront was for a long while an almost isolated pioneer in this field.

The shift which has occurred in the last few years is due to a widening of the fields of interests, and to a modification of the serial methods perfected by economic historians so that they are applicable to this new domain. These modifications include the establishment of statistical series which enable one to investigate the third level of historical inquiry, thus permitting a mathematical analysis of the series and a twofold investigation of documents, first in their own terms and then in relation to their position within the homogeneous series in which the basic information is integrated and posed.

Several strategies are possible. A literate civilisation is more easily studied than an illiterate one. François Furet,[73] Henri Martin,[74] Robert Estivals[75] and various others[76] have laid the foundations for a quantitative study of the entirety of printed matter. This approach enables one, with the aid of the computer and of quantitative semantics, to arrive at a somewhat tentative assessment of the overall content of the various levels of elaborated discourse.

It is far more difficult to assess the content of traditional cultures, and to define the degree of access enjoyed by those who are illiterate, to thought and to taste. Yet the methods of economic history may be adapted and transposed here too. Victor-Lucien Tapié[77] and his pupils have convincingly shown the value of a serial treatment of images that recur in the altar-pieces of the country churches of the seventeenth and eighteenth centuries, for they tell us a great deal about the religious sensibility of the period and about the content of the faith. Jacques Bertin's *Sémiologie graphique*[78] contains a range of graphic procedures through which one may analyse the content of such images. His pioneering study serves as a point of departure for what will in the end be a systematic investigation of the nature of the image. In the case of furniture, the church and the peasant habitat, this chain of reasoning is still more manifest.

One inquiry in economic history of a fairly classic sort[79] culminates nowadays in massive inventories of a fundamentally novel kind. These investigations do not stop short at a study of a particular object, and of its overall significance, but aim to identify the content of a non-literate civilisation. Yet it is clearly the studies of sexuality, of life and of death which go furthest in this direction.[80] A mastery of quantitative methods, in the past through economics and latterly through information theory, has enabled Michel Vovelle, in his great pioneering work,[81] François Lebrun, in a fine book which is more classical in spirit but contains some very acute analyses,[82] and a number of others, in their recently published works, to complete a key section of a history of these fundamental matters.[83]

A global history of systems of civilisation is gradually emerging. There is obviously some connection between this development and the crisis in civilisation which, since 1962, has more and more affected, sector by sector, those countries which are entering the post-industrial epoch. This crisis undermines the transposition of Christian values into lay terms which was formulated during the Enlightenment and which had involved an eschatological transposition of Christianity on to a long-term self-activating process of growth. It was thus almost inevitable that the history of ways of acting should have been replaced by that of ways of thinking and feeling, and that history should have come to be concerned with motivations.[84]

However useful quantitative researches concerning the emergence of the couple, or concerning collective attitudes to death, may be, they should be regarded as provisional stages in a larger investigation. If we are to codify accurately those signs of panic which indicate that we are touching upon what is essential, we must attend to the whole of discourse. Serial history teaches us that the most sophisticated ideas of an elite must also be reconsidered across a long stretch of time. Seriality does not merely concern quantity, it also enables us to produce more refined analyses of quality. Serial history thus has a part to play in one of the most vital of our tasks, that of writing a history of systems of civilisation.

NOTES

1 Ernest Labrousse, *Histoire économique et sociale de la France* (2 vols., Paris, PUF, 1970), vol. 2, p. v.
2 Emile Levasseur, *Histoire des classes ouvrières et de l'industrie en France avant 1789*, 2nd edn (5 vols., Paris, 1900–7).
3 As long ago as 1955, we observed (in H. and P. Chaunu, *Séville et l'Atlantique (1540–1650)*, Paris, SEVPEN, vol. 1, p. 28) that: 'Of all the branches of economic

history, the history of prices is incontestably the one which, as far as measurement is concerned, has produced the best results, both for the modern period and for the Middle Ages. It was the pioneer.'

4 J. E. Thorold Rogers, *A History of Agriculture and Prices in England, from the Year after the Oxford Parliament, 1259, to the Commencement of the Continental War, 1793* (7 vols., Oxford, Clarendon Press, 1866–1902); and, by the same author, *Six Centuries of Work and Wages* (2 vols., London, Sonnenschein and Co., 1884).

5 G. Wiebe, *Zur Geschichte der Preisrevolution des XVI. und XVIII. Jahrhunderts* (Leipzig, 1895).

6 Vicomte G. d'Avenel, *Histoire économique de la propriété, des salaires, des denrées, et de tous les prix en général, depuis 1200 jusqu'à l'an 1800* (7 vols., Paris, 1894–1926).

7 D. Zolla, 'Les variations du revenu et du prix des terres en France aux XVIIe et XVIIIe siècles', *Annales de l'école libre des sciences politiques* (Paris, 1893–4).

8 Natalis de Wailly, *Mémoire sur les variations de la livre tournois depuis le temps de Saint Louis jusqu'à l'établissement de la monnaie décimale* (Paris, 1857).

9 J.-J. Clamageran, *Histoire de l'impôt en France* (3 vols., Paris, 1867–76).

10 Large collections of documents were never produced in such numbers in Western Europe as they were in the years between 1880–90 and 1910.

11 Yves Renouard, 'La notion de génération en histoire', *Revue historique*, CCIX, no. 425 (1953), pp. 1–23; and *Etudes d'histoire médiévale*, I, Paris (1968), pp. 1–23.

12 Ernest Labrousse, *L'Esquisse du mouvement des prix et des revenus en France au XVIIIe siècle* (2 vols., Paris, Dalloz, 1933).

13 Ernest Labrousse, *La Crise de l'économie française à la fin de l'Ancien Régime et au début de la Révolution* (Paris, PUF, 1944).

14 Fernand Braudel, *The Mediterranean and the Mediterranean World in the Age of Philip II*, translated by Siân Reynolds (2 vols., London, Collins, 1972).

15 In spite of the statistical lengthening of human life, which has come to a halt in the last fifteen years in the most developed parts of the world on account of dietary and other abuses, this timespan has been recognised across three millennia. In Psalm 90, verse 10, an ancient prayer attributed to Moses the Psalmist, we read: 'The days of our years are threescore and ten; and if by reason of strength they be fourscore years, yet is their strength labour and sorrow.' So there are fifty years of adult life.

16 François Simiand, *Les Fluctuations économiques à longue période et la crise mondiale* (Paris, Alcan, 1932).

17 Frank Freidel, *America in the Twentieth Century* (New York, A. A. Knopf, 1960).

18 This of course includes the religious domain too. The 'thirties were marked by a repossession and reactivation of theological and mystical thought' (Karl Barth). From 1955–60 on, a diaspora of German theologians from the United States gave rise to a neo-liberalism, which the mass media launched as a commodity, and which helped to empty Christian thought of all content and occasioned the widespread destruction of all the Churches from within in the 1960s.

19 Henri Hauser, 'Un comité international d'enquête sur l'histoire des prix', *Annales d'histoire économique sociale*, 2 (1930), pp. 384–5.

20 For France, Henri Hauser, 1936, Ernest Labrousse, 1933 and 1944; for England, Beveridge, 1939; for Holland, N. W. Posthumus, 1946–68; for Belgium, C. Verlinden and Y. Craey-Beckx, 1959; for Germany, M. J. Elsas, 1936–49; for Austria, A. F. Pribram, 1938; for Denmark, A. Friis, 1958; for Poland, S. Hoszowksi, 1934, 1938; for Russia, A. G. Mankov, 1954; for Spain, E. J. Hamilton, 1934, 1937 and 1947; for Portugal, V. M. Godinho, 1958; for Italy, A. Fanfani, 1940 and G. Parenti, 1939 and 1942.

For an overall summary of all the research devoted to the history of prices, see F. Braudel and F. C. Spooner, 'Prices in Europe from 1450 to 1750', *Cambridge*

Economic History (Cambridge, Cambridge University Press, 1967), vol. 4, pp. 378, 484, 608–75.

21 N. D. Kondratieff, 'Die langen Wellen der Konjunktur', *Archiv fur Sozial-Wissenschaft* (1926); and on this topic, see Gaston Imbert, *Des mouvements de longue durée Kondratieff* (Aix-en-Provence, La Pensée Universitaire, 1959).

22 François Simiand, *Les Fluctuations économiques*.

23 Cf. Pierre Chaunu, 'L'histoire géographique', *Revue de l'enseignement supérieur*, 44–5 (1969), pp. 66–7.

24 Fernand Braudel, *The Mediterranean*, pp. 17–22.

25 From Lorenzo Valla and fifteenth-century humanism and the Benedictines of Saint-Maur to the crisis of European consciousness during the Enlightenment, and thence to the historicist hermeneutics of the Bible studies of the German universities in the nineteenth century, textual criticism has reached a level of formal perfection which will never be surpassed.

26 Pierre Chaunu, 'Dynamique conjoncturelle et histoire sérielle', *Industrie*, 6, Brussels, (1960).

27 Pierre Goubert, *Beauvais et le Beauvaisis de 1600 à 1730: contribution à l'histoire sociale de la France au XVIIe siècle* (2 vols., Paris, SEVPEN, 1960).

28 For a study of small countries treated as the basic units of social existence, see Pierre Chaunu, 'En marge de Beauvaisis exemplaire. Problèmes de fait et de méthode', *Annales de Normandie*, 4 (1960), pp. 337–65.

29 On this question, see Pierre Chaunu, 'Les Espagnes périphériques dans le monde moderne', *Revue d'histoire économique et sociale*, XVI, no. 2 (1963), pp. 145–82.

30 Pierre Vilar, *La Catalogne dans l'Espagne moderne: recherches sur les fondements économiques des structures nationales* (3 vols., Paris, SEVPEN, 1962).

31 Emmanuel Le Roy Ladurie, *The Peasants of Languedoc*, translated with an introduction by John Day (Urbana, University of Illinois Press, 1974).

32 Pierre Chaunu, 'A partir du Languedoc. De la peste noire à Malthus, cinq siècles d'histoire sérielle', *Revue historique*, CCXXXVII, no. 482 (1967), pp. 359–80.

33 Frédéric Mauro, *Le Portugal et l'Atlantique au XVIIe siècle (1570–1670): étude économique* (Paris, SEVPEN, 1960).

34 Pierre Chaunu, 'Brésil et l'Atlantique au XVIIe siècle', *Annales ESC*, 6 (1961), pp. 1176–1207.

35 H. and P. Chaunu, *Séville et l'Atlantique*, Part 1 (8 vols., Paris, SEVPEN, 1955–7); P. Chaunu, *Séville et l'Atlantique*, Part 2 (4 vols., Paris, SEVPEN, 1960).

36 Vitorino Magalhaes Godinho, *L'Economie de l'empire portugais aux XVe et XVIe siècles* (1958) (Paris, SEVPEN, 1969).

37 Pierre Chaunu, *Les Philippines et le Pacifique des Ibériques (XVIe, XVIIe, XVIIIe siècles)* (2 vols., Paris, SEVPEN, 1960 and 1966).

38 A more inclusive bibliography touching upon this question may be found in Pierre Chaunu, *L'Expansion européenne du XIIIe au XVe siècle* (Paris, PUF, 1969); and in Pierre Chaunu, *Conquête et exploitation des nouveaux mondes* (Paris, 1969).

39 F. Braudel and R. Romano, *Navires et marchandises à l'entrée du port de Livourne (1547–1611)* (Paris, Armand Colin, 1951).

40 H. and P. Chaunu, *Séville: introduction méthodologique* (Paris, 1955).

41 'Our crucial concern must be to know, to analyse, and thereby to dominate (and thus to tame) economic fluctuations', Pierre Chaunu, 'Dynamique conjoncturelle', 1960.

42 Pierre Chaunu, 'La pesée globale en histoire', *Cahiers Vilfredo Pareto*, XV (Geneva, Droz, 1968), pp. 135–64.

43 The criticisms of the ultra-liberal American quantitativists bear a curious resemblance to those advanced by orthodox Marxists ten years before.

44 H. and P. Chaunu, *Séville et l'Atlantique*.

45 I have borrowed this term from Guy Beaujouan, who used it in the summary he wrote of my work in *Journal des savants* (1960).

46 For an overall assessment of this sector, see Pierre Chaunu, *Conquête et exploitation des nouveaux mondes*, and Pierre Chaunu, 'Place et rôle du Brésil dans les systèmes de communication et dans les mécanismes de la croissance de l'économie du XVIe siècle', *RHES*, XLVIII, no. 4, pp. 460–82.

47 F. Braudel and F. C. Spooner, 'Prices in Europe'.

48 Emmanuel Le Roy Ladurie is largely responsible for the development of this theory in France, and I have therefore devoted a large amount of space to him in my study on systems of civilisation.

49 M. M. Postan, 'England', *Cambridge Economic History of Europe* (Cambridge, Cambridge University Press, 1966), vol. 1, pp. 549–633.

50 *Les Fluctuations du produit de la dîme*, the First National Congress of the French Association of Economic Historians. Contributions assembled and edited by J. Goy and E. Le Roy Ladurie, Ecole Pratique des Hautes Etudes, Sixth Section, *Cahiers des études rurales*, III (Paris–The Hague, Mouton, 1972).

51 M. Morineau, 'Les faux semblants d'un démarrage économique', *Cahier des Annales*, 30 (Paris, 1971).

52 P. Chaunu, 'Le renversement de la tendance majeure des activités et des prix au XVIIe siècle', *Studi in onore di Amintore Fanfani*, IV (Milan, 1962), pp. 221–57; and Pierre Chaunu, 'Le XVIIe siècle. Problèmes de conjoncture', *Mélanges Antony Babel* (Geneva, 1963), pp. 337–55.

53 Jean Marczewski, *Introduction à l'histoire quantitative de l'économie française* (11 vols., Paris, ISEA, 1961–9) – see the introduction to this work, especially pp. i, liv; it is reprinted in *Cahiers Vilfredo Pareto*, III (Geneva, Droz, 1964) as 'Buts et méthodes de l'histoire quantitative' – see pp. 125, 164, 177–80; cf. also Pierre Chaunu, 'Histoire quantitative ou histoire sérielle', *Cahiers Vilfredo Pareto*, III, 165–76; Pierre Chaunu, 'Histoire sérielle, bilan et perspective', *Revue historique*, 494 (1970), pp. 297–320, and *Revue roumaine d'histoire*, 3 (1970).

54 Pierre Chaunu, *Revue historique* (1970), p. 300.

55 W. W. Rostow, *The Stages of Economic Growth* (Cambridge, Cambridge University Press, 1960).

56 Pierre Chaunu, 'Croissance ou développement? A propos d'une véritable histoire économique de l'Amérique latine aux XIXe et XXe siècles', *Revue historique*, 496 (1970), pp. 357–74.

57 In recent years there have been many 'revisionist' studies of the original economic 'take-off' in England and Western Europe. Paul Bairoch's studies in particular (cf. *Révolution industrielle et ses développements* (Paris, SEDES, third edn, 1969)) have been accorded an excessively favourable reception. One recent and noteworthy contribution is François Crouzet's analysis, 'The economic history of modern Europe', in *The Journal of Economic History*, XXXI, no. 1 (1971), pp. 135–52; also R. M. Hartwell, 'The causes of the Industrial Revolution in England', in *Debates in Economic History*, ed. Peter Mathias (London, Methuen, 1967); David S. Landes, *The Unbound Prometheus: Technical Change and Industrial Development in Western Europe from 1750 to the Present* (Cambridge, Cambridge University Press, 1969); and a very remarkable analysis, which has only known a small circulation, by E. A. Wrigley, on 'Modernisation and industrialisation', distributed by the Cambridge Group for the History of Population and Social Structure. For a useful summary, the reader should consult Claude Fohlen, *Qu'est-ce que la révolution industrielle?* (Paris, Robert Laffont, 1971).

58 Phyllis Deane and W. A. Cole, *British Economic Growth, 1688–1959* (Cambridge, Cambridge University Press, 1962).

59 Maurice Levy Leboyer, 'La New Economic History', *Annales ESC*, 5 (1969), pp. 1035–69.
60 Marcel Couturier was the first to popularise this expression amongst French-speaking historians. See his 'Vers une nouvelle méthodologie mécanographique. La préparation des données', *Annales ESC*, 4 (1966), pp. 769–78.
61 E. Le Roy Ladurie, *The Peasants of Languedoc*.
62 J. P. Aron, P. Dumont and E. Le Roy Ladurie, *Anthropologie du conscrit français d'après les comptes numériques et sommaires du recrutement de l'armée, 1819–1826* (Paris–The Hague, Mouton, 1972).
63 Emmanuel Le Roy Ladurie, *Histoire du climat depuis l'an mil* (Paris, Flammarion, 1967).
64 Pierre Chaunu, 'Le climat et l'histoire à propos d'un livre récent', *Revue historique*, CCXXXVIII, no. 484, pp. 365–76.
65 Pierre Chaunu, 'Les enquêtes du centre de recherches d'histoire quantitative de Caen, bilans et perspectives...', Colloque du CNRS de Lyon (October 1970), *Industrialisation en Europe au XIXe siècle, cartographie typologie* (Paris, CNRS, 1972), pp. 285–304.
66 Pierre Gouhier, *La Population de la Normandie du XIIIe au XIXe siècle*.
67 See my chapter, 'La dimension de l'homme', in Pierre Chaunu, *La Civilisation de l'Europe des Lumières* (Paris, Arthaud, 1971).
68 For the first time between 1847 and 1851, and almost uninterruptedly from 1896 onwards.
69 There is a very brief summary in *La Civilisation de l'Europe*, pp. 95–170.
70 See *Population and Population Studies* (1946 onwards) and *Annales de démographie historique* (1964 onwards), and the joint publication of the INED by the Sixth Section of the Ecole des Hautes Etudes, by the Centre at Cambridge and by the CRHQ at Caen.
71 Amongst other possibilities there is the set of beliefs and practices surrounding eagerness for baptism; cf. also Pierre Chaunu, 'Une histoire religieuse sérielle', *Revue d'histoire moderne et contemporaine*, 1 (1965), pp. 5–34.
72 Pierre Chaunu, 'Un nouveau champ pour l'histoire sérielle, le quantitatif au troisième niveau', *Mélanges Fernand Braudel*, II (Paris, Privat, 1972), pp. 105–26.
73 François Furet and others, *Livres et société dans la France du XVIIIe siècle* (2 vols., Paris–The Hague, Mouton, 1965).
74 Henri-J. Martin, *Livre, pouvoir et société à Paris au XVIIe siècle (1598–1701)* (2 vols., Geneva, Droz, 1969), which follows on from L. Febvre, H.-J. Martin, *The Coming of the Book: the Impact of Printing, 1450–1800*, translated by D. Gerard, edited by G. Nowell-Smith and David Wootton (London, New Left Books, 1976).
75 Robert Estivals, *Le Dépôt légal sous l'Ancien Régime de 1537 à 1791* (Paris, Marcel Rivière, 1961); by the same author, *La Statistique bibliographique de la France sous la monarchie au XVIIIe siècle* (Paris–The Hague, Mouton, 1965), and also a duplicated thesis on 'Bibliographie bibliométrique' (Sorbonne Library, 1971).
76 Jean Quéniart, Geneviève Bollème..., who have recently established a *Revue d'histoire du livre*.
77 Victor-L. Tapié and others, *Enquête sur les retables* (2 vols., Paris, Centre de Recherches sur la Civilisation de l'Europe Moderne, 1972).
78 Jacques Bertin, *Sémiologie graphique* (Paris, Gauthier-Villars, Mouton, 1967).
79 Jean-Pierre Bardet, Pierre Chaunu, Gabriel Désert, Pierre Gouhier, Hugues Neveux, *Le Bâtiment, enquête d'histoire économique, XIVe–XIXe siècle, I, Maisons rurales et urbaines dans la France traditionnelle* (Paris, Mouton, 1971).
80 P. Chaunu, 'Un nouveau champ pour l'histoire sérielle, le quantitatif au troisième niveau'.

81 Michel Vovelle, *Piété baroque et déchristianisation: attitudes provençales devant la mort au siècle des Lumières* (Paris, Plon, 1973).
82 François Lebrun, *Les Hommes et la mort en Anjou aux XVIIᵉ et XVIIIᵉ siècles: essai de démographie et de psychologie historiques* (Paris–The Hague, Mouton, 1971).
83 In the wake of Michel Vovelle's achievement in analysing some 50,000 of the 500,000 wills preserved in Provence for the years 1680 to 1790, Jean-Marie Gouesse has attempted something similar regarding the emergence of the phenomenon of the couple, by making a serial treatment of the hundreds of thousands of requests for a dispensation that have been preserved in the West.
84 I have tried to demonstrate this in my *Histoire science sociale – la durée, l'espace et l'homme à l'époque moderne* (Paris, SEDES, 1974).

3. Constructing Marxist history

PIERRE VILAR

The history business has one thing in common with selling soap powder: mere novelty in both can easily pass as innovation. The only difference is that our trade marks are not nearly so well protected. There is nothing to prevent anybody at all from calling himself a historian, nor from adding the qualification 'Marxist' if they want to. In fact anybody can call anything 'Marxist'.

History, however, is a difficult discipline, and true historians, particularly Marxist historians, are rare and exceptional. The word 'Marxist' ought properly to imply the rigorous application of a theoretically formulated method of analysis to the most complex areas of knowledge – men's social relationships and the nature of the ways in which they have changed. It is doubtful whether any historian has ever satisfactorily resolved the problems posed by this definition. As Ernest Labrousse was fond of saying, 'History is yet to be written', which is a notion both intimidating and salutary. Louis Althusser has added the reminder that the concept of history has yet to be constructed.

From a less ambitious perspective, however, I would argue that, in scientific practice as in life, the results of the dialogue between thought and action, theory and experience, are only recorded slowly. I would even maintain that the concept of history entertained by most contemporary historians (if we except M. Castelot) more closely resembles Marx's (or Ibn Khaldun's) version of it than that of Raymond Aron, which derives from Thucydides.

I have in mind here the rarely mentioned but important fact that the absurd objections that used to be advanced against Marx are scarcely ever heard now outside low-level polemic. Contemporary historians are not concerned with creating oppositions between terms like chance and necessity, freedom and determinism, or the individual and the masses (as Jacques Monod did in a recent attempt to revive the old debates), but with deploying the varying combinations of these terms. Of all the new modes of analysis, whether derived from linguistics, psychoanalysis or economics, not one is exempt from the fundamental hypothesis employed in the writing of history, namely that the material of history is both structured and thinkable, and as accessible to scientific inquiry as any other reality is.

This is what Marx had always said. When criticisms are made, moreover, they tend to be of a 'hypermaterialist' or 'anti-humanist' kind, and are therefore at the opposite pole to the former sorts of objection. These criticisms are nevertheless part and parcel of vulgar (or, if you prefer, dominant) ideology. The consequence of this is that some historians are more Marxist than they believe, while others are less Marxist than they imagine themselves to be.

It may be felt that, in these circumstances, history is an odd 'science'. Yet while it is true that it is still establishing itself as a science, all sciences are constantly in the process of establishing themselves. The notion of the 'epistemological threshold' is a useful one if it helps to distinguish between the ways successive constructions of the mind are rendered adequate to the structure of reality, but the phrase 'epistemological break' is dangerous if it suggests that there can be a sudden transition from 'non-science' to 'science'. Marx was well aware of this, which was why he scoured the distant past so intensely for the slightest anticipations of his own discovery, and why he did not consider that the possibility of earlier or partial scientific developments was less important than his own discovery:

Science, unlike other architects, builds not only castles in the air, but may construct separate habitable storeys of the building before laying the foundation stone.[1]

This sentence from the *Contribution to the Critique of Political Economy* should act as a reminder to all those who claim to date everything from Marx but who would probably prefer to see everything as dating from their own work, and therefore, having endowed the 'foundation stone' with almost magical powers, hasten to offer new justifications for building storeys in the air.

The problem as Marx saw it, and as it faces all those engaged in trying to cast light on the mechanisms of human society in the hope that they may one day be controllable, is to construct a science of society that is *coherent*, in that it has a solid, shared, theoretical schema; *total*, that is, able to include all useful areas of analysis within its jurisdiction; and *dynamic*, since, as no stability is eternal, the most important thing to discover is the principle of change.

1. Marx as historian

The obvious first question is to what extent Marx himself can be taken as the prototype of Marxist historians. Everybody knows that Marx liked to say he was not a Marxist, but it does not follow from that that giving Marx lessons in Marxism is not a risky thing to do. It is difficult to imagine him working as a historian and not conforming fairly closely to the norms of his own thought. The only valid question to be asked is whether he ever wanted to be a historian, and whether he ever set out to write a 'history'.

In the articles he poured out on current affairs, and in his correspondence,

Marx was continually writing 'history' in the ordinary sense of the word. He talks history, as he talks politics, with the sole purpose not of establishing certainties but of putting together clusters of probabilities which might, as they say nowadays, be operational. For Raymond Aron the historian's defining pleasure lies in 'giving the past the uncertainty of the future'; Marx, on the contrary, worked in the hope of reducing the extent of uncertainty in both. But he was not under the illusion that this already constituted a 'science'. It is obviously not enough to say that because somebody thinks correctly in political terms they are therefore thinking correctly in terms of history.

This is solely an empirical exercise, shifting repeatedly between example and reasoning, and it is the method historians and politicians have always used (though more often badly than well). When it has been handled with genius a few have acted effectively and a few others have put forward strong and convincing arguments. But such examples are rare. In Marx's case, his genius is beyond dispute; the problem is to know whether he went further than that.

The suggestion I should like to put forward, at the risk of being misunderstood, is that we should stop locating Marx's work as a historian solely in *The Class Struggle in France*, *The Eighteenth Brumaire*, and *The Civil War in France*, which is the current tendency, especially in France. These, rather than the less carefully thought out newspaper articles are, of course, the works that contain the high points of 'Marxist' reflection, bringing together as they do commentary on current affairs and events with acute observations on the structure of society. There can be no question of their exemplary importance for a type of analysis that I have defined as issuing in action, in the same way that every scientific analysis can and should result in action. But to write history in that way you have to be somebody like Lenin.

No analysis, however, can be written without a foundation in historical fact, and the professional historian, the indispensable, ordinary, everyday researcher who provides it, would come a cropper if he tried to write essays in that genre. On the other hand there is a great deal to be learned about the job itself from Marx's work as a whole, in particular even the parts the historian finds least accessible because (outwardly at least) they do not correspond to the traditional forms.

Let us take, as an example, Chapter 2 of the *Contribution*, which comes as he breaks off the first draft of what was to become *Capital*. He is concerned at this point, between his account of 'the commodity' and his explanation of 'capital', to clarify the role of money, the enigmatic intermediary. Marx has just concluded the previous chapter by setting out the four areas which, in the aftermath of Ricardo's work, call for immediate theoretical attention: wage-labour, capital, competition, and rent. Money is not included. Indeed, he begins the chapter on money with some ironic observations about the enormous number of lucubrations, all mistaken, to which the nature of money has given rise. From the outset, therefore, he appears to be avoiding any rigorous conceptualisation in this area. He refuses all those definitions that are no more than tautologies (such as that money is any means of payment), and he is aware that no partial definition will cover all the functions and forms of money, which he prefers to examine one by one. He remains undogmatic, not saying, for example, that money must be a commodity, but merely that 'The principal difficulty in the analysis of money is surmounted as soon as it is understood that the commodity is the origin of money.'[2]

Yet despite this reference to the origin of money, Marx rejects the classic pseudo-historical account pioneered by Aristotle, who ignores the real reasons for its development in favour of the simple logic of money's superior convenience over barter. And although one might then expect a scholarly account of the nature of primitive money and the transition to minted metal coins, Marx is very scornful of mere scholarship as soon as there is any risk of it being taken as explanation.

Finally, if one reads the beginning of the chapter, and the opening paragraphs of each of its sections, and then turns to the same chapter in a condensed form as it appears in *Capital*, one might be tempted to believe that Marx, writing as an economist, although not confining himself to abstraction and the pure logic of his hypotheses, likewise rejects a historical account as the source of his thinking, and therefore offers few lessons to the historian. But he anticipated this when he wrote:

Of course the method of presentation must differ *in form* from that of inquiry. The latter has to appropriate the material in detail, to analyse its different forms of development, to trace out their inner connection. *Only* after this work is done, can the actual moment be adequately described. If this is done successfully, if the life of the subject-matter is ideally reflected *as in a mirror*, then it may appear as if we had before us a mere *a priori* construction.[3] (The first and fourth emphases are Marx's, the other two are mine.)

There can be no doubt that the inquiry stage constitutes the work of a historian. And, I hasten to add, not merely superficial or second-hand work but direct absorption in the historical material. That applies to all those impatient Marxist literary critics and sociologists who are arrogantly disdainful of the 'empiricism' of historical work but base their own (lengthy) analyses on a (sketchy) historical knowledge gleaned from two or three textbooks. At the other extreme, Marx sometimes writes for twenty pages without alluding to history, although the writing itself may be the product of twenty years historical research. It is nonetheless necessary to be aware of that historical perspective and that means being a historian.

So in order to deal with the problems of money in 1859, Marx not only examines the monetary aspects of the 1857 crisis in the light of the specialist works produced in 1858, and the most recent numbers of *The Economist*, he also looks at the rival arguments of Plato and Aristotle, Xenophon and Pliny. It is neither academic history nor journalism. Marx was deeply involved in the life and culture of his own time, but every stage in the long history of money fascinated him. He was an enthusiastic observer of the debates in Parliament in 1844 and 1845 on the Bank Acts, and was familiar with all the arguments about currency principles and banking principles. He read Fullerton and Torrens, admired Tooke's *History of Prices*, devoured both good and bad writing on economics (he never gave vent to his sometimes ferocious criticism before he had read a book very attentively), and followed the dispute back to its source in Bosanquet and Thornton, as well as in Ricardo. He was then able to grasp, and to demonstrate, exactly what it was that linked the monetary events in England between 1797 and 1821 with those between 1680 and 1720; and the debate between Locke and Lowndes sent him back to Petty and Child, and forward to Berkeley, Steuart and Hume. As far as seventeenth- and eighteenth-century England is concerned he read everything, and read it in contemporary texts. Nor did he confine himself to England. He knew Vaubon and Boisguilbert, and he defines one of the possible forms of monetary inflation by means of a brief reference to *assignats*. Custodi's anthology made available the Italian economists, Carli, Verri, Montanari and Galiani (whom he justifiably preferred). For sixteenth-century attitudes to money he cites Luther, but also Pedro Martyr and the Cortes of Castile. He read old treatises on the German and Bohemian mines. He knew about the mediaeval handling of money. And although he made fun of those who tried to discover the ideal form of money in Barbary or in Angola (his principal accusation in fact was that they did not know what they were talking about), he himself had found out about Inca accountancy systems and Chinese paper money.

Marx did not, of course, approach all this material for its own sake, 'historically', so to speak. It almost entirely disappears when he comes to write the chapter on money in *Capital*. And as far as *Capital* as a whole is concerned, whether or not the history in *Theories of Surplus Value* was intended to form part of it or not, it is conventional (too conventional even) to follow the famous hint in the Preface and acknowledge that 'historical facts' are only referred to as 'illustrations'.

2. Economic theory and history: Althusser's critique

This brings us to a central problem, the relationship between historical knowledge and economic knowledge, between historical research and the economist's attitude to theory.

Althusser himself, although he stresses the purely philosophical (i.e. theoretical) nature of his intentions, also considers what he writes about to be of interest to historians and economists. And in fact it certainly does concern both them and the legitimacy of their disciplines when Marx is enthusiastically acclaimed as the first to uncover the scientific foundations of these disciplines and yet at the same time respectfully but firmly shown to have been incapable of knowing it, let alone saying it.

This is another one of those cases where the word 'new' is used with a special emphasis, as in 'new quantitative history' or the 'New Economic History'; the fact that in Marx's case there is a hundred-year time-lag is apparently irrelevant precisely because a hundred years ago his novelty was so 'new' that even he himself failed to grasp it. I imagine this must mean that it responded too soon to criteria suggested to the philosopher by recent 'histories of knowledge'.

Scientific knowledge must be, like Caesar's wife, above suspicion first, of ideology, and second, of empiricism. Althusser easily demonstrates (though unfortunately by allusion rather than by recourse to examples) that non-Marxist economists, empirical in their reliance on concrete examples, on 'historical facts', have simply elevated naive anthropology into a theory. And, just as easily (although still by allusion), he shows that historians, with their traditional concern for the 'precise' facts or their pride in full-blown reconstructions of the past, have never constructed theoretically the object of their knowledge, particularly time, which they have treated as a simple, linear, 'datum'.

This is not yet the place to consider the elements in Althusser's powerful contribution to the creation of a Marxist science that are constructive and useful to historians. At this point it is just as helpful to distinguish the limitations of an approach which rather too readily demolishes the 'habitable storeys' which have developed at the various stages of scientific advance, none of which should be treated as god-given but which Marx dealt with rather more circumspectly.

A basic concern for consistency must prompt anyone, whether they are Marxists or not, to ask Althusser a preliminary question. If he accepts the foundations of a critique of knowledge derived from Marx, if he suspects any construction that does not fit in with it of being 'precritical', 'empirical' or 'ideological', if he is entitled to be equally suspicious of Marx, inasmuch as he did not complete his intellectual revolution, then why can he not be as scrupulous when it is a question of what he calls 'the studies of the history of knowledge we now have at our disposal' (he leaves us to guess which he means, but that is not difficult) or the 'adequate philosophical training' which, according to him, a productive reading of Marx requires? This reminds me of the attitude of economists like Joan Robinson, who are certainly willing to 'read Marx', but only in the light of an 'adequate economic training', which of course turns out to be their own. I hope I shall not be misunderstood here; I am not protesting in the name of Marxism about the *ignorance* of 'modern' economists or epistemologists. It just seems to me that fidelity to Marx is not guaranteed by searching through *Capital* for signs of Foucault or anticipations of Keynes, but rather by approaching Keynes or Foucault with the habitual scepticism that Marx himself would have brought to them.

As for economics, Althusser apparently knows the subject so well that he can treat the greatest of the early classical economists and the most learned modern econometrists with equal scorn. This, it must be said, is a bit much. On the other hand, he is prepared to borrow from the 'histories of knowledge' the theories of a 'philosophy' charged, he says, with watching over dialectical materialism as Lenin did in the years after 1900 during the crisis in physics. But Lenin's attack was directed not at the physicists but at their interpreters, and one wonders, to say the least, what he might have had to say about some of the current trends in epistemology, which have for several decades tried constantly to replace all dialectic with neo-scholasticism, set up an anti-humanist neo-positivism against Marx's consistent sense of purpose, and which erect an anti-historicist, neo-idealist structuralism in opposition to what Althusser rightly recognises as a 'theory of history'. That is not to mention, either, the criticisms of empiricism or common sense, which although they are nominally made in a scientific spirit choose to base themselves on individual psychoanalysis without taking account of the existence of class, of class struggle, and its illusions.

A Marxist study of these trends ought to put both historians and philosophers to the test. They are evidence of the (existential) ideological reaction of a threatened class. Each spontaneous 'anti-historicism', each 'critique of historical reason' is eagerly grasped as the antidote to Marx's true discovery, the historical critique of reason.

I am quite prepared to admit, indeed I will go further than Althusser and say that it seems self-evident, that the object constructed by Marx in *Capital* is a theoretical object. I admit that it does not help to confuse thought with reality, nor reality with thought; that thought only has a 'relation of knowledge' to reality (what else could it have?); that the process of knowledge takes place entirely in thought (where on earth else could it take place?); and that there is an order and a hierarchy of 'generalities' on which Althusser has made observations of major importance.

But I cannot quite see, I confess, what 'astounding' sin Engels can really have committed by writing (merely as an image, in a letter, and so quite off the cuff) that conceptual thought progressed 'asymptotically' to reality, when according to Althusser the law of value, in connection with which Engels used the image, 'is, in fact, a concept perfectly adequate to its object, since it is the concept of the limits of its variation and therefore the adequate concept of the field of its inadequacy.'[4]

This subtlety indicates the real difficulty we encounter, as we define our proceedings or carry out our research, in not 'falling into empiricism' by keeping too close to the object described, too close to our 'example'. But only a razor's edge separates the two pitfalls of empiricism and idealism. Anybody who abhors examples, or dwells too much on 'that holy of holies, the concept' (an expression I came across in a recent 'Althusserian' work on the idea of economic law in Marx) risks being 'precipitated' (or catapulted) into a world that is no longer Marxist. For if we are to 'hear the silences' in

Marx's 1857 *Introduction*, we shall have to be careful not to silence these words:

The totality as a conceptual entity seen by the intellect is a product of the thinking intellect which assimilates the world in the only way open to it, a way which differs from the artistic, religious and practically intelligent assimilation of this world. The concrete subject remains outside the intellect and independent of it – that is so long as the intellect adopts a purely speculative, purely theoretical attitude. The subject, society, must always be envisaged therefore as the pre-condition of comprehension even when the theoretical method is employed.[5]

This contains the essence of Marx's thought. The world only remains 'independent' as long as the mind stays 'speculative'. *The subject is society*. The theoretician only 'assimilates' it if it is always 'envisaged'.

Althusser argues that in the *Introduction* (which is unfortunately one of those works which people only remember selectively) Marx failed to distinguish the proper hierarchy of abstraction. But in this passage Marx does indicate different ways of 'assimilating the world': the empirical mode ('the practical intelligence'), the religious mode (myths and cosmogonies), and the artistic mode (which Bachelard, Foucault and even Althusser make ample use of). The scientific mode grows out of these, and is also different from them. It grows out of them, since it could not exist without 'the practical intelligence' ('technology'), and it gradually 'corrects' cosmogonies and traditions. But it is also different from them, and it is here that any serious work in epistemology can be of help in indicating the 'thresholds' between types of knowledge. On the other hand, merely to describe one abstraction as 'good' and another as 'bad' (as Ricoeur did with 'subjectivities'), sets one just by the choice of vocabulary on the slippery path towards philosophical dogmatism, and a tendency for the slightest distraction to lead to ill-considered ideological condemnations.

This quarrel between empirical observation and theoretical construction is not, in the end, very different from the *Methodenstreit* between the 'historical school' and the mathematical economists, which was contemporary with Engels's controversy with Schmidt and has close affinities with it. And if this debate now appears cut-and-dried, superseded, it is only so in relation to Althusser's definition of the 'new', which of course reflects the current imagery of theoretical objects, combinatory patterns and logical matrices. So that if what was innovative in Marx's work, which did indeed prefigure all that, had done nothing else besides, then there would be a strong argument for saying that the most recent trends in economic science represent the full expression of Marx's discoveries. Their response to hackneyed objections about the gap between their model and reality, and about reality's unfathomable 'richness', is to offer the same defence as Althusser does (most justifiably) of Marx, that different 'objects' are in question. For them, the utility/scarcity approach is a theoretical model adequate to its object. What is more, modern macro-economists now take the argument much further from the same premisses; their operative concept 'the formation of capital' is simply another name for 'surplus value'. Some economists even go so far as to say that this indicates the belated triumph of Marx's discoveries.

Despite their assertions, however, it would clearly not be 'Marxist' to accede to this line of argument, since the essence of Marx's discovery is neither economic, nor theoretical, but socio-historical. It lies in the unveiling of the social contradiction involved in the free, unfettered formation of surplus value ('accumulation of capital'), and in the coherent ensemble of the mode of production which ensures it and which is characterised by it.

3. The mode of production and the unity of history

At this point we can return to Althusser. The central concept in Marx, the coherent whole, the theoretical object, is indeed the mode of production, as determining and determinate structure. But its originality does not lie in its being a theoretical object but in its having been – and having remained – the first theoretical object to express a social whole, whereas the first attempts at theory in the social sciences were confined to economics, and saw social relations either as immutable data (as the physiocrats saw the ownership of land) or as ideal conditions to be fulfilled (as in liberalism's view of juridical freedom and equality). The second original quality of the mode of production is that it is a working, developing structure which is neither precise nor static. The third is that the structure itself implies the (economic) principle of (social) contradiction, bringing with it the necessity of its destruction as a structure, or its 'destructuration'.

If, on the other hand, this proposition is accepted it prevents non-Marxist theory from being dismissed out of hand, which would clearly be an absurd thing to do. In fact it seems perfectly well able to exist as theory, not given scientific status by any except its own adherents (and Althusser), and at the same time be an ideology, not because of inconsistency or empiricism, but because it claims universal application for what are only the laws of one sphere (the economic) in one particular mode of production (capitalism).

Yet this is precisely the criticism Marx made of Ricardo's formulations, which Althusser deems inadequate, but which in fact is exemplary. We can and must recognise and make use of intellectual genius and the logic of systems, provided we can be clear about three things: first, the logical field in which the hypotheses are applicable; second, the thresholds which bourgeois theorists cannot cross without repudiating their own basic assumptions (thresholds that Walras, Keynes and Schumpeter saw very clearly); and third, the practical areas which, rather than demonstrating the gap between the model and reality (which is a factor in all knowledge), will show the true limits of the scope of the theory under consideration, in this case modifications in the structure of capitalism, socio-political problems, treatment of pre-capitalist societies, and the historical appearance of different kinds of socialism.

This is where the need for a historical approach is most crucial if we wish, as Marx liked to say, to 'understand the facts'. In that way, we can come to understand how a theory, because it is partial, in that it only expresses one level of one mode of production, yet claims to be universal, can be both a practical and an ideological tool in the hands of one class and for a specific period of time.

The period of time has admittedly to be constructed, since it consists of alternations between failures and successes, and between pessimism and optimism. It alternates in fact between moments when the existence of profit seems to camouflage the real nature of things, and moments when the true state of affairs, the extraction of surplus value, can be intensely felt, even though it may not be perceived in the next period of expansion when it reappears under the name of investment or as the basis of expanded reproduction. The most important thing to grasp, however, is the existence of the factors which, because they are part of an unquestioned hypothesis, are permanently camouflaged. For the physiocrats, this was the ownership of land; for the capitalist mode of production it is both the private ownership of the means of production and the fixing of values through the market.

Given these 'relations of production', it is possible to theorise effectively at the economic level, throwing light at the same time upon 'economic history' in the countries and periods where these relations are in fact dominant. But this is precisely why the would-be Marxist historian should not confine himself to 'economic history', save for the empirical study of individual instances. I have said before that I am convinced that so-called 'quantitative history' is no more than retrospective econometrics, and that I do not believe that the 'New Economic History' deserves to be called cliometry. For, as Colin Clark admits, history is higher than economics in the hierarchy of the sciences because it includes it. To which I should add, following Marx, and also because it cannot be divided up.

One reason why I feel strongly about this is that for me it has always represented the meeting point of Marx and Lucien Febvre. The major weakness of history as Febvre saw it, in his time, and which he fought particularly hard to combat, was the widespread respect for 'watertight compartments' in academic work, with one person studying economics, one politics, another ideas, and so on. So I must confess to being amazed and disappointed when I saw that Althusser's proposals about the 'Marxist conception of social totality' concluded by talking not only of the 'possibility' of returning to the division of history into a number of separate 'histories', but even of the 'necessity' for it.

If anything savours of empiricism it is this notion of plural 'histories'. For where the status of history as real knowledge is concerned it gives credence to all the traditional claims of specialists to know best. And as far as social practice is concerned – and this is a tragedy for the building of socialism – it forces the separate worlds of science, economic technocracy, politics, ideas, and art to exist each at their own 'level' and at their own 'tempo'. While at the same time, beneath the surface, spontaneous processes harmonise and unite these different 'tempi'.

When the 'specific dependence' of these levels on each other has been positively stated in Althusser's previous paragraph, I refuse to join him in asserting the relative independence of their histories. We all know what happens to clever phrases like 'independence in interdependence' when the meaning of the two terms is not fixed. We may conclude that our task should be to fix what they mean, but the example that (for once) Althusser offers fails to reassure us about the purpose, from a Marxist point of view, of distinguishing all these 'histories'.

It is an example concerned with the history of philosophy. Philosophers, we are told, follow one another chronologically. This sequence, however, does not constitute the history of philosophy. Who would wish to disagree with that? There are no works or textbooks that still confuse the two, though perhaps some might just as well. A dictionary is always useful, but it does not contain every single construction. But how are we to know what 'history' is?

For Althusser, a rigorous definition of the historical requires that three different sorts of condition be met. It must be defined philosophically (i.e. theoretically); its own 'peculiar time' must be identified; its 'differential relations' and its 'peculiar articulations' with the other levels must be located.

This is all very well, but he wishes to elicit what he believes to be a 'rigorous' definition of 'facts' or 'events' from one particular 'relatively autonomous' history. The 'philosophical fact' is that which 'causes a real mutation in the existing . . . theoretical problematic'. The 'historical fact' is that which 'causes a mutation in the existing structural relations'. He even speaks of 'philosophical events of historic scope', which demonstrates that the language of theory suffers from the persistent weight of the sensationalised treatment of 'naively gathered' history.[6]

4. Events, breaks, and historic process

In fact there are no events that are not, in one sense, anecdotal. Even when figures of the stature of Spinoza or Marx appear, they possess 'scope' (except in the eyes of idealist history) only in terms of the period, however close or distant, when their ideas are taken up. Until that point it is actually the *repression* of those ideas which constitutes their history.

We may wonder, then, whether 'structural relations' have ever been changed by 'a fact'. Even the most conscious of revolutions has only changed them imperfectly. And this is even more true of technology. Papin 'sees' the power of steam, and Watt harnesses it, but his 'innovation' must be 'established' in order to be a true 'productive force'. And there are a number of factors that should be taken into acount. Where is the 'break'?

The dealers in sensation will go on multiplying 'events', the latest moon-landing or the newest barricades providing 'historic facts' which are all the rage for a day or two. The task of the theorist, of course, is to choose between them. But by what criteria? The housewife who does not want to pay ten francs for a kilo of French beans, or who cannot afford to, is acting as 'historically' as one who does pay that price; so is the conscript who responds to the call of his class, and the conscript who refuses. Conjunctures depend on them. They either reinforce or undermine structures. The only possible basis for a materialist history is the objectification of the subjective through statistics, however imperfect the interpretation of them may be; only in that way will it be a history of masses, aware both of mass facts to do with the infrastructure, and of the human 'masses' that theory needs to 'penetrate' if it is to become a force.

One is led to wonder whether theorists of the concept of history have been attacking such an outdated notion of history that they have become imprisoned by it, first parcelling history out among 'specialists', and then looking for 'historical facts' and 'events'. Events are of course important, especially the manner in which they fit, naturally or by chance, into a sequence, but Marxist historians, even if they are uneasy about the reaction against the importance of events which has transformed history during the last forty years, will not abandon the basic assumptions they share with Marx. It is impossible to compromise, even in the choice of words, with myths like 'the days that made France' or 'the days that shook the world'. At the end of Eisenstein's *October* somebody says, 'The revolution is over.' But we know that it was only just beginning.

The difficulty cannot be evaded by extending the meaning of the word 'event', especially when the idea of the 'break' has been suggested by the word 'mutation'. Science and theory both suffer from their vocabulary these days, with esoteric words invented for quite commonplace ideas and familiar names used to designate esoteric subject matter. Words like 'event' or 'time series' pass into the language of mathematics as historians become suspicious of them, and genes can be said to make decisions when heads of state only have the illusion of making them. 'Overdetermination' and 'effect of an absent cause' are both terms drawn from the vocabulary of psychoanalysis, just as 'mutation' is taken from biology.

It is questionable, however, whether a word created for one structure is appropriate to all. Marx and Engels were certainly not happy with that sort of comparison. In Schumpeter's words, Marx did not just link economics and history in a mechanical way, he created a 'chemical' mixture of them. I have always found this image attractive, having learned long ago, at school, that in a mixture the substances remain separate, while in a combination a new sub-stance is formed (in this case, the Marxist totality). But I am not sure how valuable such a comparison is for modern science, nor what I can learn from it about the job of the historian. Balibar would like to replace the word 'combination' with 'combinatory', but he never quite goes that far, always qualifying it, as in 'pseudo-combinatory', 'almost a combinatory', or 'by no means a combinatory in the strict sense'.

If, therefore, I decide – as Marx is still 'new' – to use his terms where they exist and to create new ones where necessary, but without borrowing from other sciences which cannot speak on behalf of history, history could surely be constructed quite adequately.

It is no more possible to provide a satisfactory explanation of the nature of history in terms of theory alone than in purely practical terms. Yet one can try to do it, as Marx did, by a twofold absorption in 'making one's own' a complicated matter which always demands a certain amount of theory, and in 'constructing' the object of thought which corresponds to it, which simultaneously demands detachment from the material and 'envisaging' it. There should be no research without theory, and philosophers are quite justified in being irritated by historians' lack of attention to it. But by the same token there should be no theory without research, or theorists will very quickly be accused, as the economists recently were, of dealing in nothing but 'empty boxes'.

On closer inspection, in fact, the boxes may turn out not to be so empty as they appear, because historians are less empiricist than they seem to be. Rather than getting pleasure out of making negative critical pronouncements – which is well and truly part of the ideological trap – it would probably be more sensible to take account of the progress historians have made, just as it would be more scientific to attempt, as historians, to make a historical evaluation of Marxism, not considered in the light of our own political preferences or our moral imperatives, but 'thought' as a phenomenon to be resituated in time.

5.   Is historians' time 'linear'?

In the discussion of 'historical time' Althusser refers to two equally dangerous pitfalls, 'homogeneous and continuous' time, which is the time of common sense and historical research, and Hegelian time, with its 'essential sections' and 'historical present', the continuity of time and the unity of the moment. Taking the latter first, there is surely no historian who could be so unhistorical as to accept the 'absolute horizons' that have started reappearing in philosophy; and, for the former, when it is in terms of thousandths of a second it is the time-scale physicists use, and as tenths of a second it is time as used in sport. Time as it is actually lived is measured in days and nights, winters and summers, seed-time and harvest, fat cattle and lean cattle, the intervals between births and expectations of death. There is much to learn about differential temporalities from historical demography. A man of seventy does not see time in the same way as a man of thirty, any more than time in the Caribbean is the same as Eskimo time.

I would even go so far as to say that it is traditional history that 'constructed' time. The old annals, even the school chronologies, with their events, their reigns and their periods, all constitute an ideological construction, but not a 'homogeneous' one. Indeed when that concern for chronology became critical of its subject matter, look how many myths it demolished and how many texts it demystified. That process too is part of the 'history of knowledge', part of the 'production of knowledges'.

Dating for its own sake is merely a tool of scholarship, albeit a useful one. The full complexities of dating remain the task of historians. An awareness of sequences in time and the scale of different durations is very different indeed from simple data. It does not emerge out of nature and myths, but is formed in opposition to them. And yet Althusser ends by identifying the concept of history with the concept of a time, as if he had never realised the full meaning of the term 'chrono-logy'.

On the other hand, having read Hegel, he sets too much store by the term 'periodisation', when he writes:

On this level, then, the whole problem of the science of history would consist of the division of this continuum according to a *periodisation* corresponding to the succession of one dialectical totality after another. The moments of the Idea exist in the number of historical *periods* into which the time continuum is to be accurately divided. In this Hegel was merely thinking in his own theoretical problematic the number one problem of the historian's practice, the problem Voltaire, for example, expressed when he distinguished between the age of Louis XIV and the age of Louis XV; it is still the major problem of modern historiography.[7]

Let us say that after it has freed chronology from myths, history tends spontaneously to systematise it. It is strange that it should be criticised for this. Ever since just after the French Revolution, the French school has been trying to get to grips with the concept of social class; and the division of history into the periods of antiquity, middle ages, modern, and contemporary worlds, represents the sequence of the three dominant modes of production, with the modern period corresponding to the preparation for the third through the triumph of the mercantile economy. It is Eurocentric, badly conceptualised, naively divided by the 'mutation-events' so dear to Althusser such as 1492 and 1789. Yet it is nonetheless reassuring in the light of the anticipated convergence of practical 'approaches' and the 'constructions' of theory.

It is true that Marx, in *Capital*, gives us a 'construction of time', for economics, 'a complex and non-linear time – a time of times' that cannot be read on the clock of everyday life, but which fits each properly conceptualised operation such as labour, production or the turnover of various sorts of capital. But people often affect not to perceive his discovery. Despite this, modern economists might seem to have taken this construction of the time of capitalism as far as it will go, so that once again if their work was based on, and included, the real discovery of Marx we could say that it was here perfected and superseded.

But Marx's discovery is missing from their analyses. It consists in showing that 'turnovers', and 'cycles' (and of course 'revolutions', despite various plays on the two meanings of the word) never come back to their point of departure but create new situations, not only in the economy, but in the social whole.

Here is the difficulty which the philosophers seize upon. It is quite meaningless to speak (as I was once unwise enough to do) of 'creative time'. Lévi-Strauss proposes 'cumulative history' and 'hot history', but as a way of avoiding the problem. It is not easy to put a name to whatever it is that makes the new emerge from the old.

The physicist may make fun of it, and the biologist may be reduced to philosophising, but their materials do not change with the rhythm of human lives. The historian's field is change, not only at the level of individual 'instances' but at the level of structures. Any temptation a historian might feel to identify stabilities would be an ideological one, stemming from his distress at change. For there is nothing one can do: people in society, apart from a few isolated groups who will not survive very much longer, do not still live as they did in pre-history, a word whose very coinage argues a more complex history of the concept of history than Althusser's version admits. 'Historical time' spans six thousand years or more; our own horizon reaches back several centuries, and our economics and our science has an ancestry of two or three hundred years. The *longue durée* is not very long. It is the medium time, between *longue durée* and 'event', which is the enigma.

Althusser does admit that 'a few historians are beginning to pose these questions', even adding 'in a very remarkable way'. But, he goes on to say, they are content to observe 'that there exist' long, medium and short time-scales, and to note their interferences as products of their intersections rather than as products of the whole that governs them, the mode of production. A ten-line critique, with three names mentioned in parentheses (those of Febvre, Labrousse and Braudel) is hardly an adequate basis on which to situate contemporary 'historical practice' either in relation to the historical period, or in relation to Marx.

My impression is, quite honestly, that Althusser only mentions these historians out of a sense of scruple. His criticism is aimed at all historiography from its beginnings to practically every historian living. This is not an entirely unjustifiable attitude. It implies a large-scale inquiry, which would certainly be very welcome, into the place occupied in class and national culture – from academic history to televised sport – by what Althusser grandiloquently terms 'the elegant sequences of the official chronicle, in which a discipline or a society merely reflect its good conscience, i.e. the mask of its bad conscience'.[8] But that calls for an inquiry on a world scale. And there would also have to be a more difficult one to discover the final place of a 'true history' and the sites where it might be established, if, indeed, it could be defined in the first place and could actually be written. On this point Althusser's hopes on the subject of the construction of historical time, and of a construction in the sense that Marx intended, differ from my own. I shall explain my reasons for this by discussing the work of the three historians mentioned by Althusser, and on the basis of my own experiences. I am, however, fully aware that this is a very narrow foundation for the two questions I want to examine, namely what was, and is, the historical role of history as ideology; and what the present, and possible future, roles of history as science are.

A. Michel Foucault or Lucien Febvre? The time-scales of knowledge

The one historian who prompts Althusser to write positively for a page is Foucault, whom he sees as the discoverer of a 'true history', containing nothing that allows it to be read in the ideological continuum of a linear time-scale that just needs to be divided up, and as the discoverer of 'completely unexpected temporalities' and 'new logics'; an effort, in short, not *of* abstraction but *in* abstraction, that has constructed an object of history by identifying it, and from this constructed the concept of *its* history.

If at the time he wrote that, Althusser only knew Foucault through *Madness and Civilisation* and *The Birth of the Clinic* I would be prepared to share his enthusiasm. Yet if there has to be a 'peculiar time' for each 'cultural formation' of this type, when will the time of the whole be? Even when I first read Foucault's work I had an uncomfortable sense of being shut in, appropriate enough to the subject but also a consequence of its demarcation. My feeling was that this sense of discomfort was Marxist.

Since then, in a series of major works, Foucault has generalised a method which shows his weaknesses to better advantage than his strengths. He starts by asserting hypotheses, and, in the course of the proofs that follow, any reader with some knowledge of the subject soon discovers muddled dates, texts chosen to fit the argument, and such obvious lacunae that one is forced to believe that they are deliberate, and, most disturbingly, historical misconceptions. But, above all, when he has unveiled the *episteme*, Foucault is quite prepared to replace it without warning, not with concepts which he has constructed (which one would congratulate him for) but with his own set of images. Althusser writes of Michelet's 'delirium'; all in all, Foucault's talent is not dissimilar. Yet if historians had to choose between the two, they would opt for Michelet.

Lucien Febvre seems to me to be much closer to Marx. Yet Althusser treats him as one of the assemblers of 'linear time', with no proper conception of history as a whole. Nothing could be further from the truth. It would be absurd to number him among the propagators of elegant official sequences, since nobody has done more than him to demolish them. Taking everything else into account, I cannot think of a better place than his work to look for 'unexpected temporalities' 'antipodal to the empirically visible history' and 'the identified objects of history'. Unbelievers are surely as valuable as objects of history as madmen are, and 'mental capital equipment' cannot be without use for the 'production of knowledges'.

It is characteristic of our time that Althusser, in his discussion of history, should mention Lucien Febvre in passing, after condemning Michelet and praising Foucault, as one of those 'beginning to pose questions'. We are all so worried about communication that we are only capable of hearing one kind of language, that of our training, our 'formation'. It is no coincidence that we attribute so many closed 'cultures' to the past. It would be very useful to discover what other periods of crisis in the past have shared a similar concern for compartmentalisation.

Febvre's writings on the sixteenth century certainly do not reveal a closed period. Luther, Lefèvre, Marguerite d'Angoulême, Rabelais, des Périers, are all disclosed to the precise extent allowed by the cohesion of the 'overdetermin-ing' whole. Yet 'it does move'. Just as 'a revolutionary epoch cannot be judged in terms of its own consciousness of itself', so historians have to establish their view against the ideology of their own time and their own teachers. Febvre's success is due to his approach to sixteenth-century society, 'making it his own' at every level and 'envisaging' it all the time by means of research which was concrete but not empirical, systematised as it is by his struggle for the problematic against historicist positivism, for the mass fact against the mere point of detail, and for true scrupulousness against pseudo-scholarship. It is a struggle that frequently strikes a note reminiscent of Marx in a bad mood.

'True history' therefore can emerge from a practice and a critique, not because of some affected 'rigour', but out of a correctness to be seen in the complete absence of misconceptions. Febvre never considered himself to be either a theorist or a Marxist, yet he would never have imprisoned Marx in the nineteenth century in the way Foucault does, in passing, in *The Order of Things*.

B. Structure and conjuncture: the time-spans of Labrousse

Ernest Labrousse's more obvious kinship with Marxism is not enough to warrant different treatment by Althusser, who seems to be aiming his criticism at all conjunctural history. Yet the criticism seems ill-judged when he is seen to take no account at all of the long line of commentators, from Vico to Kondratieff, from Moore to Akerman, from Levasseur to Hamilton (or to Simiand, if we wish to keep the focus on France) who have claimed that their observation of indices casts light on the relationship between cycles and development, and between natural time, economic time and historical time; and that, after all, is the question at issue.

The real difficulty here comes when we have to consider whether the question was posed in terms of time in the 'ordinary' sense, or in terms of the time of the Marxist 'whole', the 'mode of production'. As a result of their mode of presentation, premature commentary, and popularisation in schools, conjunctural historians often appear to be saying that history is a product of time (which is meaningless) rather than that time (in its non-homogeneous distribution, its differential forms) is a product of history (or the moving set of social relations within structures). A Marxist objection has already been advanced against that notion by Boris Porchnev, but his important survey mistakenly extends the criticism to include Labrousse's work. There is therefore a need for a closer definition of the relationship between the conjunctural and the Marxist approach.

Marx himself can be of assistance in this. If we consider various factors, such as his assessment of the boom of the 1850s ('the new stage of development which this society seemed to have entered after the discovery of gold in California'),[9] the hopes he shared with Engels at each capitalist crisis (a forgivable naivety in a man of action), the frequent references to the long economic boom which, after the discovery of America, became the take-off ramp for bourgeois societies, the interest he showed in Tooke's *History of Prices*, his criticism of Hume for constructing arguments about the monetary economy of the ancient world without any basis in statistics, and, finally, his systematic analysis of the 'cycle', which is far more 'modern' than is often realised, then these all make it impossible to present Marx as an opponent of conjunctural history, any more than conjunctural history can be seen as innovative in relation to Marx. What should really be compared are the theoretical foundations that underlie the various approaches, and their sometimes hasty historical conclusions.

Observation of the real rhythms of economic activity must start from a strict conceptualisation of what is being observed. There has been too much unsystematic examination of nominal prices here and silver prices there, volume of production here and market rating there, or long term here and short term there, without adequate examination of which was the index and which the object, and what theory linked one to the other. I long ago criticised Hamilton for having confused, over the long term, the formation of capital with the gap between nominal prices and unit wages (which does not mean that Marx was unaware of the category 'profits of inflation'). A concept, or a standard, is only valid for one period; I still do not agree, despite Marczewski (and Fourastié), that there is any point in trying to discover the 1970 equivalent of a 1700 income, because in the end, by eliminating one movement in order to isolate others, one creates a statistical mirage. There are also traps in 'construction'.

This is why the most classic cyclical movements can be contested, and one needs only read Imbert to gauge the dearth of theory in the face of Kondratieff. The medium time-span has not been mastered, as we can see from the monetary crisis, whereas, since the failure of Harvard empiricism, capitalism has been able to control the intradecanal cycle, and there are some who would like to jettison it altogether. But as the economic time-span of a long stage in the mode of production, it forms a part of the corresponding historical time-span. There is no way out of the conjunctural labyrinth for the historian.

Nor does Althusser offer any clear help to anybody taking Marx as their guide. Replacing 'varieties' with 'variations' and 'interferences' with 'inter-twinings' is no more than a verbal change if there are no examples in support of it; and if *Capital* only contains economic time-spans, what are we to do about 'differential temporalities' and the other 'levels'? The question has been anticipated:

we must regard these differences in temporal structure as *and only as* so many objective indices of the mode of articulation of the different elements or structures in the general structure of the whole . . . it is only in the specific unity of the complex structure of the whole that we can think the concept of these so-called backwardnesses, forwardnesses, survivals and unevennesses of development which *co-exist* in the structure of the real historical present; the present of the *conjuncture*.[10]

The structure-conjuncture seems here to have become a blueprint in the practice of history, which guarantees nothing in itself but which is as far removed from quantitative empiricism as it is from those traditional 'elegant sequences'.

The place where this 'break' between the conjunctural economism of Simiand and a structural conjuncturalism closer to Marx occurs, is in the work of Ernest Labrousse. What can Labrousse tell us about 'temporalities'?

If one were simply to present the following argument, it would seem very mechanistic: the French Revolution develops out of an 'encounter' between a long time-scale (economic growth in the eighteenth century), a medium time-scale (the intercycle of depression between 1774 and 1788), and a short time-scale (the critically high prices of 1789, which culminate almost too neatly in the *seasonal* crisis of July). It appears merely mechanistic in that it is putting forward a simple set of linear time-scales as a causal sequence. But that is not all there is to it.

The statistically observable 'short cycle' which provides the rhythm of economic *and social* reality in eighteenth-century France is in fact the original cycle of the feudal mode of production in which agriculture is still the basis of production, but where the basic techniques of production no longer govern the stochastic cycle of production; in which taxes on producers *ought* to be adjusted according to production; and where charity and price-fixing *ought*, in a bad year, to mitigate the worst hardship.

But from the eighteenth century onwards this pre-capitalist 'tempo' coexists with others which, while not yet typical of the future mode of production in the way the 'industrial cycle' will be, share some of its characteristics and pave the way for it. First, there is a long period of primitive accumulation of money-capital, which is directly or indirectly of colonial origin, which creates a money-bourgeoisie and embourgeoisifies a section of the nobility; second, there is the possibility in the medium term of trade depressions (market crises, falling prices) which affects and unsettles a growing number of farmers, landowners and businessmen, whose products are now entering the commercial circuit and becoming 'commodities', in consequence of which they tend to become interested in equal rights, a free market, and the end of feudal structures; and finally the short-term exasperation of the 'old-style crisis', less deadly than in times of famine, but occurring when speculation and scarcity, no longer held at bay by official price-fixing and redistribution by the Church, pauperises and proletarianises more than ever, setting the poor peasants in opposition simultaneously to feudal levies, royal taxes and free trade.

This encounter of 'specific temporalities' issues, in July and August of 1789, in the 'event' which overturns the whole judicial and political structure of society, and there could scarcely be a better example of the 'intertwining of times' in the form of the 'process of development of a mode of production', or even in this case the process of transition from one mode to another.

I realise that Althusser, in addition to his professional interest in scientific and philosophical time, has a quite legitimate concern about the current usage of terms like 'backwardnesses', 'forwardnesses', 'survivals' and 'unevennesses of development', and that by prefacing these words (when he was defining 'conjuncture') with an ironic 'so-called', he wished to emphasise the absurdity (and the ideological danger) of a terminology which, in its implications of models and ends, has something, as he says, of the air of a railway timetable. And there is a certain amount of support for this impression in the graphs that statistical yearbooks like to print, with their network of lines indicating dollars per capita, investment rates, or the number of scientific journals published, down which some countries seem to take the high speed train while others potter down a branch line.

Although this is fair criticism of the verbal bragging of economies and ruling classes, and of the distorted image that some quantitative criteria provide, we should not let it make us forget certain essential Marxist principles, such as the primacy of the industrial–economic synthesised in the productivity of labour; the necessity for quantification in order to avoid inexact descriptions; and the major reality constituted by inequalities of material development. Marx always 'envisaged' the forwardness of England and the assets of the United States, and Lenin always kept hold of the concept of 'uneven development'. It is not sufficient to condemn linear time-scales, we must be able to escape from them too.

Suppose there is a time-lag between a type of institution, a mode of thought, an economic attitude, a social morality and the mode of production which we deem to exist (all of which are so many theoretical hypotheses). Should one then maintain that there is 'forwardness', 'backwardness', 'survival' or 'autonomous rhythm' in these moralities, attitudes, thoughts and so forth? Or would it not be better to ask how closely the mode of production we deem to exist functions in accordance with its model, and to discover across what geographical space, over what period of time, and in which sectors the totality is effective, and if it is already there, whether it is in the process of constitution, and if it is still there, whether it is in the process of being destructured?

This then is what is meant by 'conjuncture' in the full sense of the word (rather than Simiand's 'meteorological' sense).[11] Several 'specific times' contribute to it. In my work on Spanish history I have always found that structural contrasts are based in the specificity of economic rhythms. In the relatively small space of Catalonia I identified as many as three rhythms in the process of the modification of the mode of production. In the subsistence crisis of 1766 the insurgents, the priests, and the agitators who organised unofficial price-fixing, all invoked concepts of rights, morality and property which stemmed from the twelfth century, whereas the correspondence of quite unimportant wholesalers about free trade or true prices was couched in the vocabulary of Samuelson. Here the specificity of time is a specificity of class. It is equally instructive to look at the 'industrial cycle'. It disappears from socialist economies, even though the slowness at which agricultural techniques are transformed means that the 'old cycle' continues for a long time. Yet any attempt to re-establish the 'regulatory' power of the market causes a swift reappearance of the 'industrial cycle', with inflation as its symptom. And when that cycle becomes less marked in capitalism, it is because capitalism is deviating from its model. The sectorial establishment of transformations, the class establishment of superstructures and the spatial establishment of 'totalities' are all revealed by their corresponding 'objective indices'.

C. Structure and the longue durée: Fernand Braudel's time-scales

The third historian whom Althusser mentions was an inevitable choice because of his justly famous article, 'History and the Social Sciences: the *Longue Durée*' (1958). When Braudel, having written history for thirty years, decides to theorise about it, the philosopher's response is to say that he is now *beginning* to ask *himself* some questions about it. But this is quite wrong: Braudel in fact concludes by addressing questions to others because he is annoyed, if not actually angry, at their indifference to the new ideas appearing in the work of historians.

The other social sciences are fairly ill-informed as to the crisis which our discipline has undergone in the past twenty or thirty years and they tend to misunderstand not only the work of historians, but also that aspect of social reality for which history has always been a faithful servant if not always a good salesman: social time, the multifarious contradictory times of the life of men . . . All the more reason for indicating very strongly . . . the importance, the usefulness of history, or rather the dialectic of duration as it arises from the exercise of our profession, from our repeated observations.[12]

'Profession', 'observations', 'work', 'servant' and 'salesman' are words likely to offend theoreticians, and there are still other terms which might encourage them to place Braudel among those not yet freed from their servitude to linear time: phrases like 'accumulation of days', 'narrative of conjuncture', 'the earth's rotation', 'time-scale' and 'time identical with itself', and, in the plural, 'times which all fit neatly into each other because they are measured on the same scale'. All of which are counterposed to Bachelard's sociological conception of time. Yet underneath this emphasis it is not very hard to detect the stirrings of criticism, faint traces of irony.

Braudel in 1958 was wondering about the fate of his own contribution to this branch of knowledge, the long time-scale, 'geo-history' conceived as the projection of space through time. When he speaks of the 'narrative' of the conjuncture there is an implicit irony as he is afraid of seeing it as a return to the 'event'. Labrousse moved from his 'long eighteenth century' of 1933, to his 1943 highlighting of the pre-revolutionary 'intercycle' of less than fifteen years, then, in 1948, to a brilliant outline of revolutions seen in the 'short time-span' – 1789, 1830 and 1848 – and this earns him some friendly teasing about the 'tricks' of the profession, and remarks about 'the historian as theatrical producer'. The historian, Braudel believes, must be *above* 'the clamour of events'. If one points out to him that the proper purpose of the profession is to relocate events within the dynamic of structures, he hints that if one sets out with that intention one always ends up sacrificing structure to event.

He should not be so worried about the 'long time-span'. But that is no longer the issue. One kind of anthropology decides to look for permanence in the logical structure of sociological 'atoms', and economists discover the 'communication' properties of qualitative mathematics. Braudel, always responsive to the latest ideas, would like to be convinced, and these innovations share his own emphasis on resistance to change. But he is a committed historian. The 'long time-span' is fine for historians: but when there is no sense of time at all, the historian's role disappears.

He proposes therefore to define 'structure' as 'of course a construct, an architecture, but over and above that it is a reality which time treats badly and transmits very slowly over long periods'.[13] At which the theorist grumbles again that phrases like 'of course' and 'over and above that' are hardly rigorous. And whatever the reality may be it is not 'time' that treats it, but 'something' which treats it unevenly in accordance with reality. The problem is to define that 'something'.

But there is still the point that a reality that lasts longer than another envelops this one, and 'envelopes' is the word Braudel uses in something approaching its mathematical sense to designate the geographical and biological overlays, those powerless technologies, on the basis of which he constructs the 'long time-span', and, within which, prefiguring Foucault, he includes 'spiritual constraints' and 'mental frameworks', both of which he refers to as 'prisons of the *longue durée*'.

It would surely be a great omission not to set these ideas in relation to Marx, especially when Braudel explicitly mentions him as the first creator of 'historical models', and indicates the places where he has tried to follow his example, even if he has not taken the same path. It is not an entirely convincing reference, but Marxist historians will certainly have to take account of the problems Braudel poses both in his work generally and in this article: the question of how historians should deal with nature, space, resistant structures and, if there are such things, with ahistorical structures.

Let us consider nature first. In the only piece Marx wrote that can be said to have been planned as a work of history, the 1857 *Introduction*, he reminds us briefly that 'The starting point is of course the naturally determined factors; both subjective and objective.' And his basic definition of productivity mentions, just as briefly, 'natural conditions'. Last but not least. For the dialectic of man and nature cannot easily underestimate 'natural conditions'.

Against that we need only set technical progress (followed by science). Between the victories of those two the limits that are revealed are the framework of the mode of production.

Thinking history in geographical terms, then, is not contrary to Marxism, but it would be more Marxist to think geography in historical terms. It is difficult to know how to define where in these 'permanences' are the poles where man's hold was most successfully established. The Mediterranean has an abundance of them but they are 'enveloped' by mountains and deserts. It seems to me that 'identifying' and 'constructing' something that Althusser has not even bothered to discuss is a desirable (and dialectical) 'object of history'.

Space is likewise an object to be constructed. Theories have been sketched out and developed about it, and Braudel, unlike Althusser, has paid careful attention to them. The old temptations of geographers, economists and logicians are outlined, and sometimes caricatured. Since men, villages, towns, fields, factories and so forth are not set down 'anyhow' it must, they argue, be possible to discover a logic for their arrival. This provides inspiration for a host of mathematical, graphical and cartographical exercises which there is no call for anybody to condemn. But while the historian may learn from them, they also have lessons to learn from historians.

It is possible to imagine the organisation of space for the benefit of man, a kind of 'willed geography', but this is not exactly on the cards yet. It is also possible to imagine a new capitalism, on a new space, establishing itself with no global plan at all save its own logic, which (as Marx often pointed out) is almost the situation of the United States. The tendency is a powerful one, in fact; as people are beginning to realise, it is monstrous, which is why ecology is becoming a mystique there.

But in the old world the problem is more complex. History is not only the intertwining of times, it is also the intertwining of spaces. The logic of a village in Brittany is not the same as the logic of Nuremberg, which in turn is different from Manhattan. The nineteenth century rips the heart out of mediaeval Paris and turns the Marais into a slum: the twentieth century rescues the Marais and demolishes Les Halles. For five hundred years the city of Barcelona stays within the confines of its walls, then it comes up with the Cerdá plan and is immediately ruined. The American city carries the cancer of *favelas* and *barriadas*. The areas surrounding the Mediterranean have become a playground and waver between skyscrapers and tents. The Vedel plan proposes to treat two-thirds of the cultivated land in France as pleasure gardens. The *longue durée* is no longer part of this world.

But landscape historians and urban historians tend to lose themselves in pre-history or collective psychology. While space, even if it is saved from property developers, passes into the hands of empirical sociologists or technocrats.

The concept of space is of little use to the old world if it is taken together with the concept of time, for each stage of production and each social system here has had its towns and its fields, its palaces and its cottages, with each historical totality living after a fashion in the legacy of another. A 'true history' that adjusted balances and dismantled mechanisms would help in the construction – this time in the concrete sense – of a thought combination between past and future. Socialism has had a certain amount of success in this area. It would be interesting to know how much, if anything, this owes to the Marxist conception of this combination.

Historical time and group struggles provide yet another combination. The apparent treatment by Marx and Engels of history and class struggle as one and the same thing has long been an ambiguous element in their thought, leading some to believe that they failed to take into account the ethnic foundations of political groupings. And at first there was a certain value in this interpretation in the struggle to overturn a concept of history ideologically founded on the power of kings and wars between nations.

In the correspondence between Marx and Engels, however, and in their articles on current affairs, words such as German, French, English, Turkish and Russian appear just as frequently as 'bourgeois' or 'proletarian'. This is not an abandonment of theory. Class contradictions are the motor of history, as technology and the economy are at the root of the contradictions. But the 'last instance' operates through quite different aspects of reality as well. In the 'points which . . . should not be forgotten' in the 1857 *Introduction*, the first word Marx used is 'war' and the last words are 'tribes, races, etc.'[14] And if we look at the twentieth century in the light of this, and see nationalities and supranationalities, fascist and revolutionary nationalisms, centralised states opposing the demands of ethnic groups, and resistance on the part of independent monetary systems to multinational economic links, then everything shows that the second half of the twentieth century is clearly just as sensitive, if not more so, to the existence, or the requirements, of political formations that involve group consciousness. And here, too, Marxism has a theory to offer, authoritatively formulated by Stalin in 1913 and based on 'differential time-spans' related to the central concept of the mode of production (as well as, I should add, to the concept of class).

The political formation that corresponds to competitive capitalism is the market nation-state of the bourgeois ruling class, which comes into being out of overnarrow feudal frameworks (as in Germany or Italy) or tends to come into being at the expense of large, heterogeneous empires (such as Austria, Russia and Turkey). But the condition of their creation is the pre-existence of 'stable communities', not timeless, but constituted historically out of very diverse elements and over a very long time-span. Marxism does not view these communities as absolute ends or as determining factors: they are the proposed framework, the tools offered to a class to enable it to forge its own state. The feudal world provides examples of its own. The mercantilist stage of the bourgeoisies of France and England directly prepared the way for the nation-state.

This projection back into the past implies that it may be possible to make a similar projection for the future. Given the existence of a stable community, other classes, too, may be able to take it as a basis for action: their success will depend upon their capacity to create a new mode of production. There is also the fact that capitalism tends to become less and less effective as an instrument of nationalism. Lenin criticised Rosa Luxemburg for relying too heavily on the long-term tendency of capitalism to construct multinational links and forge superstates. Today this tendency is quite apparent, and national bourgeoisies are not easily able to resist it. What resistance there is comes from nations to the extent that their own class struggle creates revolutionary situations. In the end it is socialism's task, in the reorganisation of multinational space as well as of economic space, to construct (as scientifically as possible, and, of course, on the basis of a concept of history) the combination of past and future. Everything depends on fidelity to theory in the analysis.

There is thus a triple dialectic – firstly between the long time-span and the specific time of the mode of production, secondly between the small spaces of ethnic groups and the large expanse of space occupied by modern economic activity, and thirdly between class struggle and group consciousness – which I have found so valuable in my research into the past, and so illuminating about the present, that I was very sorry not to find it mentioned either by Braudel in connection with the 'long time-span' or by Althusser in connection with the intertwining of specific time-spans. Marxist theory probably becomes more obscure as it penetrates further into developing history.

A few words about ahistorical structures. Historians, particularly Marxist historians, are likely to be wary of the concept as, for them, everything changes, and nothing is totally independent of a global structure which is itself in a constant process of self-modification. Yet if one is prepared to accept the idea of the 'long time-span' and the 'stable community', there is also an argument for including with them, where necessary, the enduring networks of the oldest structures – those of the family and of myths – when the ethnologists to whom we owe our understanding of the logics of these networks have discovered something closer to their pure form. The aspect that historians may be particularly interested in here is the intensity, the modalities and the roles of these resistant, enduring networks in societies undergoing transformation. The 'intertwining of times' again.

The argument would be different in the face of two claims that structuralism, or structuralisms, have made – frequently in the days when they were new, but less forcefully of late. The first concerns the autonomy of areas of research. Each area is concerned that its own internal structure should render it self-explanatory, and therefore all attempts to put what is studied into a historical perspective are seen as unhelpful, ineffective and even discreditable, and while, in the study of literature for example, this may be a desirable reaction against a superficial use of history as background, to dismiss it out of hand means that a whole dimension of the work is ignored (as I have tried to show in the case of Cervantes). The other 'structuralist' claim is that it is global. In this view the social sciences together make up an 'anthropology', which, taking as its basis all formalisable structures, especially those concerned with communication, sees them as revelatory of psychological and intellectual mechanisms. The whole project is ideological, exhuming the old metaphysic of 'human nature', and proposing to study the 'atoms' of human societies before examining them at the macro-economic and macro-social level.

Reducing all social relations to a 'language', and all economic relations to 'communication of goods' (thus taking no account of production, the relationship with nature) is akin to 'naive anthropology' and its equilibrium of exchange. A games theory in which everybody makes rational choices will always fail to explain why there are losers.

This all stems from confusion over the science of language, which after a long period of mistaken historicisation was given a new lease of life by the discoveries of structuralism. It is therefore already quite clear that the autonomy the structuralists lay claim to is not a complete one. If a new field has opened up in historical semantics it is because changes in words are an indication of changes in things; given that 'stable communities', for example, are separated by a language barrier, why is it that some endure longer than others? Questions of that sort, of interest to the historian, are the ones to which structuralism provides no answer.

It is strange that when Marx was discussing production he should have believed that a comparison with language might be illuminating:

Of course although the most highly developed languages share certain laws and properties with the least developed ones, it is precisely this divergence from these general and common features which constitutes their development. It is necessary to distinguish those definitions which apply to production in general, in order not to overlook the essential differences existing despite the unity that follows from the very fact that the subject, mankind, and the object, nature, are the same.[15]

As Balibar has rightly pointed out, the distinction Marx is making here is not between the generality of the concept and the particularity of the real, but between two types of abstraction, two types of association between concepts in the theory of history, neither one more significant than the other for the establishment of the theory of knowledge. This comment is of crucial importance for the debate between history and structuralism. Furthermore, Marx issued a warning, in economics at least, against any recourse to 'generalities' about man or nature which turn into the 'commonplace in delirium'. We frequently encounter the commonplace and the tautological, and not always unhelpfully, as we try to establish the logic of things: all we have to do, both as scholars and in our everyday lives, is to make sure the commonplace is not in delirium.

6. Some persistent difficulties on the way ahead

I have deliberately chosen to be optimistic in a period of demoralisation. I wanted to demonstrate that history is not so impoverished as some Marxist theoreticians imagine in their (rather un-Marxist) quest for an absolute of knowledge. Rather than taking achievements that have been reached without any great reference to Marx's theory and forcing them into a Marxist mould, my intention has been to indicate the possible uses Marxist historians might make of all those elements in contemporary historical research which reject a simple, partial approach to a fragmented reality in favour of an attempt at a global apprehension of the social. And I did not want to overlook anything which might be of service to science (in the Marxist sense of the term) in an interdisciplinary approach to the social – structuralism, like empiricism, being ideological only to the extent that it aspires to universality in immobility, or to a fragmented isolation from other disciplines.

It remains for me to indicate some of the serious difficulties that persist, and the many and various ways forward that are open to us.

A. A look at the persistent difficulties

I do not see any way forward, basically, in the 'theory of transition' that Althusser longs for but fails to find in Marx. As he is a philosopher, and has therefore remained more Hegelian than he would wish, Althusser's concept of the mode of production has grown so closed and so crystallised that how it is to be entered or left has become a worrying problem for him. And he is quite right to be worried if there is any question of the 'transition' *as such* being erected into a new object of thought.

But Marx, after all the time he spent looking at the workings of the capitalist mode of production, scrutinising it carefully, considering it from all angles, did not only put forward a cogent theory of capitalism, including a forecast of the process of its destruction. He also spent a great deal of time scrutinising the transition from feudalism to capitalism, a process of thought which started characteristically when the debates in the Provincial Assembly of the Rhine, in 1842, revealed an overlap, in fact a conflict, between two sets of laws, two conceptions, two quite distinct ways of thinking about a problem as common-place as the gathering of fallen wood. (This characteristic starting-point is something people often forget when they are trying to decide whether a work of Marx's is 'economic', or 'political' or 'philosophical' when of course the fact that it is all of these is precisely what makes it interesting.)

There is a wealth of suggestions in Marx's work, therefore, and in Lenin's, on the subject of the transition to capitalism. There is also the old, but still important, debate between Marxist historians like Dobb, Sweezy and Taka-hashi, and a great deal of work on the early modern period in relation to analyses of the middle ages and contemporary periods, not to mention my own research experience which, whatever value it may have, I can use as evidence here: all of which, I believe, shows that we are making progress in the 'true history' of the transition from feudalism to capitalism, and that this can help us think other transitions theoretically.

There is a more urgent need to develop methods for moving from theory to the analysis of individual instances (those frameworks for possible action), which do not as a rule involve a single mode of production, nor a transition towards one, but a complex, sometimes quite stable, combination not just of two, but of several modes of production.

The distinction between the real 'economic and social formation' and the theoretical object, the 'mode of production', should now be quite clear. What we need to find out, and what I have often pondered, is whether a complex structure, a 'structure of structures', has in itself, like the mode of production, a certain determinative power, an 'efficacity'.

In his work on Latin America, where the individual instance is almost the rule, Celso Furtado has constructed economic models with multiple para-meters which combine a set of sectors with differentiated 'fundamental laws', but he confines himself to the economy. Another example, and one I am more at home with, would be nineteenth-century Spain, which it would be equally absurd to call either feudal or capitalist; semi-feudal is a poor compromise, and 'bisectorial' suggests too simple a juxtaposition. And even if, *grosso modo*, one does find a juxtaposition of two modes in one space, the interdependence that will result is enough to constitute something substantially different and original, characterised precisely by the juxtaposition with its contradictions, its conflicts, and its consciousness of them. Will it be necessary to construct a theoretical object to correspond to each 'formation'? It is what they do in chemistry.

Causality, though, is still the main problem, and it will not be resolved by talking about 'efficacity'. The proposal that Althusser puts forward certainly requires some consideration, with its notion of 'structural causality' internal to the mode of production. They key concept is Marx's *Darstellung*, which designates the presence of the structure in its effects. Or, better, that 'the whole existence of the structure consists of its effects'.

This is an attractive formulation, and reinforces the conviction which I have already expressed, that a global structure cannot exist unless all its effects are present. But I do not like the arguments Althusser uses. They rely too much on images, like the image of *Darstellung* or (theatrical) performance. It is an image that Marx used, but while I can admire its suggestive power, I can also see that it is vague and inconsistent, as when the mode of production is compared to a 'general illumination' which modifies all the other colours, and then to 'a special ether which defines the specific weight of every existence arising in it'.[16] It is a powerful idea, but the expression is not Marx at his best.

In my view Althusser's main reference point is psychoanalysis, and this may be the reason why so many of his comparisons are not convincing, as there is no reason why the social whole should behave in the least like a physiological or psychological whole. Like everybody else, Marx chooses words and comparisons to communicate his meaning, and sometimes the choice is a good one and sometimes it is not. For that reason I would rather try to understand his thought by taking his work as a whole, looking at the kinds of analysis he makes, and the 'illustrations' he uses.

And in its applications, too. A psychoanalyst is a practician, so that if he speaks of 'the effectivity of an absent cause', the concept will evoke for him a certain number of individual cases. If a creative Marxist, no matter what importance he may or may not have as a theoretician – Lenin, Stalin, Mao, Ho Chi Minh, Castro – tries out the efficacity of the mode of production he wants to create on a society that for a long time has been determined by a different structure (or several different structures), then that is the way in which he tests the validity of the concept. Historians see a similar experiment, which is less conscious but certainly not blind, in France in 1789. It is history that provides the evidence.

The final difficulty is this: Althusser sometimes, under other influences, defines structural causality as a simple logic of positions. The 'relations of production' would appear to result solely from the *place* of men in the system. They would be the bearers, not the subjects, of these relations. And it is true that Marx did not see social relations as exclusively 'intersubjective' in the way that vulgar economics does, first, because they have relations with things (which is what is meant by the primacy of production), and, second, because it is not a matter of denouncing individual exploiters, but of revealing social exploitation. Marxism cannot, therefore, be reduced to a theory of 'human relations', any more than it could be reduced to 'public relations'!

To express that, however, simply by saying that a 'reduction' of that sort 'would do damage to Marx's thought' is to allow too much weight to an anti-humanism which is in danger of doing itself damage. History as seen by the author of the *Communist Manifesto* is not a chess board, nor is class struggle a game, or even a 'strategy': it is a battle.

B. A look at the ways ahead

The difficulties that I have outlined show that the field is open to whoever wants to do the research to resolve them. For Marxist historians, two approaches would seem to be excluded: first, the repetition of theoretical principles in order to produce constructions that are skeletal as far as content goes; and second, the kind of writing that is so much confined to fumbling with technical innovations that it in fact remains at the least creative empirical level.

No, if a 'true' Marxist history is to be constructed, it must be ambitious. And this it can be if it moves all the time from full, patient research work to a theory which stands up to rigorous investigation, and also moves back from theory to the individual 'instance' in order that the theory does not simply remain as useless knowledge.

Let us look first at the movement from research to theory. We have seen too many inadequately resolved problems already not to define one important way ahead for historians: the use of comparative history to examine these theoretical problematics. And if we are ever puzzled by the exact nature of a structure, or a structure of structures, or an intertwining of differential time-spans, or an articulation of the social on the economic, or of the spiritual on the social, or a class struggle, or an ideology within a class struggle, or the relation between the place of an agent in production and the human relations that place implies, or the combination between class struggle and the struggle of ethnic or politically-defined groups, then the problems they involve, being both theoretical and historical, impose on us the simple duty of looking for the answer, like Marx, by taking account – sceptically where necessary – of the economic, political and social research being carried out around us, yet refusing to believe that the last twenty years are historically unique: we must go back into history, and we must examine *all* countries.

Research will do no harm to theory. It is worth recalling Marx's chapter on money again in this connection. It is only because of the vast quantity of historical information, attested by the range of facts, periods, places and theories Marx examines, that the chapter achieves its theoretical originality, and – probably for the only time in the endless, inexhaustible literature concerning money – demystifies the pseudo-problem of the quantitative theory of money. It might be objected that we are dealing here with economics rather than 'history', but that would be wrong; there is no 'pure' economics, and money, and all sorts of history – political, psychological or whatever – are constantly bound up with each other. On the other hand, it would seem pre-eminently sensible to apply the same method to certain other concepts, equally theoretical and equally historical, such as, for instance, class, nation, war and the state, all of which have become cocooned in ideological narratives and discourses, and in as many 'commonplaces in delirium' masquerading as theory.

Althusser, who can simultaneously assert that there is no such thing as 'history in general' and that we need to 'construct the concept of history', says nothing at all about these intermediary concepts, which are constantly being used but seldom thought. There is need for a constructive critique of this area, for which Marxists should, and sometimes do, take the responsibility.

The second element was the move from theory to individual 'instances', which is as demanding a requirement as the first one. It is necessary, though, because there is not much use in a theory which neither helps the historian to a better understanding of one country, or one period, or one conflict that was previously unintelligible to him, nor helps the man of action (no matter who it may be, as everyone is involved) to a better understanding of his country, or his period, or his conflicts.

It is not an easy task, unfortunately. Marxism has its great achievements, which must certainly be indicative of some adaptation of theory to individual 'instances' – Lenin during the Revolution, Stalin in the period of construction and during the War, Mao during the toppling of a traditional world – but alongside these we are all aware of wavering between a schematism that relied on simplicity for correctness but that was too 'all-purpose' for its application always to be welcomed, and, on the other hand, 'revisions' undertaken in the name of the complexity of reality, but which in fact risk turning into an empirical treatment of each individual 'instance', or else into pure speculation that leaves reality 'independent'.

What then is the proper historical 'approach' to individual 'instances'? First, there are some kinds of 'theoretical instances' which occur simultaneously in different places, and therefore require to be interpreted together. Take fascism, for example, or enlightened despotism: both are forms of authoritarianism which seek to establish a certain type of state in order to save a mode of production which is approaching its end, by adopting (or pretending to adopt) part of the mode of production whose time is coming. A theory of modes of production, a theory of transition, and a theory of the state are thus brought to bear on the analysis of real instances, while their combination can provide the outline of a theory of the phenomenon itself.

Next, at the other end of the spectrum, lie the incoherent 'episodes' of historicist history. I must confess to having no theory to account for the articulation between the global working of societies and the incubation of 'events'. Subjects like state theory and conflict theory demonstrate the need for a science of these areas, as well as demonstrating a tendency to fragment what ought to be one subject. It is not really possible to develop a political theory of fascism without also having a theory of war. And the theory of war needs to be much more than mere strategic schemas, or the 'commonplace in delirium' muddling Salamis and Hiroshima together. 'Conflict theory', to be truly historical, needs to bring together modes of production, types of state, kinds of army, kinds of tension, and kinds of class struggle, in order to set every conflict – past, present or to come – within a global framework as well as describing it in its own situation.

Third, there is the pre-eminent example of an individual 'instance': the socio-economic formation within a political framework that is historically stable – a nation or a state – one of the problems being the extent to which those two do or do not coincide. Here the Marxist historian's task is to discover how to pass from general sociological theory to an analysis, which must explain the past and be efficacious for the present, of a 'body' that is defined juridically and politically, but which also affirms its existence through quite different associations (sometimes destroying itself in the process).

The ninteteenth century gave such a potent ideological role to both written and taught history that the Marxist tradition has been one long attempt to break its national, or nationalist, framework; the task of any 'new history' must be to provide alternatives. But that old-fashioned historiography is the expression of a whole period of history, and, in fact, forms part of that history itself: revealing it as ideology takes us one step nearer to scientific status. This is not to say that the ensemble of changes in the world should no longer be examined through the study of individual national 'instances'; it is only to insist that each instance needs to be thought and situated in relation to those changes, and that we need to remain aware of the totalising effects of each 'instance'. As I have said elsewhere, since the global social structure is determinant, the 'regional' structure of society, which is a complex combination, a structure of structures, should be visible in its effects as well. This brings us close to the notion of 'total history', an idea I have frequently defended, and one which tends to provoke sarcastic remarks about people who know everything about everything.

The point, of course, is simply to show what the whole depends upon, and what is dependent upon the whole. That in itself is quite a task, but it is not on quite such a daunting scale as those endless accumulations of useless fact in the old-fashioned histories, or those books nowadays where each chapter is written by a specialist in a different subject in the vain hope that all of them taken together will cover everything.

Let us look at the example of a human group, a 'nation'. From the common-sense point of view, its superficial aspects like national characteristics, language or culture, make nations seem natural. Yet the deeper problem, the reason for the group, remains. How should nations be thought?

The reply comes back once more, by 'penetrating' the material, by 'making it one's own'. In 1854, Marx received a request from the *New York Tribune* for a series of articles on a typically commonplace 'event', a Spanish pronunciamento. In response, Marx taught himself Spanish out of translations of Chateaubriand and Bernardin de Saint-Pierre, which he appears to have found very entertaining. Before long he was reading Lope de Vega and Calderón, and was eventually able to write to Engels that he was deep into *Don Quixote*. When the anarchist militant Anselmo Lorenzo called on Marx in London in 1871, he was amazed at the profound knowledge of Spanish culture that his conversation revealed; admiring, but not to be outdone, he concluded that so much learning was 'bourgeois'. What Marx did in the series of articles he wrote between 1854 and 1856 was to provide a historical perspective on Spain, the lessons of which were not properly heeded until this century. He outlines all the main features without a single misconception, and some of the articles on the War of Independence have never been superseded.

It may be true that Marx was a genius, but there is still a great deal to be learned from his method. I began this essay by wondering whether Marx had ever wanted to 'write a history': here, then, is the answer. He does not write a history of Spain just in order to produce an article on a *militarada*, but he does believe in the necessity of *thinking Spain historically*.

Thinking everything historically is really the essence of Marxism. It is just a quibble about words, as in the similar case of humanism, whether that makes it a 'historicism'. I merely tend to distrust passionate denials. It is important to know, it seems, that England is not the subject of *Capital*. This seems obvious enough, since capital itself is. Yet the pre-history of capital goes under the names of Portugal, Spain and Holland. Or to put it another way, history is thought over space as well as over time.

'Universal history', wrote Marx, 'has not always existed. History in its universal aspect is a consequence.' This is another key sentence. Capitalism, born out of colonisation and the world market, universalised history. It did not unify it, of course, but that will be the task of another mode of production.

And here I come to the remaining ambition of the historian. Universal history is relatively recent, and the notion of it is still relevant. There is something ridiculous about the sort of remarks one often hears to the effect that we know too much, there are too many specialists, the world is too big for one book, or for one man, or for one teaching system to tackle universal history. The encyclopaedism implicit in it is at the opposite end of the scale to 'considered history', 'total history', the whole 'concept of history', in fact.

We may dream, therefore, of three sorts of undertaking. First, 'historical treatises', which would not be any more absurd than psychological or sociological ones. Second, national histories clearly periodised in accordance with modes of production, which themselves should be studied systematically, starting with productive forces and social relations, differential time-spans, and combinations of regional structures. Third, universal histories, which would contain sufficient information to delineate adequately all the essential features of the modern world, but which would be schematic enough to make the explanatory mechanisms perfectly clear. At every level Marxist history is yet to be written. And Marxist history is, simply, history. In that sense all 'true history' will be a 'new' history. And any 'new' history which has no ambition to be total in its scope is a history that is obsolete before it even begins.

NOTES

1 Karl Marx, *A Contribution to the Critique of Political Economy*, with an introduction by M. Dobb (London, 1970), p. 57.
2 *Ibid.*, p. 64.
3 Karl Marx, *Capital*, vol. I (Moscow and London, 1961), Afterword to the second German edition, p. 19.
4 Cited in L. Althusser and Etienne Balibar, *Reading 'Capital'*, translated by Ben Brewster (London, 1970), p. 82.
5 Karl Marx, *1857 Introduction* in *Contribution*, p. 207.
6 L. Althusser and Etienne Balibar, *Reading 'Capital'*, p. 102.
7 *Ibid.*, p. 94.
8 *Ibid.*, p. 103.
9 Karl Marx, *Contribution*, pp. 22–3.
10 L. Althusser and Etienne Balibar, *Reading 'Capital'*, p. 106.
11 Translator's note: Simiand used to say that explaining situations by the use of conjuncture was like saying 'the storm can be explained by meteorology', i.e. it is a purely verbal explanation.
12 F. Braudel, 'History and the social sciences: the *longue durée*' (1958) in *On History*, translated by Sarah Matthew (London, 1970), p. 26.
13 *Ibid.*, p. 31.
14 Karl Marx, *Introduction*, pp. 214–15.
15 Karl Marx, *Contribution*, p. 190.
16 Cited in L. Althusser and Etienne Balibar, *Reading 'Capital'*, p. 187.

4. The history of climate

EMMANUEL LE ROY LADURIE[1]

I

In recent years, extremely interesting developments have taken place in the historical study of climate. Before analysing these, I shall however review the main methods employed in the study of the climate of the last thousand years.

1. As far as the last two hundred years are concerned, the historian's task is quite simply to collect, verify, tabulate and publish meteorological series. From the eighteenth or the beginning of the nineteenth century onwards, there is no shortage of such information. The temperature series covering the last three centuries published by Gordon Manley and various Dutch historians may be taken as a model.[2] Temperature series from neighbouring geographical areas may be tested against each other: new information may thus be verified against existing statistics. The purpose of such information is to enable the historian to detect, on a regional, national or even European scale, warm and cold periods ranging from a decade to a century in length. Future work should not neglect rainfall and barometric pressure statistics, which exist for the nineteenth and even, in some cases, for the eighteenth century. Less reliable than temperature series, they are nevertheless of great use in helping to create a picture of past climates. Much of this precious information still lies untouched in the files of observatories, medical and provincial academies, and learned societies.[3]

2. For periods before the eighteenth century, the study of the growth rings of trees gives us precious information concerning degrees of drought in arid and subtropical countries, rainfall levels in temperate regions, and temperatures in northern regions. These three phenomena will be considered in terms of their fluctuations for the purposes of this article.

3. Phenology, the study of the yearly dates at which plants flower and bear fruit, is so far limited to the grape harvest: these dates, for which archives exist, indicate average tendencies in temperature for the period from March to September in a given year. If a whole series of such figures is available for an area or group of areas, they indicate temperature fluctuations from year to year

and from decade to decade but not, at least at present, from century to century.[4]

4. 'Event-based' or non-statistical methods in this area mean the systematic collection of empirical and qualitative remarks on climate made by contemporary observers in their correspondence, diaries, parish registers, etc. A model of its kind is Titow's famous article in 1960 in the *Economic History Review*, concerning the English climate in the fourteenth century; but as early as 1949 D. J. Schove had published work on the European climate in the sixteenth century and the cold period between 1540–60 and 1600.[5]

5. The glaciological method has recently been illustrated by J. Grove in an article on Norway in the seventeenth and eighteenth centuries.[6] The techniques involved represent a combination of textual work (for example, the Chamonix archives, registers concerning subglacial farming in Norway, Icelandic sagas) and direct scientific evidence of three types: geomorphological study of moraines, palynological study of marshes and peat-bogs situated below glaciers, and, finally, the use of carbon 14 to date the remains of trees found in moraines or in layers of rocky debris revealed by the recent retreat of glaciers. Such methods reveal glacial fluctuations over periods of a century or even several centuries. Information is available, in the West, for the last millennium; it is a precious but distorted indicator of climatic variations, particularly temperature.[7]

However, various remarks seem necessary concerning both the methods and the substance of the research which has been outlined.

1. The aim of the history of climate is not to explain human history, or to furnish simplistic parallels with one particularly marked historical episode (for example, the crises of the fourteenth and seventeenth centuries, and the expansion of the eighteenth century), even if such parallels are a valid object of the historian's curiosity. The aim, in the first instance, is quite different: to trace the broad lines of overall meteorological change, in the spirit of what Paul Veyne calls 'a cosmological history of nature'. Certainly, this 'chronological cosmology', modestly restricted to the study of the climate of one region, may eventually lead to another, altogether more ambitious project directly linked to human history, particularly the history of famines and perhaps of epidemics. But these are indirect consequences, and, however important and exciting, remain secondary. The strategy for the historian of climate, beyond immediate tactical considerations, must be one of front-line research in interdisciplinary collaboration with natural scientists. If the latter see the disciple of Clio as a useless intruder incapable of teaching them anything, the historian must swallow his pride and try to show that his contribution is unique and indispensable. Pierre Chaunu said some years ago that the economic historian's first task was the modest one of providing the professional economists with primary material. In the same way, the historian of climate is there to supply the specialists in the sciences of the earth and the air (meteorologists, glaciologists,

climatologists, geophysicians etc.) with archive material. The reasons for this division of labour are obvious and banal: the historian possesses special skills (palaeography, knowledge of Latin, and above all 'the historian's trade') which are necessary if information is to be extracted from the illegible archives where it was buried several centuries ago. The meteorologists long ago ceased to be able to read Latin, and they never were palaeographers (not that we should hold that against them!), not to mention 'historio-metricians'.

2. My second remark concerns the necessary climatological background knowledge which the historian of climate must possess. If such history is to be more than a chronicle of bad weather, the historian must have a general understanding of air masses and atmospheric circulation. General theoretical syntheses on this subject exist, and are constantly evolving. The most up-to-date is that of H. H. Lamb; I summarised it in 1970, but that is no substitute for consulting the original.[8]

These, then, are the essential presuppositions upon which my work over the last fifteen years, and that of other historians on the recent history of climate, has been based. In the second part of this article, I shall simply point out more recent developments, some of which do and some of which do not represent new directions. I shall note in passing the most obvious gaps, in the hope that new hands will one day set about filling them.

II

1. The first method I described was the collection and tabulation of old meteorological series, which the historian must sometimes try to complete by judicious interpolation. Here, recent results have not always measured up to the work of Gordon Manley, who in the 1950s constructed his British temperature series for 1690–1955.[9] Since Manley, the most remarkable contribution has come from von Rudloff (1967): in an important book little known in France, this German meteorologist has used a whole range of published series to construct a table of European climate from 1700 or 1750 to the present day.[10] The characteristic phases are picked out in von Rudloff's work: a cold period, followed by a fluctuating and irregular increase in temperature of one degree centigrade at most after 1850 or 1900; and, finally, a cooler period since 1953–5. But the greatest value of von Rudloff's work lies less in the exposition of these overall trends of which others were conscious before him, than in the subtle, precise and seasonally oriented way in which he describes them.

Restricting my view to France, I must express a regret which is also a *mea culpa*: we are still waiting for a historian to construct a reliable and continuous series of monthly temperatures from the beginning of the eighteenth century to the present day. This task could be done, thanks to the superb daily meteorological records of the Paris Observatory and other archives. It would probably concern the northern half of the country, more specifically the Paris region and the Nord, since these possess the best old records. But our professional meteorologists are too absorbed in the daily prediction of tomorrow's weather to provide us with such data. Even Dettwiller,[11] in his fine work on the Parisian climate, did not see fit to continue beyond the nineteenth century. It is to be hoped that either a professional historian or an interdisciplinary group will soon undertake to provide us with a series on this scale.

In the meantime, the exploration of the vast meteorological archives has begun, and has given some interesting partial results. The example of the archives of the Académie de Médecine in Paris is pertinent from a methodological point of view: the results of a collective investigation launched by Vicq d'Azir, between 1775 and 1790, are conserved in the archives: they include more than 150 series of daily meteorological records for 'the whole world' (of the period), but above all for France.[12]

The use of computers has in the last few years enabled us to sift the enormous mass of records, to separate the wheat from the chaff, the reliable series from the unreliable ones. All series which are sufficiently long and cover more than four years have been cross-checked: a statistical test which is now an everyday tool in history and the social sciences enables us to select those series which, when compared with other series for the same region, show a correlation rate of at least 0.8 and preferably 0.9, over a wide range of monthly data. The research group at the Sixth Section of the Ecole Pratique des Hautes Etudes thus eliminated the series from the south of France: they are inadequate, correlate badly and are the work of observers who were neither keen, conscientious nor scrupulous. On the other hand, some local series from the Paris region, western France and above all the very north (Arras, Montdidier etc.) came through our computer test with flying colours: they show mutual correlation rates exceeding 0.95. They provide a very solid basis for a picture of the climate during the last two hundred years of the *ancien régime*.

As far as the applications are concerned, this piece of research sheds some light on the agricultural slumps which, as Ernest Labrousse has already shown, are part of the pre-Revolutionary 'intercycle': our team showed that at least as far as its climatic aspects are concerned, this phenomenon of overproduction of wine leading to falling prices is largely due to a succession of warm years, and more particularly hot springs and summers, from around 1780. In the same way, precise meteorological reasons can be given for the bad harvest of 1788, which in turn contributed to the *Grande Peur* and other social disruptions in the critical spring and summer period of 1789. Among these reasons we should of course mention the hailstorms of July 1788 which have been known about for a long time; but our team also discovered the fact that crops were scorched by hot weather just before the harvest of 1788, and that there was heavy rain at seed-time in the autumn of 1787. All these little facts represent an important element of chance in the causal analysis of 1789.

2. Let us now turn to the second discipline mentioned in the first part:

dendrochronology. I believe that the methodological advances which have only recently been offered to the historian have led to progress in two directions. Firstly, we have gone beyond the old, well-proven, but one-sided formula used by dendrologists of yore: it consisted, as readers will remember, of correlating a dendrological series (based, for instance, on a given type of pine in a particular part of Arizona) with one particular meteorological parameter – either rainfall or, at a pinch, dryness (the latter being a function both of the degree of precipitation and of evaporation and therefore temperature). The new generation of American dendrochronologists, notably Harold Fritts, have sought to replace this old method with broader, synthesising techniques. The approach now is to map, over time, yearly or ten-yearly growth in conifers over vast continental areas such as the south-west of the United States. This gives a chronological sequence of maps – almost a film – each one made up of lines of isochronism and forest 'isogrowth', geographical variations in tree growth being, of course, the variable which interests us. This provides a spatial representation of the evolution of climate, and of ten-yearly movements of atmospheric masses, over the continental area studied. Harold Fritts's series of maps for the whole area between San Francisco and Los Angeles is eloquent in this respect: they show alternating waves of hot, dry, and cool, wet weather affecting the Pacific coast and its hinterland over periods of several decades since the sixteenth century.

Secondly, instead of studying a single parameter (aridity in desert zones or summer temperature in Arctic forests), Fritts analyses the whole range of weather types in a given year, made up of rainfall, temperature and seasonal components. This annual set is linked to a 'concomitant mean annual tree-ring' which varies in thickness. When the correlations between one particular group of weather-types and a tree-ring type have been established, the historian can write the history of the overall climate of an area, in all its complexity and temporal variations.[13]

These new directions in dendrochronology, in which Harold Fritts occupies a seminal position, are specifically American. In Europe, we are not so far advanced, and it is a pity, especially in view of the important questions which could be posed, and answered, by such research – questions affecting both human history and, more abstractly, diachronic cosmology.

Over the last decade European dendrochronology has, nevertheless, produced some new results which, in themselves and from the point of view of method, are not lacking in interest. The essential references are Huber's work on Hesse and Hollstein's on the western regions of West Germany (annual oak series, AD 820–1964). Hollstein's series is exemplary in its techniques for establishing data: the recent sections are based on about fifteen living trees, varying in age between a hundred and several hundred years. For early periods ('modern', Middle Ages, early Middle Ages), Hollstein's curve uses scores of samples taken from old beams, themselves originating from old buildings, historical monuments and even archaeological digs. Precise dating of these samples[14] has enabled the German tree-ring series based on living trees to be extended considerably further back in time. Beginning 45 years ago, Huber and Hollstein have used hundreds of thousands of tree-rings, and their work contains confirmation or discovery of certain essential episodes in the climatic history of western Europe. They provide brilliant proof of the *Sägesignatur*, or saw pattern, which had already been quietly suggested in a previous publication. Over the eleven years between 1530 and 1541, in western Germany and in the French and Swiss Alps and Jura, hot, dry summers follow cool, wet ones in a regular biennial cycle. This cycle shows up in the zig-zag of tree-ring graphs and in 'Franco-Swiss' grape-harvest dates, early and later vintages alternating systematically. Seen in the longer term, the biennial alternation which marks these years represents one of the few regularities to be observed in Western meteorological history. But it is extremely rare for this alternation to manifest the clockwork regularity which has been established on both sides of the Rhine during the 1530s.[15]

A further advantage of the *Sägesignatur* of 1530–41 is, therefore, that it provides one of the surest signs allowing historians to date beams, previously undatable, to the sixteenth century. From the point of view of climatic and agricultural history, Huber and Hollstein's work also represents a step forward both in terms of methodology and of content. They confirm, for instance, the high rainfall of the period 1310–20, which rotted grain crops in seed and in ear, and caused the great famines of 1315–16. This rainfall is reflected in thick tree-rings (indigenous west European trees are frequently lovers of rainfall, unlike wheat crops, which are immigrants from the dry east and have never quite come to terms with the leaden skies of temperate Europe). All German dendrochronological graphs show the decade from 1310 as a rising dome, reflecting tree-rings gorged with water. The history of wood and the history of wheat (or of the lack of wheat) thus complement and confirm each other by their opposite trends.

Following the example of the two German historians already mentioned, some researchers in Germany are working on annual dendrochronological series for the last thousand years in other areas of Germany. Following the example of P. de Martin at Nancy, similar work should be done on France, particularly the eastern provinces. There, comparison with German series already in existence and which are geographically not far removed should mean that work proceeds fast, with some stages even being passed over.

A final method of tree-ring analysis should be mentioned. It is important for the historian, even if the latter cannot practise it personally, since it provides a precise breakdown of seasonal components in the climate of very early periods. It involves microscopic and X-ray examination of a particular dated beam. The growth-rate and size of the cells which constitute the rings vary appreciably with the season, and even with the variations from month to month and week to week, of rain and shine, heat and cold. It is therefore theoretically possible to gain first-hand information on changing climatic conditions in the spring, summer and autumn of 1284 or 1558, in Lorraine or Württemberg. It must be said that work using these methods (Fletcher at Oxford and Polge at Nancy) has often reached the laboratory stage, but has rarely been published.[16]

The conclusion as far as dendrochronological methods are concerned is that the constitution, using the techniques proposed by Huber or Hollstein, of thousand-year or longer series for Germany, France, or Great Britain, will be of much use to historians of climate, but of even greater interest to archaeologists working on the Middle Ages or the modern period and seeking to date beams from old buildings, whether intact or in ruins: they will be able to date these oak beams with confidence, by correlating the growth graphs drawn from the beams with the master diagram for the history of all oak trees in the area in question or nearby: P. de Martin has been able to date houses in Lorraine to the period of reconstruction after the Thirty Years War, using this method.[17] The dendrochronological method, then, is crucial for dating purposes, and important, but secondary, as far as the central preoccupations of historians of climate are concerned.

3. The dates of the grape harvest, on the other hand, remain central to our concerns. The refinement of methods, coupled with the discovery by Mme M. Baulant of perfectly usable archives in the Paris region, has enabled us to extend our phenological series further into the past. Previously, they were reliable from 1600 onwards: now they are satisfactory back to 1490–1500 and for the whole of the sixteenth century. Methodologically, it is worth noting how this reliability was first established. Mme Baulant had found phenological sources for the sixteenth century, but they were far from complete. They concerned grape-harvest dates in the area around Paris. The gaps in the series, luckily, were different in each case, so that it was possible to fill them in by reference to the other series from the same area around the capital. Concomitant series existed for sixteenth-century Burgundy, Franche-Comté and Switzerland. They were less fragmentary, generally speaking, than those for Ile-de-France. The first stage of analysis was to take as a basis for reference the most complete of the Ile-de-France series, Chartres. Appropriate corrective procedures were used to make the rest of the series comparable with this one.[18] Then a mean series for the whole of the region could be established, with hardly any gaps, synthesising all the available information. The next stage was to compare the Parisian diagram with the picture in Burgundy, Franche-Comté, and Switzerland, and this comparison produced reciprocal correlations which in terms of yearly, intradecennial and ten-yearly movements were entirely satisfactory. This meant that it was legitimate to average out all these series, from Lausanne to Paris, giving one single diagram for the whole northern vineyard (the so-called 'Franco-Swiss' vineyard). Close scrutiny of the overall graph shows that it is not artificially distorted by a century-to-century tendency

towards later or earlier vintages. If such a tendency had been present, it would have been of human origin: we know that Burgundian vine-growers in the seventeenth and eighteenth centuries harvested the grapes later and later, in an attempt to produce a riper grape with a higher sugar content and thus a stronger wine; this *pourriture noble* means that we cannot attribute any climatic significance to the progressively later vintage dates revealed by Burgundian series for 1650 to 1780.

Our new sixteenth-century graph shows no human symptoms of this type, and we are therefore free to interpret it climatologically. It contains clear evidence of the overall movement of spring and summer temperatures throughout the sixteenth century: not just short-term fluctuations, and certainly not fluctuations attributable to the whim of vine-growers, which would have no bearing on the climatic debate. The most interesting conclusion is the lower temperature of springs and summers in the second half of the century, and especially after 1560: and this drop in temperature correlates perfectly with the considerable advance of Alpine glaciers, caused by reduced summer melting, over the same period. Archival study of grape-harvest dates, then, confirms Alpine sources which have been known to glaciologists for a long time: this is a real case of the interdisciplinary research which is often preached but more rarely practised.

But let us tarry awhile with our wines, bottles and casks: Bacchus certainly is an inexhaustible source of climatic information! Grape-harvest dates are now well-known to historians:[19] but the quality of the wine is also an invaluable climatic document. The following law, based on the statistical work of Angot, is valid for the northern vineyards of France, and for Germany, where the amount of sunshine is often insufficient for the grapes: a good wine in a given year means a hot summer. The example of the excellent vintages of the post-war years (1947, for instance) illustrates this proposition, which finds exact confirmation in meteorological records. Conversely, cold, cool or wet summers mean that the grapes dry out or rot before they have had time to ripen and produce enough sugar for a good alcohol content: hence the undrinkable wines of 1675 or 1968. Angot was the first to stress the remarkable potential for a history of summer temperatures offered by the systematic annual study of the quality of wines in past centuries: in 1895 he published an excellent annual series on the quality of Burgundian wine, going back to the seventeenth century. Unfortunately, French historians failed to follow Angot's example: access to archive material put them in an excellent position, but they neglected the history of the changing quality of wines. But in Germany and Luxemburg, Müller and Lahr, respectively, constituted remarkable series on the quality of wine from vineyards on the Rhine, the Neckar, and in the Black Forest, etc. Von Rudloff used these series in his history of Western climate from 1670 to the present day.[20] A few words concerning them will not come amiss.

The adjectives used to describe the quality of a wine in a given year ('acid', 'undrinkable', 'delicious', '*extragut*', etc.) have none of the precision and objectivity of harvest dates. The Lahr–Müller method, for all its qualitative nature, nevertheless lends itself to the quantitative, serial treatment so dear to *Annales* historians, and it provides remarkable evidence on climatic tendencies. Returning to the case of the sixteenth century because of its illustrative clarity, we see that the quality of the wine confirms the century-long tendency. The years between 1453 and 1552, seen as a whole or split into ten-year blocks, are generally good years in Germany (although of course individual years produce bad wine in this century favoured by the gods). On the other hand, and subject to the same reservations, the five decades from 1553–62 to 1593–1602 are all, generally speaking, years of bad wine in Germany.[21] This evidence, stretching over more than a century, is particularly reliable since the German vineyards on which it is based are, on the whole, northern ones, where the amount of sunshine, rarely excessive and often insufficient, is in any case critical. Furthermore, no methods for improving spoilt wine and turning a *piquette* into a *grand cru* by the addition of sugar or chemicals were known at the time. We can therefore conclude that information drawn from glaciological studies concerning a cold period between 1560 and 1600 is corroborated by two series based on wine production: grape-harvest dates and wine quality. Springs and summers between 1553 and 1602 were considerably cooler than in the period 1452–1553, and this resulted in later harvests, poor wines and more extensive, not to say more dangerous, glaciers: between 1595 and 1605, a few hamlets in Chamonix and Grindelwald were swallowed up. Counter-examples might be the frequently delicious wines of the 1860s and the period 1940–53 in both Germany and France, in each case corresponding to the culminating years of warm periods.

Let us conclude with the wish that the Lahr–Müller method be applied in France, the home of fine wine since the Middle Ages: a truism, but a useful one to recall, since it means that over the years *connoisseurs* faithfully noted, in all sorts of contexts, years of good and bad wine. All these sources should be tabulated and serialised, more completely than by Angot nearly a century ago. Let us have reliable and up-to-date series for Burgundy, Champagne and Ile-de-France, since the sixteenth century: they represent a powerful research tool which, coupled with other methods, would answer some outstanding questions about the climate of the modern period.

4. At the beginning of this article, I mentioned the potential of the 'event-based' method, at least as far as regions such as ours, with its high density of archive material, are concerned. A recent and powerful example of this method is François Lebrun's *La Mort et les hommes en Anjou aux XVIIe et XVIIIe siècles*, in which details of hot, cold, wet or dry weather are listed for every month, together with approximate indications of the intensity of the phenomenon described. Lebrun's sources are parish registers, family bibles, etc. The author concludes by giving us a kind of visual summary of his findings:

his series of *histogrammes* provides a visual history of the climate in Anjou over almost two centuries. This visual representation makes it possible to establish a typology, valid for northern latitudes, of famine in the seventeenth century and wheat shortages in the eighteenth century, both phenomena, but especially the first, being seen as results of the unfavourable weather conditions of this 'little ice-age'. We therefore now know the two combinations of weather which are most likely to produce famine.

(a) A combination, over one or several consecutive years, of very cold winters and cool, wet springs and summers. This is the typical 'little ice-age' combination, and seems to have occurred in 1660–1, 1692–4, 1709 to some extent, and finally 1740.

(b) The alternative is a slightly more complex combination of a very wet, but potentially mild winter which drowns the grain in seed, followed by a cold, wet spring and summer. In this case, only the spring and summer fit typically into the 'little ice-age' pattern (A). The wet and perhaps mild winter is part of a different climatic tendency (B). It is this combination of A and B which causes (1630) or extends (1662) certain major seventeenth-century famines, and also those of the 1310–20 period. It is a rare combination, as the infrequency of major famines in the classical age would suggest.

In methodological terms, then, Lebrun's work is doubly interesting: for the historian of climate proper and for the historian of famines. But this work on Anjou, and de Martin's similar work collecting all the meteorological references in the work of Mme de Sévigné, will only yield their full potential[22] when brought together in an 'archive bank' or data base which assembles findings by different historians. These series would be indexed by century, or by region, country, or part of continent.

5. As for the glaciological method, it should ask itself whether it has not quite simply reached the end of the road. It is certainly the case that many useful texts have already been identified, published, tabulated and serialised, and productivity will perhaps decrease from now on. But archival scoops are still to be made: Jean Grove[23] has published new details, drawn from tax archives, concerning destruction of and damage to farms caused by glacial activity in the Jostedal mountains in Norway between 1695 and 1750 and, perhaps, as early as 1340. In the Alps, new texts discovered by ordinary archive research suggest that a mediaeval historian should go to work on the municipal and ecclesiastical archives of Chamonix, which, despite their richness, are little known, at least as far as the fourteenth and fifteenth centuries are concerned. In German-speaking Switzerland, the absence of centralisation – beneficial in other fields too – has meant that village, canton and diocese archives in glacial areas (Grindelwald, Aletsch, Rhonegletscher, Allalin, etc.) are untouched, and that new discoveries are possible here even for the classic period of the 'little ice-age' (1570–1850). It goes without saying that such research requires not only the skills of an archivist in the best Benedictine tradition, but also

those of a geomorphologist, capable of field work. Such demands will not daunt French historians, traditionally trained in geography from an early stage.

New breakthroughs in this area may, however, be provided by two other methods, quite different from those I have just touched on. Both, further-more, take us far away from our familiar stamping-grounds to that paradise lost of climatic history close to the frozen wastes of Greenland. The first of these two methods is specifically cartographical in nature, as well as being uncertain and debatable, to say the least. It concerns a controversial document which a fine piece of research by the librarians at Yale University has brought to the attention of Nordic historians.[24] The sensational Vinland Map, drawn up perhaps in the middle of the fifteenth century,[25] is thought by some to summarise information gleaned by Scandinavian explorers between the tenth and the twelfth century. It contains a fairly accurate representation of the Greenland coast. If it is authentic, it might confirm Ivar Baardson's well-known two-part chronology:[26] in the first period, running from the end of the tenth to the end of the twelfth century, the southern part of the east coast of Greenland, around Gunnbjorn's Skerries, is relatively free of pack-ice, thus allowing Icelandic mariners coming from the east to approach Greenland in a straight line.[27] More generally, this warm period of the Middle Ages is said to correspond to the exploration by Nordic settlers and mariners of the whole of the Greenland coast, giving them empirical and almost cartographical know-ledge, of which the Vinland Map, the theory goes, is a distant echo.[28] In the second period (the thirteenth and fourteenth centuries, but perhaps reaching back into the twelfth),[29] the ice-floes from the north gradually block the old route via Gunnbjorn's Skerries, forcing Icelandic and Norwegian navigators to steer a course further south: the result is that circumnavigations of Greenland, if we accept that they ever took place, at this point ceased.

This periodisation squares with recent American and Danish discoveries[30] concerning mediaeval fluctuations in the Greenland climate, measured by means of 'ice-cores'. This does not, however, settle the question of whether the Vinland Map is an authentic document. G. R. Crone[31] denies this: his scepticism should at least counsel caution until new evidence is found. For Crone, the very fact that the Vinland Map contains a representation of the whole coast of Greenland is a further reason for doubt: his argument on this point is exactly the opposite of Skelton's, one of the 'inventors' of the map:

Another difficulty of the Vinland Map is the apparent accuracy of the outline of Greenland, which was not circumnavigated until the nineteenth century. It is generally accepted that firstly, this great island could not have been circumnavigated at an early period despite a somewhat milder climate; secondly, that there seems to have been no motive for the Norsemen to have undertaken such a voyage; and thirdly, that the Norsemen did not use or make charts. It is possible that the map was reconstructed in or before 1448 from oral tradition and a study of the sagas, though even this hypothesis would not explain the Greenland outline. For the present, it remains an enigma.[32]

Turning aside from this enigma, let us look for a moment at the certainties provided by the ice-fossil method, the second and last glaciological approach which I shall examine. In 1966 the American Cold Region Research and Engineering Laboratory (CRREL) succeeded in extracting from the Greenland ice at Camp Century an ice-core running the full depth of the ice. This was 12 cm in diameter and 1,390 metres long. The approximate age of the different sections of this core was established by the application of a complex formula, taking into account the speed of accumulation of the ice (35 cm per year), and its progressive compacting under the weight of the upper layers. More than a thousand centuries of ice were thus made available for systematic analysis by Dansgaard and other authors.[33]

Such evidence is clearly of primary interest to historians of climate. O 18, an isotope of oxygen contained in varying proportions in the ice, is a first-class indicator of temperature conditions in the past, since the concentration of O 18 in the rain or snow which subsequently becomes incorporated into the ice-cap, is principally determined by the temperature at which this precipitation condensed: 'Decreasing temperature leads to decreasing content of O 18 in rain or snow; and vice versa.'

The upper levels of the Camp Century ice sample contain large amounts of O 18, corresponding to the well-known warm period of 1920–30. Below this, and before 1900, lie layers of ice with low O 18 contents, belonging to the little ice-age, in other words from the thirteenth to the nineteenth century. Three waves of cold can be discerned within this period. The first, 1160–1300, is followed by a fluctuating but essentially moderate period from 1310 to 1480. The cold returns from the sixteenth century, reaching record lows in the seventeenth and again between 1820 and 1850. By contrast the eighteenth century (1730–1800) can clearly be seen as a warmer period.

Obviously, this periodisation is not definitive. Other ice-cores from other ice-fields will refine and correct these results. The important point at this stage is the precise confirmation in Greenland of the long cold period indicated by glacial extensions in the thirteenth, seventeenth and nineteenth centuries, and proceeding in a cycle of roughly 120 years – and this in spite of the large distance separating the two regions.

Continuing our descent into the ice-cap, we finally come to the record of the relatively warm early Middle Ages. Suddenly, in the five centuries up to 1125 (from approximately 610), the curve climbs and then remains steady: O 18 content for this whole period remains constantly higher than for the little ice-age of the thirteenth to nineteenth centuries. This is, then, a period of intense and continuous warmth; and it is clear that the people of the north enjoyed easier access to these shores than the ice-flow normally permitted.[34] There was considerable traffic to the Isle of Thule, and the climate certainly favoured the settlement of Greenland in the tenth century and perhaps that of Iceland in the ninth. Two high points are revealed by the Camp Century graphs: the first in the first third of the tenth century, the second in the first quarter of the twelfth. The only comparable peaks are situated much later, at the end of the eighteenth century (1780–1800) and, especially, 1920–30. It is to be noted that the two peaks in the early Middle Ages closely reflect two central episodes in the history of the Arctic subcontinent. Between 978 and 986, Snaebjorn Galti and then Erik the Red took advantage of the relatively ice-free sea and sailed directly west from Iceland to Gunnbjorn's Skerries; from there, Erik continued south to found the eastern settlement and his farm at Brattah-lid.[35] Two and a half centuries later, at the height of the climatic and demographic prosperity of this far-northerly settlement, a bishopric of Green-land was founded at Gardar in 1126.[36]

The Camp Century ice-core thus confirms the patient research of those Danish archaeologists who as early as 1925 suspected and showed the existence of this early mediaeval warm period in Greenland.

Let it be added that the CRREL sample sheds light on and confirms many other important episodes of the yet more distant past. Thus the maximum extension of the Alpine glaciers, which the Fernau peat-bogs suggest can be dated between 400 and 750, seems to have its counterpart in the cold period between 340 and 620 which the Greenland sample reveals. Like the little ice-age of 1570 to 1850, this is probably an intercontinental phenomenon, affecting at the very least Europe and America: John Mercer, in his great article of 1965 on 'Glacier Variations in Patagonia', shows by carbon 14 dating that the glaciers of Alaska and Patagonia, already showing signs of advancing around AD 250, have reached maximum extension by 450. Going still further back,[37] to the beginnings of our era (50 BC to AD 200), the Camp Century graph forcefully demonstrates the scale of the subatlantic cold period, covering the whole of the last thousand years BC and reaching a climax between 500 and 100 BC. Here again, Mercer allows us to draw a more general conclusion: a whole series of glaciers, in Greenland, the Alps, Iceland, Sweden, New Zealand and Patagonia – the dating of the latter by Mercer is magnificent – shows evidence of the culmination of this subatlantic cold period between 500 and 300 BC.[38]

Last but not least, the Camp Century core definitely confirms a prehistoric warm period. The high point in Greenland is between 5200 and 2200 BC, and more particularly the period 4000–2300 BC. In Europe as in Greenland, the fourth millennium (4000–3000 BC) is indeed the 'sunny millennium' which pollen analysis from the Nordic countries has for a long time suggested.

Through the workings of O 18, then, the ice-cap's elephantine 'memory' preserves evidence of climatic fluctuations from the great ice-age[39] right through to the most recent warm periods.

Oxygen 18 offers another promising method to historical research on climate. In 1967, Labeyrie and his colleagues analysed O 18 variations of the calcium carbonate (CO_3) found in the concentric rings of a white stalagmite of extremely pure calcite found in the Orgnac swallow in the Ardèche region of France. The stalagmite is nearly 7,000 years old. The variations in O 18 content, as above, indicate temperature changes within the cave. These are the results:[40]

10th century AD	12.1°C
circa 1150	11.5°C
circa 1450	11.0°C
circa 1750–1800	12.3°C
circa 1940	11.7°C

Subject to the usual reservations concerning the partial and preliminary nature of these results, the Orgnac swallow shows optima around 1000, and in the eighteenth and twentieth centuries, together with a late mediaeval cool period. Unfortunately, Labeyrie has nothing to say about the culmination of the little ice-age in the seventeenth century. But his work opens up new perspectives, which are also accessible for historians.

I shall conclude this short review of the different methods developed recently in the history of climate with a general statement: a central truth emerges from these diverse techniques, some of them belonging to the province of the historian as that science is now defined, and some of them, at least initially, outside that field. That truth is that the only worthwhile history of climate for the last one or two millennia, the period which usually concerns the producers and consumers of history, is an interdisciplinary and comparative history. Through widely differing techniques – from the study of ice to that of grape harvests, from O 18 to tree-rings, from mediaeval chronicles to rigorous temperature records – the history of climate seeks to establish a single, unified body of knowledge.

NOTES

1 This article first appeared in *Le Territoire de l'historien,* Paris, Gallimard, 1973.
2 See Manley and Labrijn. (Unless otherwise stated, references are to the works listed in the bibliography at the end of the notes.)
3 Angot, 1895.
4 Angot, 1883; Le Roy Ladurie, 1967 and 1971.
5 Titow, 1960 and 1970; Schove, 1949.
6 *Arctic and Alpine Research,* 1972.
7 Le Roy Ladurie, *ibid.*
8 Le Roy Ladurie, 1970, and especially H. H. Lamb, 1966. Lamb proposes two models for the broad climatic fluctuations which have been observed over the last one or two million years. In model 1, atmospheric circulation spreads southwards, but loses in intrinsic energy. The 'crest and trough' structure of the upper westerlies manifests closer spacing, particularly towards the west. The whole model correlates, through a set of related factors, with periods of cold and bad weather in North America and Europe (for instance, between 1550 and 1850).
    Model 2, on the other hand, is characteristic of warm periods and peaks, ancient and recent. Instead of spreading towards the equator, the 'circumpolar vortex' of the

westerlies contracts around the pole. The trajectory of depressions becomes predominantly a south–north one: in summer, they leave Scotland and Denmark, passing instead much further north, via the tip of Greenland, Iceland, Lapland and the Kola peninsula. A warmer climate then predominates, particularly on the western edge of Europe: the summers become hotter and more luminous, since the absence of cyclones opens the continent up to the warming influence of southern anti-cyclones. Winters, too, in model 2, become warmer as a result of intensified atmospheric circulation: western winds become stronger, bringing mild, wet weather from the Atlantic. These two sets of features, for winter and summer, merge, and thus define optimal periods, long and short, past and present, as the paradoxical result of an 'oceanic and summer-anticyclonic regime'.

9 G. Manley, article in *Quart. Journal of the Roy. Met. Soc.*, 1946 and 1953, pp. 242–52, 358; and in *Archiv für Met. Geophys. und Bioklimatol.*, 1959.
10 H. von Rudloff, *Die Schwankungen und Pendelungen des Klimas in Europa seit dem Beginn der regelmässigen Instrumenten-Beobachtungen*. See my long summary in *Annales*, September 1970.
11 J. Dettwiller, 'Evolution séculaire du climat de Paris', *Mémorial de la météorologie nationale*, no. 52, Paris, *Météorologie nationale*, 1970.
12 See the study based on these archives by the author and other historians: J. P. Desaive *et al.*, *Climat, médecins, épidémies*, Mouton, 1972.
13 Fritts.
14 On the problems of the precise dating of old beams by cross-dating with living trees, see my *Histoire du climat*, 1966, ch. 2; and also articles by Huber and Hollstein.
15 Le Roy Ladurie, 1966 and 1967, ch. 6.
16 Polge.
17 De Martin.
18 For details on these corrections, see the article by M. Baulant and E. Le Roy Ladurie in 'Mélanges en l'honneur de Fernand Braudel'.
19 See F. Lebrun, *Les Hommes et la mort en Anjou*, Paris–The Hague, 1971.
20 Angot, Müller, Lahr, von Rudloff.
21 See the table, pp. 371–5 of the English edition of my *Histoire du climat*, New York, 1971.
22 Lebrun; de Martin, in *Météorologie*.
23 Article in *Arctic and Alpine Research*, 1972.
24 Skelton, Marston, Painter and Vietor, 1965, p. 3.
25 *Ibid.*, pp. 156, 230.
26 *Ibid.*, pp. 169–70 (map) and p. 186; the Baardson text is in Le Roy Ladurie, 1971, pp. 253–8.
27 Skelton *et al.*, 1965, p. 170; and *Graenlandica Saga*, 1965 edition, p. 16.
28 That at least is Skelton's view.
29 From the thirteenth century onwards, according to the text by Ivar Baardson. From 1140 onwards, if the Camp Century ice-core datings are to be believed. See Le Roy Ladurie, 1971, pp. 257–64.
30 Dansgaard, 1969.
31 Crone, 1966, pp. 75–8. Mr George Kish, whom I interviewed on the subject, considers that the Vinland Map is genuine. But he reserves judgement on the extreme eastern edges of the map (Vinland and Greenland). Once again, caution seems to be the best policy.
32 Crone, 1969, p. 23.
33 Dansgaard; and Le Roy Ladurie, 1971, pp. 257–64.
34 Dansgaard *et al.*, 1969, p. 378.
35 *Graenlandica Saga*, pp. 17–18, 50.

36 *Ibid.*, pp. 21, 52.
37 Dansgaard *et al.*, 1969, Fig. 4.
38 *Ibid.*; Mercer, pp. 410–12.
39 The Camp Century ice-core, of which the bottom part is more than 100,000 years old, also allows us to corroborate the four major quaternary glaciations.
40 Labeyrie, Duplessis, Delibrias and Letolle.

BIBLIOGRAPHY

A more complete bibliography will be found in my *Times of Feast, Times of Famine: A History of Climate since the Year 1000*, New York, Doubleday, 1971, and London, Allen and Unwin, 1972. This is an English version, completely revised and updated, of my *Histoire du climat depuis l'an mil*, Paris, Flammarion, 1967.

Angot, A., 'Etudes sur les vendanges en France', *Annales du bureau central météoro-logique de France*, 1883.

  'Premier catalogue des observations météorologiques faites en France depuis l'ori-gine, jusque'en 1850', *Annales du bureau central météorologique de France*, I, 1895.

Crone, G. R., *The Discovery of America*, London, 1969.

  'How authentic is the Vinland Map?', *Encounter*, February 1966, pp. 75–8.

Dansgaard, W. and Johnsen, S. J., 'A time scale for the ice core from Camp Century', *Journ. of glaciol.*, 1969, pp. 215–23.

Dansgaard, W., Johnsen, S. J., Moller, J. and Langway, C., 'One thousand centuries of climatic record from Camp Century on the Greenland ice sheet', *Science*, vol. CLXVI, pp. 377–81, 17 October 1969.

De Martin, P., 'Dendrochronologie et maison rurale', *Annales*, 1970.

Fritts, H. C., 'The relation of growth rings in American beech and white oak to variation in climate', *Tree-ring Bull.*, vol. XXV, 1961–2, nos. 1–2, pp. 2–10.

  'Dendrochronology', in *The Quaternary of the United States. A Review Volume for the VII Congress of the International Association for Quaternary Research*, Princeton, 1965, pp. 871–9.

  'Tree-ring evidence for climatic changes in western North America', *Monthly Weather Review*, vol. XCIII, 1965, no. 7, pp. 421–43.

  'Tree-ring analysis: for water resource research', *HD Bulletin, US National Com-mittee for International Hydrological Decade*, January 1969.

  'Growth rings of trees and climate', *Science*, no. 254, 25 November 1966, pp. 973–9.

  'Bristlecone Pine in the White Mountains of California', *Papers of the Lab. of Tree-ring Research*, 1969, no. 4, Tucson, Ariz.

  'Growth rings of trees: a physiological basis for their correlation with climate', *Ground-level Climatology* (Symposium, December 1965, Berkeley), Amer. Assoc. for the Advancement of Science, Washington DC, 1967.

Fritts, H. C., Smith, D. G., Cardis, J. and Budelsky, C., 'Tree-ring characteristics along a vegetation gradient in northern Arizona', *Ecology*, vol. XLVI, 1965, no. 4.

Fritts, H. C., Smith, D. G. and Holmes, R. L., 'Tree-ring evidence for climatic changes in western North America from 1500 AD to 1940 AD', *1964 Annual Report to the United States Weather Bureau*, Washington (Project, Dendroclimatic History of the United States), 31 December 1964.

Fritts, H. C., Smith, D., Budelsky, C. and Cardis, J., 'Variability of tree-rings', *Tree-ring Bulletin*, November 1965.

Fritts, H., Smith, D. and Stokes, M., 'The biological model for paleoclimatic interpre-tation of tree-ring series', *Amer. Antiquity*, vol. XXI, no. 2–2, October 1965.

'Graenlandica Saga', in *The Vinland Sagas, The Norse Discovery of America*, edited with an introduction by M. Magnusson and H. Palsson, Penguin Books, Baltimore, 1965.

Hollstein, E., 'Jahrringchronologische Datierung von Eichenholzen ohne Waldkante (Westdeutsche Eichenchronologie)', *Bonner Jahrbücher*, vol. CLXV, 1965, pp. 1–27.

Huber, B., 'Seeberg... Dendrochronologie', *Acta Bernensia*, 1967.

Huber, B., and Giertz-Siebenlist, V., 'Tausendjährige Eichenchronologie', *Sitzungsberichte der österr-Akademie der Wiss., Mathem. naturw. Kl.*, Abt. 1, vol. 178, nos. 1–4, Vienna, 1969.

Huber, B. and von Jazewitsch, W., 'Tree-ring studies', *Tree-ring Bulletin*, 1956, p. 29.

Huber, B., Niess, W. and Siebenlist, V., 'Jahrringchronologie hessischer Eichen', *Budinger Geschichtsblätter*, vol. V, 1964.

Huber, B. and Siebenlist, V., 'Das Watterbacher Haus im Odenwald, ein wichtiges Bruchstück unserer tausendjährigen Eichenchronologie', *Mitteilungen der floristischsoziologischen Arbeitsgemeinschaft*, NF, no. 10, 1963.

Labeyrie, J., Duplessis, J. C., Delibrias, G. and Letolle, R., 'Températures des climats anciens, mesure d'O 18 et C 14 dans les concrétions des cavernes', *Radioactive Dating and Methods of Low-level Counting*, Monaco Symposium, 1967 (International Atomic Energy Agency, Vienna, 1967).

Labrijn, A., 'Het klimaat van Nederland gerudende de laatste twee en cen halve feuw' (with summary in English), *Koninklijk Nederlandisch Met. Inst.*, no. 102, *Meded. Verhandedligen*, Gravenhage, 49 (1945).

Lahr, E., *Un siècle d'observations météorologiques en Luxembourg*, published by the Ministry of Agriculture, Meteorological Service, Luxemburg, 1950.

Lamb, H. H., *The Changing Climate*, London, 1966.

Le Roy Ladurie, E., 'Pour une histoire de l'environnement: la part du climat', *Annales*, 1970. See also titles at beginning of bibliography.

Manley, G., 'Temperature trends in Lancashire', *Quart. Journ. of the Roy. Met. Soc.*, 1946.

'The range of variation of the British climate', *Geog. Journ.*, March 1951, pp. 43–68.

'Variation in the mean temperature of Britain since glacial times', *Geologische Rundschau*, 1952, pp. 125–7.

'The mean temperature of central England (1698–1952)', *Quart. Journ. of the Roy. Met. Soc.*, 1953, pp. 242–62, 558.

'Temperature trends in England', *Archiv. für Met. Geophys. und Bioklimatol.*, 1959. (The most important items here are the 1946 and 1953 articles.)

Mercer, J., 'Glacier variations in Patagonia', *Geog. Rev.*, 1965, pp. 390–413.

Müller, K., 'Weinjahre und Klimaschwankungen der letzten 1,000 Jahre', *Weinbau, Wissenschaftliches Beiheft*, Mainz, I, 83, p. 123 (1947).

Geschichte des badischen Weinbaus (mit einer Weinchronik und einer Darstellung der Klimaschwankungen im letzten Jahrtausend), Lahr in Baden, 1953.

Polge, H. and Keller, R., 'La xylochronologie, perfectionnement logique de la dendrochronologie', *Annales des sciences forestières*, 1969, vol. 26 no. 2, pp. 225–56.

Rudloff, H. von, 'Die Schwankungen der Grosszirkulation innerhalb der letzten Jahrhunderte', *Annalen der Meteorologie*, 1967.

Die Schwankungen und Pendelungen des Klimas in Europa seit dem Beginn der regelmässigen Instrumenten-Beobachtungen, Braunschweig, Vieweg, 1967.

Schove, D. J., 'Contribution to post-glacial climatic change', *Quart. Journ. of the Roy. Met. Soc.*, 1949, pp. 175–9, 181.

'Climatic Fluctuations in Europe in the Late Historical Period', Unpublished M.Sc. thesis, University of London, 1953.

'Medieval chronology in the USSR', *Medieval Archaeology*, vol. VIII, 1964, pp. 216–17.

'The biennial oscillation', *Weather*, October 1969, pp. 390–6.

'Fire and drought, 1600–1700', *Weather*, September 1966 (correlations between narrow tree-rings and dry years).

Skelton, R. A., Marston, T. E. and Painter, G. D., *'The Vinland Map and the Tartar Relation*, Preface by A. O. Vietor, New Haven, Yale University Press, 1965.

Titow, J., 'Evidence of weather in the account of the Bishopric of Winchester, 1209–1350', *Economic History Review*, 1960.

'Le climat à travers les rôles de comptabilité de l'évêché de Winchester (1350–1450)', *Annales*, 1970.

5. Demography

ANDRÉ BURGUIÈRE

Historical demography is a young science, barely thirty years old, and yet it already suffers from the ailments of old age: recent work has become repetitive, and seems always to come up against the same contradictions. This is not so much a sign of failure as the price to be paid for a fortune made too quickly. Unlike almost all other historical disciplines, which have had to assimilate large stocks of data and gradually get to know their sources before elaborating their methods of analysis, historical demography came almost simultaneously upon the seam which was to assure its success and a rigorous method for exploiting it. It was just after the Second World War that French historians began to examine parish registers, which until then had only attracted the curiosity of genealogists. Very quickly the analytical methods which were developed, in particular the technique for reconstituting families, conceived by L. Henry, an inexhaustible creator of techniques of statistical analysis for this new type of source, put historical demography on a firm scientific footing.

Hence the current paradox of this discipline: a big head on a tiny body. It uses statistical methods almost as rigorous as economic history in a field which is much more resistant to measurement than economic facts. But, on the other hand, its data base is very poor; apart from a few dozen villages and a few towns, the rest is semi-darkness. For whole regions it is still complete night.

This imbalance is certainly an important factor in the popularity of demography amongst historians. Not only does the sophistication of the methods used confer a kind of *a priori* legitimacy on the results, but the researcher also enjoys the prestige of exploring virgin territory. It seems as though each new parish studied must lead to a questioning of all previous results: work on pre-industrial populations has been fragmented into a multitude of monographs because the nature of the sources makes this easier, and it is as though an overall vision will come not from the piecing together of these disparate elements but from competition between them.

If the interest of demographic sources were measured by their statistical quality, then the contemporary period would be both the easiest and the best known from the point of view of demographic history. Registers of births, marriages and deaths, and regular censuses provide almost unlimited material. But the study of pre-industrial populations has progressed more in the last twenty years than the study of post-industrial revolution populations. A complex phenomenon such as the drop in the fertility-rate and the introduction of birth-control in Europe in the late eighteenth century has been much better explored, if not better explained, than the opposite tendency, the baby boom of the 1940s. This is a recent phenomenon, whose effects can be seen in the world around us. It is also a mysterious one, since it appears at the same time, 1940–5, in countries unequally affected by the war, such as Australia and Czechoslovakia, the United States and Sweden, France and the UK, etc. A very recent manual of *Démographie historique*,[1] extremely well documented as far as the seventeenth and eighteenth centuries are concerned, explains this increase in the birth-rate in the mid-twentieth century as a 'sudden reawakening of the white races' under threat from world war and the growing power of the coloured races.

It is hard to know how to react to such a hypothesis. But it clearly illustrates the underdevelopment of historical demography in the contemporary period. It is the obstacles to research rather than the ease of research which make the historian. Historical research is attracted to a period where sources are scarce, not abundant. Demographic study of the pre-industrial, pre-statistical age (which in France we call the 'modern' age) has also been encouraged by the effect of a whole new school of French historiography taking as its starting-point the serial study of prices, and gradually shifting its focus from production to population, and from population to society. But, as with every important development in historical research, the major impetus came from outside. In this case the source was the Institut National d'Etudes Démographiques, whose major concern was to study the long-term fall in the French fertility-rate. To understand the causes and, more simply, the mechanisms of this long-term decline, it seemed necessary to trace its history, and therefore to go back along the graph to a change of conjuncture, to the period when the French population was still characterised by the high, stable fertility-rate of most modern agrarian societies.

The main interest of parish registers is that they imply significant changes in the nature of statistical information. Series concerning prices, gold shipments, tithe receipts or the dates of the grape harvest, and other quantitative historical sources, give a more or less exact measurement of phenomena which contemporary witnesses were able to observe directly, but whose importance they could not judge. The figures therefore in themselves express a certain direct reality, even if they must be contextualised within a wider historical analysis if they are to yield their full meaning. On the other hand, fertility statistics, which are the most original and most precious information available from family files, seem to represent a direct passage, via mathematical language, from a first-hand to a hidden reality, from behaviour to motivation. Thanks to such statistics, quantitative history has been able to entertain the hope that it may one day measure the unmeasurable, that it may, without having to make a long and tiring detour via literary sources or personal records such as family bibles, gain access to the basis of human behaviour, to motivations which remained unexpressed.

Any result is in itself significant, whence the inexhaustible attraction of monographs; but at the same time, it never means anything in isolation. Fertility-rates, birth frequencies, marriage ages and death-rates must be combined to produce a model, a simulation of behaviour. But does the model in itself represent the key to the phenomenon? These combinations are variable; they yield not one but several models, and leave us to contemplate an ambiguous cultural reality. The way in which multiple meanings can be attached to demographic statistics is nowhere clearer than in the difficult and ambitious area of parish registers. That is why this discussion will be confined to the problem of the demographic model in the seventeenth and eighteenth centuries, since that is the area of demography which has attracted the most historical attention, has added most to the historian's knowledge and, of course, has raised most difficulties.

First of all, it is difficult to see just how far back into the past the demographic model of the *ancien régime* goes. At least as far as France is concerned, the sources only allow precise observation from the middle of the seventeenth century onwards. Are we then dealing with a traditional, primary model already having a history going back over several centuries, like the agrarian-based economic system? In this case, we would be justified in seeing the two as corollaries. Alternatively, is this a model which develops precisely at the same time as the sources appear – in France this means the Counter-Reformation? If this were the case, the model in question would represent a transitional structure, developing in response to the difficult economic conjuncture of the seventeenth century: an austerity model corresponding to a contracting economy, but also preparing for industrialisation and economic take-off.

Problems also arise when one tries to project the model spatially in order to observe wider trends of migration, which remain to a large extent hidden in a monograph. The reconstitution of families and the study of family fertility-rates can really only be carried out with any ease when population groups are stable and there is little or no migration. The researcher's job is to trace all births, taking into account infant mortality (over as wide a range of families as possible), within a parish or a group of parishes. For this reason, attention was first concentrated on rural parishes little affected, in theory at least, by geographical mobility. But seeking to avoid distortion of the statistical picture by mobility leads to exaggeration of a population group's stability.

Internal contradictions revealed by a global analysis of the eighteenth-century population suggest considerable migration. In most regions except the west of France, rural parishes show appreciable drops in mortality, so that a positive balance of births over deaths has been achieved by mid-century. The towns, on the other hand, maintain high mortality-rates and a negative balance. And yet, at the same time, urban population remains stable or increases. We must therefore suppose a constant restocking of the towns (*mouroirs* according to Pierre Chaunu)[2] by the rural population. The expanding towns can therefore be seen as Molochs swallowing up part of the population surplus of the countryside. One of the new features appearing in the eighteenth century, and which can explain the well-documented but mysterious increase in physical well-being without any support from industrial or agricultural revolution, is precisely this growing circulation between town and country relieving the agricultural world of some of its dead weight and renewing the urban labour pool.

Lastly, it is very difficult to avoid underestimating the importance of social contradictions. One obstacle, of course, is the very insufficiency of the records (professions are sometimes not recorded at all); but another is the historian's excessive faith in the mean figures produced by statistical analysis. Averages conceal not only exceptional cases, but whole areas of social difference. That this essential fact should have been ignored is all the more surprising in that historical demography, through the use of statistical and serial sources, marks itself off as different from an impressionistic, descriptive conception of history which takes literary evidence and illustrious examples at their face value. Nor does a simple opposition between elite and mass demography solve the problem: it often seems as though once data concerning the mass of the population have been found, historians have reverted to considering demography as somehow neutral, whereas it is in fact fraught with the most violent social antagonisms.

'However subtle our methods of analysis, they have never enabled us to distinguish between the demographic behaviour of the yeoman farmer and the day-labourer', P. Chaunu has written of Normandy.[3] And it is indeed true that up until the end of the *ancien régime* the rural world, considered at parish level, is isolated, bounded by the limits of the village community, and manifests great demographic uniformity, which masks social differences. But we must ask whether this is a sufficient justification for claiming that 'the unity of demographic behaviour is geographical rather than economic and social'.[4] Social differences are present, but are hidden by excessive concentration on one area. Each historian works in isolation, and this exaggerates the isolation of the population groups being studied, suggesting that their development is independent and related outwards only by the fact of reproducing a general model. There are real dangers here of backyard demography. Historians must go beyond the parish framework, not only to compare overall demographic performance, but also in order to track down class relations within demographic behaviour (for instance through comparative analysis of town and country).

It is something of a commonplace that social conflicts have an important influence on demography as far as death-rates are concerned. Baehrel[5] has shown very clearly the atmosphere of class struggle which the plague created within towns. P. Goubert, working on the Beauvaisis, observes a socio-economically determined death-rate at times of crisis in 'the densely populated weaving areas such as Mouy and Saint-Quentin de Beauvais'.[6] Finally, several recent studies[7] have shown how the practice, widespread in the eighteenth century, of putting babies out to wet-nurses created a whole series of exploitations, which mirror the wider social hierarchy. There was competition between the bourgeoisie, who could choose the best wet-nurses in the nearest village, and the lower classes, who had to look further afield in order to pay less. There was competition, too, between legitimate children and *enfants trouvés*, whom hospitals had to send to the cheapest nurses and who therefore stood a poor chance of survival. The peasants were naturally drawn into this ever-widening wet-nurse market. In the villages around Lyon many families speculated on the different wet-nursing rates in the Lyon area and outlying regions, finding cheap places for their own children in areas of high mortality so as to be able to take on the children of well-to-do Lyonnais.[8]

But such conflict should not be seen as the only effect of class antagonisms. Imitation and contagion between the dominant and the dominated create tensions which in turn lead to changes in behaviour. In this respect, demographic behaviour obeys the same rules as other cultural behaviour. Thus, we can observe downward contamination in the case of contraception,[9] and upward contamination for marriage age.

Physiology and demographic behaviour: the fragmentation of demography

If the demographic historian refuses to recognise the influence of social contradictions on demographic phenomena, the reason is a deeper refusal to make biology part of historical discourse. The illusion that there was a general demographic model for *ancien régime* France – an illusion which inspired the first demographic historians – was based on a natural, common-sense tendency to overestimate physiological uniformity. Let us take fertility, which, in the traditional demographic model, is supposed to be determined solely by physiological mechanisms. The general impression is one of high fertility which, even more than death-rates, seems to be definitive of the model: fertility constitutes the economic and cultural divide between the so-called 'natural' demographic model and the Malthusian model of contemporary industrial populations.

The trouble is that an examination of the fertility of married women in five-year age-groups shows that, for those women not practising birth-control, fertility-rates vary considerably within each age bracket from one area to another. They are high in French Canada,[10] Flanders,[11] Brittany,[12] relatively high in Normandy and in the Paris basin,[13] low in the south-west.[14] How can

Table 1. *Fertility by age-group*

	15–19	*20–4*	*25–9*	*30–4*	*35–9*	*40–4*	*45*
Sainghin (1690–1739)		512	521	419	402	220	31
Scoresbyzund		496	526	452	328	241	

Table 2. *Mean intervals between births in months, no contraception*

	1	*2*	*3*	*4*	*Ante-penult.*	*Penult.*	*Last*
Crulai	24·1	26·9	27·7	31·3	32	31·9	39·7
Geneva	23·6	24·1	23·9	25·2		30	37·5
Scoresbyzund (women married before 1935)	23·7	24·7	24·1	26·1	26·6	28·8	29·8

such variations be explained, if we accept that the cases cited all belong to a non-Malthusian model, the progressive drops in fertility from one age-group to another being the effect of natural physiological changes? We know from contemporary demographic studies of the Third World that the fertility of couples not practising birth-control can vary from one ethnic group to another. Canadian women seem to be the world record holders among white races. But the biggest gap yet observed separates Sainghin women (521 per thousand) and Thezels women (335 per thousand). A study of an Ammassalimut population group conducted just before the introduction of birth-control shows fertility-rates and spacing of births similar to eighteenth-century Flanders.[15]

Given that such a gap is conceivable, what radical ethnic difference between northern and south-western France could be at the root of it? Such a mediocre fertility-rate is perhaps simply the reflection of poor health and diet, making miscarriages more frequent. Or we must accept the hypothesis of a vague form of contraception, still too faltering to introduce a real planning of families and thus to register an effect on the fertility graph.

Spacing of births provides a more precise means of observing fertility. Early demographic historians believed that they had found a revolutionary new explanation of the fact that traditional populations, without contraceptive practices, still avoided demographic inflation: births were spaced to a greater degree than had been realised – between 16 and 31.5 months, using the model proposed by Wrigley.[16] In fact, leaving aside the period between marriage and the first birth, which is always noticeably shorter, and the last three periods (in 'complete' families), which are usually measurably longer, the average spacing, in most groups studied, is between 20 and 28 months. Beyond 28 months we can suppose a certain degree of contraceptive practice. Careful analysis of these statistics provides further correctives. Two types of behaviour

Table 3. *Intervals between births in months*

	1–2	2–3	3–4	Ante-penult.	Penult.	Last
Three villages in Ile-de-France (marriages, 1740–99)	19·8	23·5	23·3	27	29·1	35·2
Canada (marriages, 1700–30)	21	22·6	22·9			
Thezels (marriages, 1700–92)	25·4	30	32·2	32·6	33·7	38·2

can be distinguished: that where average spacing remains practically stable up until the antepenultimate birth (French Canadian or 'three villages' type); and the Thezels type, where there is a progressive lengthening of the period between births. In the latter, some degree of contraception cannot be excluded.

Rural populations defined according to classical criteria as not practising birth-control manifest as much variety in the spacing of births as in fertility-rates. This is not surprising, since they both measure the same thing. But, overall, women do not have more than one child every two years. 'I have found no exception to this rule', Pierre Goubert wrote in 1965, in his assault on the myth of the yearly baby.[17] But the myth was perhaps written off too quickly. The first monographs on urban populations have revealed considerably shorter spacing with the *bourgeoises* of Geneva, for instance. At Meulan (1660–1789), the gap between the first and second child is less than 15 months in 30 per cent of cases, less than 18 months in 50 per cent. In the butchery trade in Lyon, the subject of M. Garden's systematic research on families, the average is 12 months, and families of twelve, sixteen, twenty children are typical. Is this extreme fertility peculiar to butchers' families? Among the silk workers of Saint George's parish, similarly staggering birth-rates are to be found: over the 240 families traced, the average number of children is 8.25, and marriage is no earlier than elsewhere. In the parishes of la Platière and Saint-Pierre, socially more heterogeneous, it exceeds 7.

The difference in behaviour between town and country had long been suspected. It is generally attributed to the practice of putting children out to wet-nurses. Since breast-feeding interrupts ovulation for a certain period, women in towns who did not breast-feed their babies must necessarily become pregnant again more quickly than peasant women feeding their own and often other people's children. The effects of breast-feeding have been confirmed by the 'death in childhood' test: when a child has died shortly after birth, the gap between that and the following birth is often shorter than the others. Lactation is interrupted and ovulation has begun again. But P. Goubert[18] has shown that this phenomenon is only observed in certain types of family. Doctors are hesitant to comment on this form of amenorrhoea, and the importance which they attribute to it seems to depend more on religious than on scientific conviction.[19]

Should we then suppose the existence of sexual taboos connected to breast-feeding, supplementing or replacing physiological inhibitions of dubious reality? Such taboos exist in other cultures. The idea that if a woman becomes pregnant while feeding a baby, the baby's life may be threatened, appears in the Talmud.[20] In the sixteenth century certain casuists, for instance Ledesma,[21] use the same reasons to justify their view that breast-feeding is a case where the conjugal duty may be refused. But the Church never officially prescribed sexual abstinence during lactation, and the small amount of evidence available suggests that the population was equally ignorant of the warnings of the theologians and of the danger to the newly born child of another pregnancy.

This disparity between town and country, in which breast-feeding appears to have some influence, is only one aspect of the extremely wide dispersal of data on the degree and rhythm of family fertility in *ancien régime* France. The data are supposed to indicate tendencies and averages, to create a general picture from a series of individual cases. But it seems that, while statistical analysis has managed to deal with variety at monograph level, as soon as one attempts to paint a national picture, the data can no longer help us. In a field where the exact importance of physiology and cultural conditioning is so hard to establish, it seems better to follow P. Goubert, who, for the villages of the Beauvaisis, proposes a typology of family fertility, rather than trying to establish a single collective model of behaviour.

But the whole interest of parish registers is to allow us to go beyond figures and glimpse human behaviour. The originality of this particular form of statistical analysis is that it takes account of features which are not usually measured, but which determine behaviour patterns: sexual morality and attitudes to life. D'Angeville, the brilliant forerunner of statistical cartography, drew up a departmental index of morality based on the number of illegitimate and abandoned children.[22] Parish registers allow us to observe a wider range of phenomena: deviant behaviour through pre-marital conceptions and illegitimate births, and seasonal patterns of conception. The latter area of analysis is still problematical. The aim is to measure to what extent a population group follows the Church's ruling on abstinence during Lent, and thus to glean some indication of moral and religious conformism.

There are two obstacles to such analysis. Firstly, the date of Lent changes constantly. The only solution, if one is to minimise the risk of error, is to concentrate on the figures for March. Secondly, abstinence during Lent, having been very strictly prescribed in the late Middle Ages, is already largely abandoned by the fourteenth century. Pierre de la Palud, who rewrote marriage theory at the beginning of the fourteenth century, no longer makes it an obligation.[23] Pantagruel, the true inventor of the study of parish registers,

Table 4. *Seasonal distribution of conceptions (1660–1780)*

	January	February	March	April	May	June	July	August	September	October	November	December
Canada (early 18th century)	104·6	90·1	71·1	97	107·1	134·1	107·6	109·2	90·8	97·1	97	94·3
Auvergne (16 parishes)	87	100·8	75·5	105·1	117	133·8	119·8	97·2	88·4	86·6	90·9	98
Paris (1670–1790)	98	96·6	91·3	105·7	113·1	109·1	103·5	97·9	91·9	94·7	98·8	100
French Vexin (20 parishes)	99·6	99·9	97	117·2	112·5	125·7	111	85·3	75	92·9	91·1	102·8
Brittany–Anjou (21 parishes)	80	90	93	117	130	123	137	92	90	84	71	93
Languedoc (6 parishes)	108	107·9	100·5	107·8	116·1	117·8	103·4	93·7	76·8	85·3	89·9	93·3

Table drawn up by J. Dupâquier.

observes from the 'register of baptisms at Thouars' that many children are born in October and November 'lesquels selon la supputation rétrograde tous estoient faicts, conceuz et engendrés en Caresme'. Abstinence was, however, still recommended, and the climate of Lent penitence which the Counter-Reformation reactivated may have reawakened old interdicts. In the seventeenth and eighteenth centuries, certain population groups show a marked decline in conceptions during February and March, with March sometimes returning the lowest figures for the whole year: it seems difficult to explain this in any other way. Cases in point, illustrated in Table 4, are Canada at the beginning of the eighteenth century, Auvergne, and certain towns, such as Liège and Paris.

Lent abstinence seems to be practised more faithfully in Paris than in the surrounding countryside (for instance the French Vexin).[24] This is not surprising. Paris as a second Babylon, the capital of pleasure and debauchery, is only a reality for an aristocratic minority, and literature has exaggerated the myth. The vast majority of the ordinary people of Paris still adopt austere and religious modes of behaviour. Jansenism remains a strong influence. Generally speaking, indeed, the Church has a stronger hold on the larger French towns than on the countryside. But how do we explain the fact that the drop in births corresponding to Lent abstinence is present in the south-west but absent in the west? A kind of semi-abstinence may have survived in certain cases, an inherited habit, a shell with no moral content.

The only way to substantiate the historical value of the March fall in conceptions as a sign of moral attitudes, is to see whether it correlates with indicators of deviance: pre-marital conceptions and births outside marriage. Both of these are transgressions of the religious code, Catholic and Protestant alike. Generally speaking, the rates are low compared with our own industrial societies, suggesting a relatively high degree of moral discipline. But do these two forms of behaviour represent transgressions of the same moral rule? Illegitimate births in France often represent less than 1 per cent of all births, and rarely exceed 6 per cent. Pre-marital conceptions are more variable: rare in the west and also, it seems, in the south-west, more common in the Paris basin and Normandy. Near big towns (Sainghin near Lille, Sotteville near Rouen) they may exceed a third of all first children.

It is therefore tempting to concentrate on illegitimate births as a major transgression of the religious code and therefore a good indication of marginal behaviour. But does the increase in illegitimacy in the towns during the eighteenth century indicate falling moral standards or increasing social marginalisation? A significant proportion of unmarried mothers giving birth in towns have fled a rural parish for fear of public disapproval. How can we distinguish between urban and rural delinquency as explanatory factors? We may also consider the hypothesis that this increase is partly a reflection of increased repression. Declarations of pregnancy were established as a way of tracing recalcitrant fathers, but remain uncommon until the eighteenth century.

Previously, the authorities were probably more tolerant, since society itself was more indulgent: disapproval of bastards was certainly less strong, and, in village communities, men were less reluctant to recognise their illegitimate children. The increase in recorded illegitimacy, then, far from reflecting a fall in moral standards, may correspond to a strengthening of the marriage unit.

In an extremely detailed analysis of illegitimacy in Nantes in the eighteenth century,[25] J. Depauw observes that illegitimate births do indeed increase in the second half of the century, but that they are increasingly the product of relationships which were meant to lead to marriage, rather than the result of a relationship based on inequality (mistresses, kept women, etc.). In a sense, these illegitimate births are pre-marital conceptions gone wrong. So the analysis of illegitimacy in the eighteenth century leads us to the question of pre-marital conceptions. But the rates are so varied that it is difficult to attribute any stable meaning to them. In England, where they were already high in the seventeenth century, pre-marital conceptions seem to be due to the survival of marriage contracts where physical union takes place before the religious ceremony, which is simply a belated confirmation.[26] Is such an explanation valid for France? If it were, one could relate the increase in pre-marital conceptions to the tendency towards late marriage. But the two do not correspond. At Sennely en Sologne,[27] pre-marital conceptions are relatively common (10–14 per cent) in the eighteenth century, but marriage ages remain relatively low, rarely exceeding 24 years.

What is left of our traditional demographic model? Under the microscope, each component element fragments into a multitude of variants, which in turn allow of various combinations. The result is a series of regional models reflecting the diversity of *ancien régime* France. P. Chaunu has suggested an opposition between two demographic models: the flat, open regions with high fertility and highly developed sexual discipline, extremely vulnerable to crises; and the *bocage*, more robust and resistant with its contraceptive practices and laxer moral attitude.[28] The same writer supposes for eighteenth-century Europe taken as a whole 'something like fifty behaviour types covering several thousand basic molecules of demographic behaviour'.[29] It is certainly true that in *ancien régime* France different economic conditions, different customs and traditions led to the existence and juxtaposition of several demographic models. But there is a danger that this 'molecular' theory, with its systematisation of diversity, may mistake research conditions for the state of reality, attributing the status of molecule to the area covered by one monograph. Do we not exaggerate this diversity because of our ignorance of the whole, because we can see no link between the isolated islands of our knowledge?

The key to the Western demographic miracle

A systematic inventory of all variants would lead to an endless taxonomy, and it seems preferable to focus our attention on the meaning and evolution of the traditional demographic model. Recent interest in the origins of contraception in France is highly relevant here. Thanks to statistical analysis of family fertility, there can no longer be any doubt that contraceptive practices permeate through to the mass of the French population in the eighteenth century. Interpretation of this fact, on the other hand, remains problematical: and the phenomenon which is observed through fertility statistics will only become meaningful if it is linked to deeper and more complex changes in people's attitudes.

One can, of course, isolate the phenomenon from its historical context. The transition to a Malthusian demographic model is one which every society undergoes sooner or later on the road to industrialisation. Nowadays, several Third World countries are trying to organise the transition artificially in order to speed up industrial development. But the resistance which they are meeting shows that the problem is more than a technical, demographic one, that it is bound up with the whole cultural framework of the society: why contraceptive practices became popular in France in the eighteenth century, and how they were invented or reinvented, are in fact one single question. Contraceptive practices – in reality, *coitus interruptus*, the most basic variety – were strictly forbidden by the Church, which considered them unnatural practices.[30] The introduction of such practices was for a long time considered in Catholic circles as an act of impiety: it was explained either as an effect of dechristianisation encouraging the population to ignore religious morality, or, more simply, as an example of the general decline of moral standards. Such views were not far from those of the 'political arithmeticians' of the period, lucid and regretful observers of demographic change such as Moheau: the spread of these 'fatal secrets' is for him proof that the moral corruption of the town, evident in the increasing number of abandoned children, is now spreading to the countryside.

We know how difficult it is to interpret the indices of morality which demography provides. The growth of illegitimacy can be attributed either to changes in pre-marital relationships or to increasing adultery and debauchery.[31] As for the increasing numbers of abandoned children in the towns, which were previously seen as a result of illegitimacy, it now seems that in many cases these were the children of married couples who, having been unable to limit the number of children, now sought to limit the cost of raising them.[32] But the greatest difficulty is in imagining that the ban on contraceptive practices could remain, over long periods of time, both widely known and strictly observed. Every interdict bears within it its own transgression. Moreover, in matters where unconscious drives and reflex attitudes play such an important role, more than a moral code is needed to influence people's behaviour.

That is why the interpretation offered by a pioneer in this field, Philippe Ariès, is particularly fruitful for the historian.[33] He believes that the Church's interdict on *coitus interruptus* became translated into a taboo. In other words, it was so internalised that it became the object of automatic obedience, and, simultaneously, it was forgotten. It became 'unthinkable'. This process of internalisation occurs in all forms of social behaviour where the individual's free will is short-circuited by an implicit moral code, a cultural inheritance. Contraceptive techniques did not completely disappear from reality, but they disappeared from memory. One proof among many of this process of forgetting is the fact that the sin of Onan, from the passage in the Old Testament upon which the Church based its condemnation of *coitus interruptus*, ceased, in common parlance, to mean a contraceptive practice and came to refer to masturbation.

The spread of contraception in the eighteenth century can therefore be seen, not as a sudden, widespread transgression of an interdict, but as a change in general attitudes: parents wish to enhance their children's future through education, through a better standard of living, rather than simply bringing them into the world. The new value placed on the notion of the couple, and the 'civilisation' of conjugal relations, are corollaries of this change. There is an ethical change, too: sexual pleasure and the process of procreation become dissociated, whereas the Church only accepted the former as a by-product of the latter. The apparently paradoxical notion that birth-control was encouraged by a growing concern with childhood is confirmed, for eighteenth-century France, by considerable literary and iconographical evidence. 'It was when they became interested in children that the French began to have less of them', writes Dr J. Sutter, summarising Ariès. We should add that such an analysis is consistent with the demographic conjuncture of the period. Falling rates of infant mortality lead couples to try to limit the size of their family, and are also an encouragement to invest more (materially and emotionally) in children whose birth and survival are no longer the exclusive preserve of chance.

Those churchmen of the period who seem to have realised the social importance of the phenomenon confirm this new state of mind. Mgr Bouvier, Bishop of Le Mans, observes in 1842 that contraception is common in his diocese. More often than not, it is being practised by good Catholics who do not realise that they are disobeying the Church. 'When questioned by their confessors as to the manner in which they use the rights of marriage', he writes in a letter to the Pope, 'they are usually greatly shocked', for two reasons. Firstly, because they were unaware that such practices were forbidden; and secondly, because the new value placed on married life has led them to mark off an area of intimacy and autonomy which the Church has no right to oversee.

An older text, *Le Catéchisme des gens mariés* by Father Feline, published in 1782, explains this serious deviation from conjugal propriety by 'excessive indulgence shown by husbands towards their wives... They try to be mindful of their extreme delicacy.' This last feature allows us to generalise the hypothesis, to free it from the specific religious context of eighteenth-century France. If the absence of contraception were to be explained solely by reference to the Church's interdict, it is hard to see why contraceptive practices

were introduced in France, a Catholic country, well before Protestant countries, where religious instructions on the matter were much less clear. Such an
explanation would also fail to take account of the resistance which contraception is meeting today in many non-Christian Third World countries. Comparison between two recent experiments in the introduction of contraception –
non-Christian India and Catholic Puerto Rico[34] – tends to prove that the level
of cultural attainment and above all the kind of emotional relationship within
the couple, their ability to communicate, are more determining than religious
prescriptions.

Theology has recently stated a claim to part of the historical field with the
publication of J.-T. Noonan's important book, *Contraception: A History of its
Treatment by the Catholic Theologians and Canonists* (1966). Noonan shows
clear changes in the Church's position during the period which concerns us (the
sixteenth to the eighteenth century). The tendency is to separate out, at least in
certain cases, the two purposes of marriage: sexual pleasure and procreation.
The culminating point is the Church's recognition of the inherent value of
conjugal love. Taking as evidence the arguments of the Jesuit casuist, Sanchez,
who seems to allow *coitus interruptus* outside marriage in order to limit the
opprobrium reserved for fornication, but forbids it within marriage, J.-L.
Flandrin[35] supposes that as early as the sixteenth century, two kinds of sexual
behaviour exist in parallel: in the extra-marital relations which were becoming
more frequent as marriage took place later, men had recourse to contraception. Whereas in marital relations, which according to the Church must be
moderate (theologians condemned amorous 'display' between man and wife)
and fertile, no such practices were used. The revolution of the eighteenth
century is simply the transference of extra-marital behaviour to the context of
marriage.

This hypothesis is a curious throwback to the moralising explanations of
Moheau and Father Feline. The spread of contraception is seen as a conscious
transgression of the laws of the Church, and is a sign of the abandonment of
moral values. It provokes several objections. Is such a dichotomy of sexual
behaviour conceivable? How can we avoid the conclusion that once men were
made aware of contraceptive practices, they would soon be tempted to use
them in their married life? The complete absence of demographic evidence
renders the hypothesis even more fragile. True, it is difficult to demand such
evidence for the sixteenth century. But if extra-marital relations were as
frequent in the seventeenth century as Flandrin suggests, then an identifiable
proportion of accidents would show up in baptismal registers. As far as the
sixteenth century is concerned, the authority to whom Flandrin refers most,
leaving aside the theologians, is Brantôme. A valuable and enjoyable witness
to quote, but is that a sufficient basis for generalisation? Let us imagine for a
moment that the only evidence we had for the demographic behaviour of Paris
in the second half of the eighteenth century was Restif de la Bretonne. The

impression would be one of generalised libertinage whereas the seasonal distribution of conceptions shows exactly the opposite.

Finally, what value can we attach to the work of theologians? Up until the nineteenth century the Church is certainly better informed than anyone about the population's sexual behaviour: it oversees it with obsessional attention, and the confessional is an ever-open window onto the private life of the masses. But theology is above all an abstract form of reasoning. It seeks to be faithful to doctrinal tradition rather than to social reality. The 'penitentiaries' of the late Middle Ages, for example, are an excellent source of information on the sexual morality preached by the Church, but it would be dangerous to take the multitude of exotic and preposterous perversions which they catalogue as a faithful representation of contemporary behaviour. The lack of realism, the wild imagination and the bookish quality of clerical thought are as important here as direct experience. When Saint Bernardin of Sienna, in the fifteenth century, bemoans the fact that 'out of 1,000 households, I believe 999 belong to the devil', must we conclude that almost all of Sienna was practising *coitus interruptus*?[36]

It is even more difficult to ascertain to what extent the faithful knew the Church's attitude to sex and marriage. In this field, certain religious documents (surveys, episcopal instructions) are an untapped source of information about mass behaviour. The cultured general public was still interested in theology up to the beginning of the eighteenth century. Treatises of casuistry like Sanchez went through several editions even in France, and the controversial attention which they attracted suggests, as Bayle pointed out, that such works were used for the sexual initiation of the public as much as for its edification. But such a public is extremely small. Its minority status and behaviour, demonstrated by work which has been done on the English and French aristocracy, make it marginal to the problems raised by the diffusion of contraceptive practices in the eighteenth century.

From the historian's point of view, the most interesting aspect of theological thought is not its content but its evolution. Changing doctrines reflect theologians' efforts to adapt the Church's moral code to new social conditions, as well as the pressure exerted by the 'spirit of the times'. Theology is thus predicated upon a system of values which may be in a state of change, and in this sense it can help us to reach an understanding of behaviour. In this respect, Noonan's book is both revealing and misleading. It shows the slow gestation of a new conception of marriage and a new moral code for the couple, but because its aim is to reconstruct the route by which the Church arrived at its present positions, the book presents this development in too linear a way: it pays too much attention to innovating theologians, even when unbending traditionalists had more direct influence on the clergy.

Now, in the second half of the seventeenth century, particularly in France, a strong current of theological thought, including the Jansenists but by no means exclusive to them[37] (Bossuet is part of it, for example), develops in opposition to the laxism of the casuists. It dominates the seminaries, controls the training of the clergy and therefore represents a hold on the faithful. Pierre Chaunu is quite right to point out that this movement, rather than Sanchez, is where the Malthusian attitudes of the eighteenth century found the intellectual tools they needed. It is an apparently paradoxical connection. Noonan has shown convincingly[38] that a moral doctrine never operates directly upon demographic behaviour like a propaganda system whose instructions are immediately applied; rather, it modifies mental structures, and thereby generates or represses attitudes which it could not envisage independently. Jansenism brings about the total restoration of the Augustinian conception of marriage: sexual pleasure as intrinsically evil. Its only justification within marriage is as an accompaniment to procreation. This systematic rejection of sexuality, encouraging the believer to seek asceticism within marriage, to limit his (or her?) pleasure, leads to greater control of basic drives. On the other hand, as far as confession is concerned, Jansenists and other rigorists hesitate between two attitudes: either they seek to accord a kind of inquisitorial attention to sexuality in order to prevent or condemn guilty acts; or, alternatively, they avoid all mention of the subject, for fear that the very fact of referring to it may constitute an opportunity to sin.

Moreover, eighteenth-century Jansenism includes an anti-sacramental element, the effect of which is to keep the faithful away from the confessional. Thus, by a process of deformation, moral rigorism led to the development of contraceptive practices. The ascetic control of sexual drives becomes a technique for self-restraint and controlled pleasure. The refusal to turn to the Church for guidance leads to a non-religious, private, individual moral code. Sexuality becomes hidden in the intimacy of conjugal life.

The biggest difficulty is to demonstrate the connection in geographical terms. P. Chaunu has established a concordance between areas of Jansenism and areas of early contraceptive practice in Normandy.[39] But there is every reason to believe that precise correlations cannot be found either for France as a whole or indeed for Normandy; the ideological basis is vague, and cannot be restricted to Jansenism. But the important point about this thesis is that is shows, as Weber did in the case of Protestantism, the unexpected ways in which a deformed religious ideology can act upon social behaviour. Moreover, it does not seek to explain a phenomenon which is peculiar to France (the early diffusion of contraception) by reference to a hypothetical process of dechristianisation in which no one believes any more; rather, it relates the phenomenon to the religious revival of the seventeenth century, which is specifically French in its late arrival and in its radical, Jansenist form.

There is nonetheless something not altogether satisfying for the historian in explaining a fundamental change in demographic behaviour by shifts within an ideology. The asceticism which is so deeply rooted in the moral theology of late seventeenth-century France was not simply dreamed up by some theologian. Potentially at least, it was at work within society as a whole: the ground was prepared for it by a demographic feature, late marriage, one of whose consequences was the development of sexual austerity. Between this first form of control and birth-control, religious rigorism may well have acted as a kind of ideological link. And it is justifiable to ask just how indispensable this link was.

The beginnings of later marriage are difficult to date, but there is little doubt that it became more and more firmly established over large areas of Western Europe up until the end of the eighteenth century. In fifteenth-century Tuscany,[40] the model age of marriage for men is between 30 and 32, whereas nearly all girls are married by the age of 20. The average difference between husband and wife is 13 years. In the second half of the seventeenth century, the average marriage age for a village in the diocese of Parma, Riana,[41] is 33 for men and 25 for women. Between 1700 and 1750, the average marriage age for men rises to 34, for women to 30. Certainly, even by fifteenth-century standards, an age difference of 13 years was peculiar to Italy; but the difference has practically disappeared by the eighteenth century. The average age difference in eighteenth-century Venice is one year.[42] It is important to note that the tendency towards later marriage only affects women: the function is clearly to limit the number of children. Between the sixteenth and the eighteenth century, women's reproductive activity is reduced by ten years.

As far as France is concerned, numerous monographs show the general spread of later marriage in the seventeenth and eighteenth centuries. Only in a few specific places does some particular custom restrict this process. In the countryside, men marry at 27, women at 25: the gap is small. In the towns, marriage takes place, if anything, later still: in the parish of Saint-Pierre (Lyon) in the first half of the eighteenth century,[43] the average age for first marriages is 29 for men and 27.5 for women. Much less information is available on the sixteenth century. Women in Normandy probably married on average at an age of 21 around 1550, while in Lorraine the figure is 22; a century later, the age is 25 or 26. Figures for sixteenth-century Paris are also lower. More interestingly, we can, in certain cases, trace developments in detail rather than simply extrapolate from comparisions between the sixteenth and the eighteenth century. Thus, figures for five parishes in the Vallage area of Champagne are 24.8 for men and 24 for women between 1681 and 1735, and 27.8 for men and 26.3 for women between 1735 and 1800.[44] Decade by decade, there is a constant increase in marriage age.

How can we explain the origins of this tendency? Here we are confronted with a contradiction which is inherent to historical thought. Every time one attempts to trace the origins of a complex phenomenon, one finds not one precise cause, but a whole series of possible causes locked together like pieces of a jigsaw. It is tempting to say that a demographic phenomenon must have a demographic cause, and that the tendency towards later marriage at the beginning of the sixteenth century represents an attempt to re-establish a demographic balance. Thus, early marriage was adapted to stable, short life expectancy, but when life expectancy rose at the end of the fifteenth century, early marriage began to produce excessive numbers of children. The explanation is somewhat tautological, and exaggerates the extent to which demographic models can initiate historical change. On the other hand, increased life expectancy may have had a greater influence on marriage ages indirectly, via its effect on patterns of inheritance. Whatever the legal system, and in both town and country, a sudden increase in average age at death throws inheritance procedures into disarray. Later marriage may be a response to later settlement.

But for that analysis to hold good, we must show that marriage was considered as a form of settlement. Now, parallel to the demographic take-off of the early sixteenth century, there develops a new conception of marriage and family. This development can be seen at various levels. Within theology, Noonan has clearly demonstrated that the laxist attitudes to sexuality which triumph with the seventeenth-century casuists, originate in the redefinition of marital relations and the new value attached to the notion of the couple at the end of the fifteenth century. The Paris nominalist, Martin Le Maistre, seems to have been largely responsible for this development. Amongst humanists and reformers there is also a general questioning of marriage, both as a sacrament and as an institution. The German humanist, Albrecht von Eyt, published a treatise in 1472 called *Ob einem Manne sey zu nemen ein eeliches Weib oder nit.* Rabelais' Panurge asks the same question in the comic mode. The feverish literary activity surrounding the question of marriage is a sign of a profound social malaise.

But it is perhaps in the legal field that the pressure of social demand is most clearly visible. Emmanuel Le Roy Ladurie, studying Languedoc, has shown the strengthening of lineage structures and the various forms of family amalgamation (such as *affrèrement*)[45] which seem to have been the dominant, if not the general tendency of an 'age of human scarcity'. The demographic take-off of the sixteenth century makes these amalgamations both more economically fragile and more inhibiting. It undermines patriarchal authority and leads to the introduction of formulae of legal emancipation. Agricultural and family structures fragment simultaneously; there is a progressive shift from marriage as a means of integration into the family lineage towards marriage as the establishment of a new family and economic unit. Later marriage is the result of emancipation.

A study of marriage practices in sixteenth-century Bordeaux[46] shows the progressive replacement in marriage contracts of rigorous clauses such as *affiliation* (by which the children of the first marriage are absorbed into the second) by associative formulae such as the joint ownership of property acquired in common. In the first two decades of the century, another new form of marriage contract develops, diametrically opposed to traditional lineage rights: spreading from the town and from the lower classes, the joint estate is sometimes referred to in contracts as the 'household' (*ménage*), confirming the indivisible reality of the couple. We can conclude that the development of notions of joint property in the fifteenth century favoured the growth of marriage as settlement in two ways: it released centrifugal forces which saw marriage as a means of dividing up authority and property; and it provided a model of the family as a unit guaranteeing the autonomy and settlement of the couple.

In fact, contradictory tendencies regarding marriage are at work in the sixteenth century. The indissolubility upon which the Church insists, and the poor social status of marriage, are both objects of criticism. It has widely been held that marriage was a dying institution in the sixteenth century. In fact it was an under-developed institution. In general, the Church had done no more than add baptism to the contractual marriage of Roman or customary law, and impose certain moral obligations. The Church's role was not to administer the sacrament, which was conferred by the *copula carnalis*, but to register it. This led to an imbalance between the triviality of the procedure and the gravity of the obligations which it implied, an imbalance criticised by many, and not least the State. It led to a number of abuses (kidnapping, clandestine marriages) which were a violation of the rights of the parties concerned or of parental rights. An edict of Henri II in 1556 gives parents the right to disinherit sons of less than 30 years and daughters of less than 25 who have married without parental consent. The Church, for its part, sought to strengthen its hold on the institution, for instance by making the presence of a priest compulsory, and at the same time tried to maintain the free choice of the couple. The decisions of the Council of Trent are a response to this double need. Even if they were not applied immediately – they were rejected particularly in France – they provide a legal and moral basis for late marriage.

Let us therefore risk the hypothesis of a two-stage development. The first stage is the birth of later marriage in the sixteenth century as a means of attaining two objectives: the moral autonomy and the economic independence of the couple. Up until about 1580, later marriage serves to cushion and slow down the population explosion. The second stage takes place in the seventeenth century: the consolidation of late marriage as the keystone of an austerity model. Between 1580 and 1730 population is stationary. Late marriage guarantees this stability. Austerity enters the fabric of life as society's response both to a contracting economy and to the idea of asceticism, which is the only acceptable justification for such a frustrating habit. All the Church's efforts to strengthen the celebration of marriage reflect its desire to impose its discipline on sexual activity. The strange history of the institution of betrothal is a perfect illustration of the moral rigorism which the Church progressively introduces into everyday life.

Betrothal was an old institution going back to Roman law, but was more active within certain areas of customary law. The Church had many reasons for disapproving of it. It symbolised the contractual aspect of marriage, the agreement between two families: this was for many the most important aspect of the whole procedure, the religious ceremony being seen simply as a record of a *fait accompli*.[47] The Church was particularly determined in its denunciation of two consequences of betrothal: firstly, the agreement between the two families preceded and often ignored the agreement of the couple, upon which common law insisted; and secondly, the fiancés often lived together long before the religious ceremony had taken place. The Church's response, as was often the case with pagan practices, was not a direct attack on betrothal, but rather an attempt to Christianise it more completely and turn it into an instrument for moral improvement.

In France, the post-Tridentine Church made the betrothal ceremony general and compulsory in areas where it had remained popular. Where it was on the decline, it banned or simply ignored it. Synodical ordinances show a clear opposition between northern and southern France as far as the status of betrothal is concerned.[48] It becomes a way of verifying the free consent of the couple, a preparation for marriage. But the ordinances often insist upon the fact that the fiancés must not live together or even share the same roof. This insistence is proof that the Church had to fight to impose its will. At first, betrothal was to take place before the publication of the banns; then it gradually moved closer to the date of the actual marriage, finally merging with it. Betrothal progressively disappears: like a film which turns more and more slowly until it stops completely, betrothal, part of the austerity model of the seventeenth century, gradually becomes a fossilised piece of folklore. A habit like *la nuit de Tobie*,[49] whereby the newly-weds are forbidden to consummate the marriage on the marriage night, is certainly a vestige of this institutional asceticism. This ancient mediaeval custom was encouraged by the Church after the Council of Trent. It was still to be found at the beginning of this century in some French provinces.[50] Other rituals, such as *la mariée cachée* (hiding the bride) or *la fuite de la mariée* (the flight of the bride), belong to the same family.

Is it possible for a religious institution and a set of legal reforms, unaided, to support a social habit like late marriage for so long a period? In our present societies, where the choice of a partner is not dictated by an official rule except the Church's restrictions on marriage within families, that freedom of choice is nevertheless severely limited by a whole series of economic constraints, customs and tendencies. A numerical imbalance between the sexes within a population group can, for instance, cause later marriages. Given stable age differences between partners, a sudden increase in the birth-rate will swell the ranks of marriageable women. Since their potential husbands are older, and fewer, some of these women will have to find a younger husband – thus going against social convention – or else wait for members of a younger generation of men to reach an acceptable age. The result, in other words, will be later marriage for women.[51]

This is perhaps what happened in the sixteenth century in countries, such as Italy, where the age difference between partners was very marked. But it seems difficult to believe that this particular mechanism operated everywhere and over such an extended period of time. The historian is tempted to adopt the approach of a geneticist faced with the proliferation of a genetic defect. If a defect established itself, this is to be explained by the fact that over and above its negative aspects it has been the object of natural or social selection: it has become useful. In the same way, chance perhaps generated late marriage in the name of necessity. The chance element is the demographic imbalance which may have changed the social habit in the first place. By necessity, we should understand the phenomenon of general readjustment which gradually mobilised legal practice, canon law, and religious moral codes to create a true behaviour structure. But had it not been for social demand, for the slow gestation of a new conception of marriage, which we can already glimpse in the work of fifteenth-century theologians, then the demographic event alone could not have established late marriage as a lasting habit.

We are in fact dealing with a Weberian demographic model. J. Hajnal has suggested an interpretation of the Western marriage pattern comparable to Weber's analysis of industrial capitalism:[52] late marriage, with its corollary, a relatively high proportion of unmarried people, was a historical exception. It recurs, except in the twentieth century, neither in Western Europe nor in most other civilisations. Its originality is above all that it imposes unnatural behaviour, that it broadens to its maximum extent the gap between instinct and institution. All cultures insist upon a pause, a rite of passage, but it is generally short.

Western Europe, on the other hand, and as early as the sixteenth century, chooses the road of austerity. As a determination taking place at the level of moral systems, this again recalls Weber. Despite J.-L. Flandrin's hypothesis of a double standard in sexual behaviour, it is difficult to deny, at least in the seventeenth century, the existence of a generalised mood of asceticism, encouraged by the Church and confirmed by parish registers, and reflected in the infrequency of extra-marital sexual relations and contraceptive practices. Why should we necessarily hypothesise a sexual outlet for the desires which society repressed? We know since Freud that active neuroses can quite easily absorb such desires and channel them towards different objects. And this means not only the spectacular neuroses such as witchcraft, hysteria and the other wild forms of peasant culture remarkably described by Le Roy Ladurie, but also a very broad process of sublimation which could be traced in the social dynamics of this austere age.

The other Weberian feature of this model is its social efficacy. Apart from regulating demographic flow, late marriage creates a cheap labour pool of women, so increasing productive forces and facilitating primitive capital accumulation.

But as in the case of Weber's analysis of Puritanism, the social values which crystallise around it give late marriage its social efficacy. We have seen that by delaying marriage, *ancien régime* society had increasingly identified it with settlement. In the country, this autonomy often took the form of the couple moving to a separate home. It supposes the existence of an inheritance (frequent in the world of shopkeepers and artisans), or at least of savings sufficient to pay for the new home. The spirit of enterprise gradually replaced the spirit of alliance which had traditionally inspired family strategies and the young couple's ambitions: rather than simply creating a family, the couple must know how to manage it, and to preserve and improve its social status, which is now its main goal.

Sexual austerity fulfils the same function in this matrimonial spirit of enterprise as thrift in the capitalist spirit of enterprise. Is this just an analogy? Historical demography today is discovering the common ground between mentalities and social behaviour which Weber lacked: it has placed the ideal of austerity and capitalism on the same continuum. Our claims here should be neither too big nor too small. It would be absurd to try to reduce the whole European industrial adventure to a simple demographic choice. But it is not enough to consider only the material consequences of that choice. European demography not only created the 'preconditions' for industrial take-off: a population evenly spread across age-groups, increased life expectancy. It also served as an archetype for economic behaviour. Late marriage and contraception are part of the same cultural logic, applied differently in an apparent reversal of values. Both inhibit instinct in the name of the reality principle; both are part of the strategy of prolonging life and producing happiness.

NOTES

1 P. Guillaume and J.-P. Poussou, *Démographie historique* (Paris, 1970).
2 Translator's note: 'Dying places' is a scarcely adequate translation of the neologism *mouroirs*.
3 'Malthusianisme démographique et malthusianisme économique', *Annales ESC* (1972).
4 *Ibid.*
5 R. Baehrel, 'La haine de classe en temps d'épidémie', *Annales ESC* (1952).
6 P. Goubert, *Beauvais et le Beauvaisis* (Paris, 1960).
7 M. Lachiver, *La Population de Meulan du XVIIᵉ au XIXᵉ siècle* (Paris, 1969); M. Garden, *Lyon et les Lyonnais au XVIIIᵉ siècle* (Paris, 1971).
8 M. Garden, *op. cit.*
9 Cf. L. Henry and C. Levy, 'Ducs et pairs sous l'Ancien Régime', *Population* (1960); L. Henry, *Anciennes familles genevoises* (Paris, 1956).
10 J. Henripin, *La Population canadienne au début du XVIIIᵉ siècle* (Paris, 1954).

11 R. Deniel and L. Henry, 'La population d'un village du nord de la France: Sainghin en Mélantois', *Population* (1965).

12 P. Goubert, 'Legitimate fecundity and infant mortality in France during the eighteenth century', *Daedalus* (1968).

13 E. Gautier and L. Henry, *La Population de Crulai, paroisse normande* (Paris, 1958); J. Ganiage, *Trois villages de l'Ile de France* (Paris, 1963).

14 P. Valmary, *Familles paysannes au XVIIIe siècle en bas Quercy* (Paris, 1965); A. Zink, *Azereix, la vie d'une communauté rurale à la fin du XVIIIe siècle* (Paris, 1969).

15 J. Robert, *Les Ammassalimut émigrés au Scoresbyzund: étude démographique et socio-économique de leur adaptation (côte orientale du Groenland)*, Cahiers du CRA, 11–12, in *Bull. et Mém. de la Soc. d'Anthropologie de Paris*, vol. 8, 12th series (1971).

16 E. Wrigley, *Population et société* (Paris, 1969).

17 P. Goubert, 'Recent theories and research in French population between 1500 and 1700', *Population in History*.

18 In *Beauvais et le Beauvaisis*.

19 In 1950 Dr R. Guchteneere put forward the view that ovulation is naturally inhibited by lactation. This hypothesis strengthened the position of the Church in only authorising the rhythm method of contraception. Quoted by J.-T. Noonan, *Contraception et mariage* (Paris, 1969).

20 Yebamoth, 34b (Rabbi Eliezer).

21 P. de Ledesma, *Tractatus de magno matrimonii sacramento* (Venice, 1595) (quoted by Noonan).

22 A. d'Angeville, *Essai sur la statistique de la population française*, reprint (Paris, 1969).

23 P. de la Palud, *Quartus sententarium Liber*, quoted by E. Helin in *La Prévention des naissances dans la famille*, Paris, 1960.

24 Translator's note: French Vexin, as opposed to the Norman Vexin. The *ancien régime* name for the area around Pontoise.

25 'Amour illégitime et société à Nantes au XVIIIe siècle', *Annales ESC* (1972).

26 Cf. P. Laslett, *The World We Have Lost* (London, 1971).

27 G. Bouchard, *Le Village immobile: Sennely en Sologne au XVIIIe siècle* (Paris, 1972).

28 In *Civilisation de l'Europe classique* (Paris, 1966).

29 In 'Malthusianisme démographique et malthusianisme économique'.

30 The most complete synthesis is J.-T. Noonan, *Contraception et mariage*.

31 Cf. J. Depauw, 'Amour illégitime et société à Nantes', *Annales ESC* (1972).

32 Cf. F. Lebrun, 'Naissances illégitimes en Anjou', *Annales ESC* (1972).

33 In *La Prévention des naissances dans la famille: ses origines dans les temps modernes*, Cahiers de l'INED, no. 35 (Paris, 1960).

34 See M. Brewster Smith, 'Motivation, communications research and family planning', *Public Health and Population Change* (Pittsburgh, 1965); for India: T. R. Balakrishnan, 'India: evaluation of a publicity program on family planning', *Studies in Family Planning* (1967); for Puerto Rico: Reuben Hill, J. Mayone Stycos, Kent W. Black, *The Family and Population Control: A Puerto Rican Experiment in Social Change* (University of North Carolina, 1959).

35 J.-L. Flandrin, 'Contraception, mariage et relations amoureuses dans l'Occident chrétien', *Annales ESC* (1969).

36 Quoted by Noonan, *op. cit.*

37 Leading the rigorist camp, the Faculty of Theology at Louvain with Jean Sinnigh, an Irish émigré.

38 J.-T. Noonan, 'Intellectual and demographic history', *Daedalus* (1968).

39 In 'Malthusianisme démographique et malthusianisme économique'.
40 D. Herlihy, 'Vieillir au quattrocento', *Annales ESC* (1969); C. Klapisch, 'Fiscalité et démographie', *ibid*.
41 Quoted by J. Hajnal, 'European marriage patterns in perspective', *Population in History* (London, 1965).
42 D. Beltrami, *Storia della popolazione di Venezia* (Padua, 1954).
43 M. Garden, *op. cit.*
44 G. Arbellot, 'Cinq paroisses du Vallage aux XVIIe et XVIIIe siècles', typescript (Paris, 1970); Noonan, *Contraception et mariage*.
45 Translator's note: *affrèrement* – a legal contract, common in Languedoc and the south of the Massif Central, encouraging family amalgamation after the death of the patriarch and preventing the splitting-up of the inheritance. See Cabourdin, G. and Viard, G., *Lexique historique de la France d'Ancien Régime* (Paris, Armand Colin, 2nd edn, 1981), p. 9.
46 J. Lafon, *Régimes matrimoniaux et mutations sociales: les époux bordelais (1450–1550)* (Paris, 1971).
47 For instance in the case of *matrimonia praesumptia*.
48 Cf. C. Pivoteau, 'La Pratique matrimoniale en France d'après les statuts synodaux', typescript (Paris, 1957).
49 Cf. A. Van Gennep, *Manuel du folklore français contemporain*, vol 1 (2): 'Mariages-funérailles' (Paris, 1946).
50 Particularly in Brittany and Normandy, Bresse and Savoie.
51 For a similar phenomenon affecting France today, see Louis Roussel, 'La nuptialité en France', *Population* (1971).
52 J. Hajnal, *op. cit.*

6. Religion and religious anthropology

ALPHONSE DUPRONT

Religious anthropology may be defined as the study, or the science, of religious man. Whilst it may certainly be considered to be a partial perspective upon the totality of human existence, it is nevertheless one of the most compelling, for all religious life, be it individual or collective, is a key to unity. This is true both in the sense that it demands and posits a 'beyond', and one that is necessarily linked to human existence, and in the sense that, in its definitive interpretation of the nature of the universe, it implies the most extensive participation possible in every aspect of the cosmic. Finally, no matter how relentlessly the modern mind has sought to dichotomise, and has claimed even to separate religion from other forms of existence, the need for religion has remained, whether consciously or subliminally, of real use as a form of balance for human beings and as a powerful witness. It thereby represents both creation and violence. When a man is engaged in a religious act he is thus, contrary to what now outmoded analyses imply, practising or seeking after omnipotence. Religion expresses what is virtually the loftiest and most vital measure of what it is to be human, and it does so across a very long time-span. Religion belongs to the *longue durée*, and is therefore of abiding interest to the historian. The transformations and development that it undergoes are, moreover, very gradual, both in terms of the new customs that emerge and in terms of its vision of the world.

Whether a religion is a cosmogony or is ethical and normative in structure, one should not casually alter the power of the keys to the nature of existence or the balance that it provides. For, of all the various modes of expression in human society, religion is the most deeply stable. This is in part attributable to the anthropological fact that a thing is venerable if it endures, and once its venerable nature is established, it will endure still longer. In our epoch there have been quite legitimate questionings regarding the solidity of religions, but the occasionally stormy controversies in the period after the Second Vatican Council ought not to encourage an excessively Western interpretation of things. These controversies may appear sudden, but the Catholic world has been prepared for three centuries for such things, as it has gradually assimilated the religious purities of the Reformation (notwithstanding the tenacious and even 'triumphant' liveliness of the Tridentine compromises). Through religious experience, man is able to apprehend a slowed-down time in its actual unfolding, and he is thereby given the remarkable and perhaps unique opportunity to decipher wishes and needs, as well as the double meaning both of the fight for existence and of man's interpretation of it. In collective thought, the *longue durée* and eternity (or rather, extra-temporality) are usually confused. The history of religious facts may thus legitimately be taken to provide material for an anthropologist to study.

Whilst this is the case with all history, it is particularly true of religion, since it shifts so very slowly. Its depths, which are, as it were, the entrails of history, unfold across lived time in a solemn and reverential manner. Given this double development, in space and time, history also permits quantification. To quantify is to treat an undifferentiated mass statistically, both eliciting it and apprehending it in all its density and, at the same time, dissolving it. Quantification lends yet more weight to the ancient formula, which is already so in tune with modern conceptions, of man 'at every period and in every country'. Contemporary apologetics, which are themselves complacently universalising, continually invoke the *consensus omnium*, though it is difficult to see who can be in a position to apprehend this 'everyone'. Nevertheless, figures allow one to identify the nature of needs, attitudes, practices, and visions in human society, and thereby to transcend the limits of a restricted comparativism, in which the temptation is always to argue on the basis of what are necessarily quite circumstantial correlations.

A statistical language is, admittedly, only one aspect of the establishment of an anthropological communality. Yet its derivation from history serves to justify it, for if historians were to omit the materials from which quantification is derived, they would by the same token be jettisoning any guarantee they might have that each fact was rooted in time. In spite of the natural tendency of numbers to homogenise everything, each fact considered by a historian will still preserve some trace of the soil from which it came. Quantification, when it is used in history, never obliterates specificity entirely. What it offers is a solid basis in what is 'common', and above all a grasp of similarities, an awareness of 'the same' within the extension through time of the human presence and of human perturbation. The clearest example, though a fairly crude one from the point of view of material evidence, is provided by the many authoritative studies of 'religious practice' by Gabriel Le Bras and his school, in which collective religious behaviour is firmly grounded in the study of French geography. It may be studied diachronically but, even if we disregard synchrony–diachrony relations, there is still a wide range of evidence available to us. Thus, the need for the sacramental, which is largely conditioned by social pressure, enables us to identify the relations of participation between the natural and the supernatural dimensions. We can also examine correspondences between collective liturgical life and the cosmic order and, in terms of this correspondence and the work rhythms of an agrarian society, an almost unremitting conflict between liturgical festivals and the demands of agriculture. We can examine the opposition or reconciliation between ecclesiastic society and the cosmic sacralities, which it regards as pagan, and, at a deeper level, the psychosocial components of sacral conformism or need. Finally, we can examine differences in behaviour linked to the physical milieu or environment.

Such is the solid mass of religious fact, or at least a part of it. If we do not offer an interpretation of it, we obviously cannot begin to understand what *homo religiosus* essentially is. Yet only history, i.e. a study of basic fact and basic memory, enables us to give it a treatment that is sufficiently refined that we avoid lapsing into either reductive generalisations, which are the most dangerous of all forms of abstraction, or an attractive but vacuous rhetoric, which squanders the experience of past generations.

This outline of the links between history and religion as it is lived over time, suggests that these two approaches to knowledge or perspectives on human experience, both individual and collective, may perhaps be fruitfully reconciled. But in order to be quite certain of this, it may be helpful to define more exactly than hitherto what a religious anthropology could or should be. It is obviously a form of knowledge of man's religious behaviour, itself a quest for the beyond occasioned by the mutual interaction of racial, environmental and species-related factors. It involves the analysis of myths or cosmogonies, and of their basic structures, as well as the development of the double mechanism through which the will to power so central to all religious experience is expressed. This mechanism entails a transcendence either through the beyond or through sublimation, a plenitude of the present through possession of the instant, and access to the wellsprings as a means of recharging one's energies for the quest.

Religious anthropology is thus a form of knowledge in which all the signs of religious experience or of the religious state quite naturally converge. It includes the mass of religious practices, which are themselves a measure of a vital collective force, along with the analysis of mental mechanisms, above all of those postulates which are contained in statements of doctrine. This knowledge involves defining and understanding the actual life of institutions, their relationship with the environment or even, since this is still a modern obsession, a more or less harmonious coexistence within man himself of the religious with other equally exclusive, if less fruitful universes. It is also concerned with the intellectual and verbal economy of liturgical ceremonies, with the constitution of exemplary persons (saints or heroes), with the rhetoric of sermons or with the logic of the catechism. This knowledge thus has to do with any and every manifestation, through a complex interrelation of behaviour and needs, of the mystery of man's power in his religious life; with the manner in which he manipulates boundaries in order to be able to pass from one world to the other, or to make one manifest in the other. All these signs, mutually incompatible as they sometimes are, speak of men, and it is the task of a religious anthropology to advance an interpretation of them. One must begin by carefully assembling the constituent elements of such an interpretation and then, having established its coherence, one must endeavour to grasp the pertinence of the symbols themselves, whilst at the same time avoiding overhasty induction or banally mechanistic analyses. It must be recognised, however, that at least as far as the Western world is concerned, we are a long way short of satisfying this far-reaching but fundamental ambition. We have only just begun to develop our understanding of the material, and on a very small scale at that. The anthropological perspective is quite a novel thing, and so is our consideration of a material which, though plentiful, has hitherto been used in a different manner, by historians in particular. It therefore seems a good strategy to isolate an ostensibly more accessible object of study from within the huge field of religious anthropology. An anthropology of the sacred would seem to serve the purpose here.

To define the anthropology of the sacred as a subcategory of religious anthropology may seem paradoxical or even misguided for, strictly speaking, the former may well appear at first sight more inclusive than the latter. One could restrict oneself to those elementary crystallisations which enclose the living and lived content of religion within established institutions. But religious experience involves a religious drive, and every life or quest or even basic consciousness of sacrality presupposes a religious universe or a religious approach to existence and to things. Considered as a whole, the anthropology of the sacred is virtually an immediate datum. Its material, crude as it is, is often quite manifest and openly and obviously displayed, for evidence of it is often supplied by popular cults. Within this boundless mass of data, it is practices, gestures, and rites which give the impression of being the expression of a common language derived from an anthropology that is already in place. The sacred is easily approached, and our main difficulty consists in sifting through the vast amount of material, but we should be careful not to come to premature conclusions regarding its essential nature. It may be best defined in terms of the life of objects, but there is a sacral creation which precedes objects, or which may subsist without them. If we employ the only kind of interpretation which takes the totality into account, namely, an ambivalent one, this creation is double, involving both supernatural creation – and everything which is, by whatever path, a sacralisation from above – and collective interpersonal creation, in which group, milieu and society are recognised in the instant or in time as bearers of sacral power.

An anthropology of the sacred, so construed, ought therefore to involve each of the three crucial paths by which the sacred and sacral creation are manifested in human experience. The interpersonal is often the hardest domain to subject to a scientific analysis, but through an inventory of values termed sacred, through prohibitions, memorial cults (such as the monuments to the dead of the two world wars), and linguistic habits (even of the most cursory sort), it provides the basic material for whatever is acknowledged or recognised, and therefore for what is inherited over time.

Yet one ought not to neglect sacral creation in the present either. Those grassroots communities developing nowadays within the Western European Churches undoubtedly live what is, through their reading of the Gospel, their reception of the Word and their elective affinities, a sacral creation. Around Charles de Gaulle's tomb we find a cult of the body, of historical memory and of collective idealisation emerging, all focused upon 'a particular idea of France'. When people gather at a tomb to celebrate a large-scale cult, be it a parade or a military review, they live out states of sublimation in a frenzy of demand, tension or conjuration. The mechanisms that are involved and the fervour that is expressed undoubtedly represent widespread needs, but they also express the sense of the sacred experienced by a given collectivity. These scattered insights into the nature of interpersonal sacrality all have, moreover, a common source. They stem from the drives, from the life of the irrational within the collective soul, an irrational whose 'existential' dynamic involves a search for the 'other', along with transcendence, completion, power and sublimation.

The sacred must never lapse into mere self-worship – the selfish idol is of itself separate from the flock – nor crystallise into sterile narcissism. On the contrary, it is a spring which gushes forth, which wells up towards its proper place, the beyond. The beyond is in fact always more or less immanent in present exaltations and panics, and its dynamic derives from an encounter with the other forms of sacral creation, the manifestation of the supernatural. Sites are consecrated from above by acts in sacred history, by their rootedness in a cosmogony, by the human existence of a divine being or by a celestial apparition or a message; by coming face to face with an event or with the ἐσχάτη, or with the fulfilment of the divine promise; through a collective awareness of participating in a sacred history or, at a more primitive level, through a collective sacral life, itself an expression of the need for the Presence; through an incarnation of the Book or of the Word, a fulfilment of what has been written or announced; or through sequences of myths or legends which unite, in terms of existence and collective consciousness, the natural and the supernatural, offering a wide range of different ways in which human beings may take in their search for the sacralisation of the Presence.

The human trajectory may still therefore be said to be the expression of an irrational power-drive. Manifestations of the supernatural as such are, however, of another order. Being bound as we are to revere it, our knowledge of it is little better than a record of traces, of moments of fruitfulness, of psychic charges which the collective consciousness has received from above or from beyond. Caught as it is between transcendence and immanence, the natural and the supernatural, sacral fervour is marked by a quivering intensity, by an exceptionally creative and fruitful ardour. All the signs with which it marks the human domain, from the words denoting a divine apparition to the innumerable legends by which the human imagination gives tangible form to the almost ineffable exchanges between the two worlds, are invested with a powerfully expressive sacrality.

The most immediate object of study for an anthropology of the sacred remains, however, the sacred object. Cults surrounding holy bodies or relics, cults of sacred places variously inscribed in the cosmic or in the historic, worship of images or of other objects, and oratories by the roadside or at the crossroads, all work upon the collective soul, urging us to worship or to beg forgiveness and all, like drives, have an object upon which they are fixated. A fixation obviously implies that one is aware and responsive, and by means of the object the sacral influx returns to the person who prays, multiplying his creative energy. At the very heart of silence and mystery, this dialogue has been for centuries preceded by an exchange in sacral resources, in which the object, wordlessly and without reference to reason, causes a Presence to manifest itself.

Owing to the conjuratory impulse of this dialogue, the language of the vast mass of people is an act of self-transcendence, and therefore of religion. Materialisation thus creates a life infinitely suggestive of the depths. It involves moving from the inside to the outside, in contrast to a movement which one might term intellectual or cultural and which starts from the outside and works towards the inside, tending by the same token to suppress the object. These widespread external cults, which make no distinction between Greek or Gentile, or between the educated and the uneducated, which involve everyone indiscriminately in the collective act of quest and participation, clearly represent a basic anthropological fact, but one which is also the root and sap of *homo religiosus*. Almost all of these cults, moreover, whether concerned with conjuration or with begging forgiveness, are therapeutic. A concern to cure is the commonest and also the most ordinarily poignant expression of the fundamental instinct of human beings in their display of power: the wish not to die. Soteriologies instruct human societies as to how they may overcome death or bring people back to life.

Therapeutic skills are not so much taught as cultivated, and are therefore the expression of an instinct which preserves much of its original nature as a vital, indeed an animal need. To have recourse to such skills is to strive to rid daily life of physical ills. The sacral has astonishing efficacy on those occasions upon which our vital equilibrium, and therefore the very power of existence, is undermined. Where simples and popular medicine prove insufficient, a sacral object may well cure us of our pain. It effects this cure through the agency of supernatural belief, and sometimes through that of the supernatural itself, resting upon the demand of human beings for wholeness, for normality and for an end to suffering, and upon the deployment of a boundless vital energy. The sacred objects through which such fixations occur are, in the Christian world, anthropomorphised. This anthropomorphisation enables one to employ the word, even if it is unspoken. To pray for a cure is already to effect one. Therapy is therefore as common, and as poignant, as sickness. It is the most widespread of the forms of sacrality, predominantly popular in idiom but invariably operative at the most visceral level, in the depths, as it were, of the collectivity. It offers a vast amount of material for anthropological investigation, and is, save for the actual mysteries of the therapeutic process, almost always decipherable.

If an anthropologist concerned with Western society wishes to become familiar with wellnigh all of the material, he will have to begin by constituting it. This is the more or less ethnological aspect of the inquiry, and it requires as many different strategies as there are variations in the nature of the data which go to make up the material. Such inquiries occur in the present and, as they proceed, one may be tempted to freeze them within an eternal present, so common is it for testimonies regarding an inventory of sacralities to assert that such things have been there 'for ever'. If, for instance, one makes an inventory of pilgrimages and popular cults the length and breadth of the country, even at a time when such phenomena are, persistently but randomly, under attack, one finds people quite unanimous as to their longevity. According to popular conception, the sacral is outside of time, it is 'for ever'. The collective soul, given the basic nature of its sacral energy, cannot conceive that this reality, which for it is eternal, is immersed in duration. The sacred defies time, since it is itself a means or a weapon for the overcoming of it. By its very nature it refuses history. Yet any inventory of sacred objects leads us towards history, if only because of the degree of attrition suffered by the various cults. Once a memory has survived intact for a significant period, sometimes for as much as a thousand years, its continuity is established once and for all. We then have to consider the vitality of the collective need which such cults express, the mechanisms which used to guarantee this vitality and which are now exhausted – as well as those which are still operative – and consistency or change in historical circumstances as cults move from place to place or remain where they are. All of these questions require answers in which an analysis of life through time is given, and which are therefore historical. In the case of France, for instance, an exhaustive listing of popular cults in a particular area which are therapeutic and which have the form either of institutional or of individual or of cryptal pilgrimages, would immediately reveal a number of basic features common to them all.

If we begin by considering the period from, say, 1850, to the present, we find that a 'model' of what a pilgrimage should be seems to be widespread. Not only does each French diocese have its annual pilgrimage to Lourdes but many cults of the Virgin of Lourdes have been established in other parts of France. These are either inside a parish church, or outside it when a natural cragginess or a rock opening out into a grotto (where this is not artificially constructed) can be used to good advantage. The finishing touches to this *imago* from Lourdes are very often provided these days by a sculpted dialogue between the Virgin in her grotto and, at a respectful distance, a Bernadette on her knees dressed as a humble peasant girl.

Why is this model and not another (La Salette or Pontmain, for instance) chosen? Only history can provide an answer to this question. Though a number of imponderables are involved, we must place this choice in the context of a wider phenomenon, and one which is apparent in pilgrimage cults in the modern world, namely, the Church's tendency, whether conscious or not, to satisfy the need for pilgrimage by using large urban centres, and thereby perhaps detaching a previously sedentary population from its autochthonous cults. Among the possible historical approaches, a Marxist analysis clearly has some cogency here. Thus, the development of the railways has definitely expanded the space of the sacred, whilst also weakening it to some degree – at least by altering the moods, expectations and penitential values of the pilgrim-age, and also perhaps by affecting its intrinsic energy, and therefore the reception of grace.

The extraordinary expansion of the cult of Mary in the nineteenth century was preceded – and at a deeper level the way was undoubtedly prepared for it – by the spread, at the height of the Counter-Reformation (and in the first half of the seventeenth century in particular), of numerous shrines celebrating the omnipotent intercession of the Virgin, which were regarded as idolatrous by the Reformation and therefore fiercely combated. Memories of this expansion are clearly preserved in the data which are now being analysed by researchers, such as devotional writings from the literature of pilgrimage, and contempo-rary inscriptions, furniture or the architectural detail of a shrine (which may easily be dated). Historical strata may thus be easily established, and then corroborated by the correlations that emerge as the inquiry advances. Collec-tions of legends provide still more correlations. We find that most of these cults are justified by narratives of 'inventions'. Thus, a statue or a cult object is miraculously discovered in the hollow of a tree (Virgins of the Oak or of the Elm, or of some vital element which is plentiful or, conversely, rare in the region), in a nook in the earth, or in the translucent water of a fountain or of a pool. Its discovery is invariably made by one of the simplest of lay people, by a shepherd or a little peasant girl watching over her flock, or indeed by one of the animals in that flock. It is clear that neither clergyman nor Church is involved in the actual process of discovery. This fact suggests that the laity is thereby rewarded and that a people that has faith, as distinct from the institution of the Church, is able to bestow upon itself, prior to any ecclesiastical discipline, the sacral object which it needs. We may make such an interpretation of history in the present period, as we investigate the second of the two levels of sacralisation, which is crystallised in the form of the legendaries of innumerable pilgrimages.

One of these two levels involves the existence of the Black Virgins, who are usually said to have originated in the East. To make this appear more 'natural', reference is made to the historical fact of the Crusades and it is suggested that the bearer was either a Crusader or a pilgrim. Such associations have the coherence of fact for the pilgrim mind and are therefore quite widespread. Our Western European and Christian sacralities commonly invoke the forms of sacral dependence upon the East which such an interpretation encourages. At a deeper level, there is an emphasis upon the chthonic implications of all those cults in which *négritude* and maternity are linked, the iconological type of the *sedes sapientiae* most commonly being a statue. Here we are in the presence of the mystery of birth and of the return, watched over by wisdom.

The other association, which is less widespread, involves an entire history, namely, the collectivity's need to place the origin of its cult far back in Carolingian times. This may be because of Charlemagne's mythical status, and also perhaps because of particular episodes in that same epoch, such as the struggle against Islam, with Charles Martel being the key name or figure. The fixing of a cult at such a historical level defines time as a dense thing for us, and sacralises origins by endowing them with an imaginary venerability. Thus, if we restrict ourselves to the lists available to us today, we can undertake a spectral analysis of the past which goes back – or down – to the depths of time: visionary Virgins of the nineteenth and twentieth centuries; Marian 'inventions' of the seventeenth century, which sometimes occur as late as the end of the eighteenth century; Virgins of Pity, which must be mentioned here since they reached epidemic proportions in the fourteenth and fifteenth centuries; and finally, Virgins of Majesty, of Dominion and of Wisdom, whose umbilical links with the East are quite apparent. This is a history of the depths which is transparent to the present. Through the picture which it reveals we are able to investigate the great shifts in religion, i.e. the transformations in the sacral vision and the participation of the previously silent masses, who have had a voice of their own restored to them even in this rudimentary account.

Although it hardly seems necessary to present further examples of the insistence of the past, indeed of the insistence of the eternal in the present (considered as a measure of the human), two deserve to be described here, for they are a part of our daily experience and of our ordinary sensibility. One concerns the distribution of cult sites, the other, of their titular saints. Both are inscribed in our landscape, in a countryside which, however familiar, is now indecipherable.

In a study of the distribution of cult sites, we have to take into consideration the spread of urbanisation and the varying amounts of low-lying country. We also have to take account, in both country and town, of chapels that have been transformed into garages or stables, and sometimes even, incongruously enough, into restaurants. Finally, old maps, place names, still vivid collective memories of cults, or other traces, may point to the existence of churches or chapels which have now disappeared. These facts could be considered solely from the perspective of historical geography. This approach would necessarily limit one to by now well-established facts, such as the spread of the mendicant orders to the cities, the *intra muros* rivalry between the new congregations and the old religious families who had returned from the countryside, and the passions of the rich and powerful as they used the city as a stage upon which to fight for their own cult sites and for their glory.

In addition, one would consider – once the people had begun talking to their priest during his canonical visits – the much repeated complaints about the great distance away of the church, and about the difficulties of reaching it in winter and in bad weather, about the imposition of a site for the castral cult, or about the complex but significant division of responsibilities between parish church and succursal chapel and, at a greater remove, that between the mother church and subsequent parish churches and, finally, the expansion which most often figures on the historical record, that of votive or oratory chapels.

Yet, if we begin at the most basic level, density and scarcity are themselves spiritual factors, as are the empty stretches which appear on maps showing the distribution of cult sites. Our investigation into the need for the sacred must therefore turn on the relative proximity or distance of God and house of prayer (where each may be in inverse ratio to the other); on a cultic enthusiasm which will immediately place in question the social and biological status of the faithful and the sacral supports around which their sense of reality crystallises, and will thus identify cults as being open or closed; and, at an altogether basic but nevertheless significant level, it must turn on the admission that there is an 'average' space of sacralisation which must be traversed if God and his house are to be reached. Through these faint, often barely perceptible features, we may uncover the instincts of the collective soul, a need for the church and a sense that it is the actual hub of the social order. This is still more apparent in the case of empty spaces. Thus, there are areas which it is forbidden to sacralise and which tend to be most highly marked with cosmic intensity. In them one may read the unceasing, dramatic and often fatal dialogue between man and nature. There is a profound freedom in such places, something inspiring, in the sense that this inspiration is nature, and a nature which is the basis of existence and thus a fundamental anthropological reality. This enables us to assess, in the case of societies which have been Christian for most of their history, just how far-reaching and bold their anthropomorphism has been, the Christian baptism of cult sites having almost invariably entailed the anthropo-morphisation of a cosmic *locus*.

Chapels, oratories or crosses dotted along the roadside tell us just as much as ordinary cult sites. Their number, situation or spacing all point to a complex history in which the need for an object as a support or a pretext for prayer, the rhythms of a sacred space, the demands of sublimation with regard to travelling or labour, and the necessary sacralisation of particular sites in space, such as crossroads or entrances to estates, is powerfully expressed. Having listed these signs, one may offer a first cursory interpretation of the religious habits or needs of an area, just as one may interpret the presence or absence of niches on the façades of peasant houses in terms of the range of a protective statue. Where a religious form is so deep-rooted that it assumes local forms, one may use it, provided that one analyses it rigorously, to discover another form of depth, beyond historical detail. Where an oratory is concerned, this often takes the form of an act of exorcism; where crosses are concerned, there will be a multiplicity of supplications which predate the Christian era. There is, in short, a whole network of protective devices aimed at preventing nature, which is nevertheless taken for granted, from enjoying sole, implacable and potentially annihilatory sovereignty over man.

Crosses, in particular, tell of the other form of sovereignty, that of man; erected as they are, they are the work of man and rule over space (although Christian crosses are an impoverished and reduced version of the four-branched cross, itself representing a genuine mastery over physical, and indeed psychical, extension). Being solar symbols as well, through their symbolic condensation they confirm human mastery over heavenly bodies and cause them to shine by grace, and this is true also of the actual gestures of crossing oneself used by those who pray or who pass by. A simple comparison of different types of cross shows their language to be yet more explicit (in that the choice of model expresses a state of the collective soul or, on the other hand, has moulded such a state down the ages), above all in the opposition between a cross of crude stone and a historiated one. The appearance of Christ's body, whether meticulously realist or full of pathos (as it tends to be nowadays), invests the cross with another presence. This latter choice by itself testifies to an intellectual adherence to an ecclesiastical culture, to an emphasis upon a humanist interpretation of Christ's mission and, in a sense, to a diminution in the symbolic power of the cross. For any humanisation cannot help but run counter to the meaning of the naked object, of this sovereign stone cross with no figure upon it.

The anthropology of our ancient Christian world finds, in sites marked by cosmic signs or by simple crosses at crossroads, its most startling expression. Indeed, the anthropomorphic and, at the same time, anthropocentric image is constitutive of Christian sacral society, entailing as it does an unrelenting yearning to recover the object in its raw state. In uncovering this huge endeavour, we are engaged nowadays in a kind of release either of the power of a traditional order, or of a baptismal reverence or, on the other hand, of a lost wealth (which makes it a manifestation of a form of human existence) at the outer edges of 'being'.

Any account of titulars raises the problem of anthropomorphism. For sacral power is here released from any connection with the name of man or of God made man, or, more rarely, from a theological, indeed historical, datum concerning divinities. A name obviously entails a choice. This collective choice of a patron, which often complements another, secondary one (a patron of a church or of a chapel and, as often, a patron of a parish) contains a religious meaning which has often all but disappeared over the centuries, but a trace of the choice persists in the form of the name associated with the religious building in question. Indeed, there are often two names rather than one, for popular piety will either transpose or, for a variety of contingent reasons which quickly become habitual, will use a different name from the ecclesiastic titular. Yet whether they are single names or double (where the titular and the secondary name are linked), the massive inventory of these titulars represents an enormously illuminating source of information for us, which may be interpreted in terms of both time and space. Whichever diocese in France you choose, even a crude quantification makes fascinating reading. The Virgin and the saints have been engaged in combat for many centuries and statistically, notwithstanding the powerful impulses towards Mariolatry in the present period, the saints are winning, thanks in part to the powerful position of Saint Martin, all of which demonstrates the fundamental Evangelism of black monasticism. A further sifting of the evidence provided by this somewhat haphazard list shows that recent names, as well as being theological coinages, were products of the Church in a period when its theological values were undergoing a transformation or, at any rate, a shift in emphasis, and all these occur in parishes or cult sites in urbanised zones or in zones where urbanisation was in progress.

The area formerly known as the lowlands proves to have been quite remarkably loyal to its saints. Quite apart from these objective impressions, titulars are plainly a part of the *longue durée*. A handful of modern accretions or variations do not affect the overwhelmingly monolithic nature of the phenomenon, as if it had been raised at the very beginning of time. Nevertheless, a series of comparisons, and the corroboration offered by overlapping historical studies, will bring different strata, as it were, to light, and will disclose changes in response to cults on the part of the groups of believers within a given diocesan structure.

One may, then, produce a chronology of the choices which were made and which, if one considers the correlations thereby established, will point to the major advances of the Apostolate, showing its impetus as well as the agreement, both theological and popular, between the teaching of the Church and the cultic conditioning of the masses. The significance of this agreement does not lie so much in the implicit freedom accorded to pilgrimages or to more or less developed, more or less public or secret popular cults, as in the great density of these choices, which contain, however ignorant we are historically of those who made them, a rock of the collective soul which the centuries have not worn away. To this rock, legends or historical narratives are connected which tell of the truth of a tale or of the probable or actual existence of a patron saint. The structure and coherence of these narratives enables us to date them historically, and they provide evidence of the criteria for sacrilisation or for the 'model' of sanctity operative in a given epoch or society. The features of such a 'model' may be dimly discerned even in the case of mawkish images of Saint Sulpice, and even when the statue of the patron saint has been relegated to one of the darker corners of a church. Through quantitative analysis we are able to learn still more from these models. For, in spite of the fact that modern canonisations result in the creation of very few titulars, even the most rudimentary quantitative classification reveals the existence of a large number of them. For instance, there is what one might term the obligatory 'episcopalisation' of the patron saint in those situations in which the powerful in a society strive to compensate themselves for the domination of the monasteries; there is the relative importance of the patron saint who is autochthonous, or who is reckoned to be such, and of the stranger; there is the crucial stratum of saints who have come from the East, and the role played by Apostolic, indeed by Roman, cults. These major divisions, which are readily apparent in any statistical survey, represent what is still in effect a secret history of the spread of cults, and of the succession of models, or of types of model, from one epoch to another. All of this is written into our present, although the investigator may very often find both that the collectivity in the area is unaware of the identity of the church's titular and that the diocesan Ordos have preserved a relatively large number of uncorrected errors.

Where space is concerned, an inventory of titulars allows one to chart, for a particular geographical area (and it is preferable to choose the largest that is consistent with the criterion of historical coherence), the manner in which saints' names radiate outwards from a given point, circulate or drift. A complete account would have to include some observations about stable features; what is one to make of those saints who appear to have feet of clay, and who never circulate? What historical conditions may be held to explain their fixity, whilst other saints cover the whole world? The extraordinary diaspora of the cult of Saint Martin, for example, is crucial to the cults of the Christian West; the Bourges–Trèves diagonal has served as a path for the migration of cults, and there is likewise an axis passing through the Rhône valley. Historical and geographical conditions may easily account for all these features of the inventory. Beyond these, however, we have to explain why choices are coherent, why the 'other' is so readily accepted (an acceptance which serves as a measure of the distance up to which a given collectivity will treat something as sacral), and how it is that acculturation occurs. The tag, *major e longinquo reverentia*, does not only hold for the classical period, for it will also serve as a key to interpreting the sacralising mechanisms of the collective soul.

From this picture of the limits, in terms of distance, of sacralisation, it ought to be possible to define a palette, as it were, of the soul's exigencies. In gaining access to the sacral by way of space, one is adopting an anthropological approach, and one of the most effective of such approaches, to the mysterious process through which the energy of the sacral contained in the collective soul is focused upon an object. It is, moreover, the case that any study of the circulation of sacral objects in terms of titulars in, for instance, Europe allows one an understanding of the basic features of an exchange of sacralities, which in some epochs overlap and in others are quite separate. We are thus concerned with a system of religious language which, beyond the vernacular languages or indeed, the sacred language, demands to be deciphered. All the more so given that the spread of cults, along with the crucial act by which a patron marks a cult site, is closely linked to the circulation and veneration of relics. These latter, in the form of the cult of the holy body, testify to another sort of Christian anthropomorphism. Whether authentic or artificial, these relics are invested either naturally or psychically with sacralities, and for at least a millennium trade in them has served to assuage the Christian West's hunger for the sacral.

This trade in relics often conformed to ties of descent, or to relations between groups and relations forged by the circulation of objects, and analysis of these ought to enable us to identify both some of the psychic dimensions of the need for the sacral and the paths by which this need is satisfied. Once things are materialised or, as one ought to put it, are humanised, the geographical effects of a cult's expansion prove that states of the collective soul often resemble each other and, where societies of different ethnic composition are involved, give rise either to an irrational drive towards unity, or to anthropomorphic fables concerning the respective virtues of the objects compared, or (as a kind of heritage 'common' to all traditions) to a demand for the sacral that is an absolutely essential feature of the Christian condition.

Hitherto my account has kept to the level at which the inquiry itself is pursued, yet even when it is limited to the most superficial aspects of the present, history has a way of intruding. In fact, one could put it that the conducting of such an inquiry releases history. For this to occur, three conditions must, however, be met. We ought not to restrict ourselves at the outset, as ethnologists too often do, to isolated cases. Nor should we rest content with hasty comparisons between such isolated cases, basing inductive arguments upon more or less superficial similarities. Comparison should involve confrontation and the discovery of connections within the data, which themselves suggest more deep-rooted links rather than a deceptive parallelism which reduces everything to identity. Bearing these two cautionary observations in mind, let us now proceed to the third condition, which concerns the use of quantification. As long as it is feasible to employ it, and as long as it is applied to things of the same kind, this approach is enormously productive. It enables one to differentiate between objects and therefore, through its juxtaposition of the undifferentiated and the specific, to arrive at a more nuanced description, highlighting both the choices that are made and the inner necessity of history (inasmuch as every specific fact is also historical).

It is also the case that the wide range of evidence produced by the use of a large sample takes historical inquiry to an altogether deeper level than is achieved by writing a series of overlapping monographs. History is not obliterated by such a massive use of evidence; it is forced, rather, to dig still deeper. It releases kinds of statement that have hitherto been silenced. Thus, the statistically attested remanences of surviving cults of the Virgin of Pity serve on the one hand to bring out their great age and, on the other hand, enable one to ascertain the level at which they first arose (we know, again through statistical information, that this was in the fourteenth century). This allows us, in borderline cases, to risk an inductive argument. Last but not least, we are obliged to analyse the extent to which this cult is informed either by the part played in the collective psychodrama by relations with the mother and with the dead son, or else by the staging of a matriarchal exaltation which has become plaintive rather than imperious, and involves the imperious play of a pacified grief instead.

Another example, which may serve to justify the employment of exploratory forms of inductive argument, concerns the statistically proven fact that Easter Monday or Pentecost pilgrimages are very longstanding institutions. The celebration of a feast day in the fields may be taken to be a more recent cult, but a very limited amount of research will usually serve to bring out the super-imposition of modern upon more ancient celebrations.

We all know that history presents things to the present but, nevertheless, through the very multiplicity of its approaches, history reinforces and deepens any analysis of the anthropology of the sacred. First of all, since we should begin with the most obvious approaches, what we are nowadays able to establish regarding a cult's duration derives from some historical inquiry, from a document, a building, or from an overlapping of pieces of information by means of which past and present become entangled materially and objectively. Vague oral testimony, on the other hand, only tells us about the sheer density of duration and may in one sense definitely be said to be an anthropological property of the *longue durée*. Yet it does not enable us to measure it. The definite attribution of historical dates, when it is possible (and this is more often the case than one might at first suppose), allows one to discern a hierarchy of different durations. This in itself represents an addition to the range of historical documentation, for comparison of what endures with what passes sheds light on the hidden nutriments of history.

Cults do disappear. Thus, it would be a gross error to treat the cult of Joan of Arc as a thriving one, even though the majority of French churches contain a statue of the Maid of Lorraine. A need for this cult did once exist and for a brief period it was fashionable. We cannot say whether the need disappeared or whether the object or image ceased to answer to that need, but we do know that the ubiquitous statues of Joan of Arc are all but dead to us. This maid in armour, with her banner rippling in the breeze, her angelic face and uplifted eyes, and represented, as she sometimes is, with her hands joined together and holding the blade of death vertically aloft, can no longer be said to inspire much religious enthusiasm. There is, admittedly, a somewhat intellectual pilgrimage to Domrémy-la-Pucelle, but there are hardly any *ex-votos* beside the statues of our churches. The Maid of Lorraine and Thérèse of Lisieux are often to be found together in churches, on the opposing pillars or walls of the nave, and it is the rose-crowned nun who comes off best. But how long will she, in her turn, prevail? These modern cults, founded half a century ago, already seem worn out, or all but so. Is there something intrinsically fragile about their sudden emergence, or do these necessary creations represent an organic need, in line with the frenzied nature of our times, for something else, for something better? A vigorous cult does not automatically emerge from every model of sanctity. To acknowledge this is to recognise the ways in which the quest for perfection or for the power of the depths is expressed. It is also to recognise the nature of their conditioning, for how far can the cult of Saint Antony of Vienne, strangely modified, admittedly, by that of Antony of Padua, be said to correspond still to a model of sanctity, the age of hermits being long since gone? But, in the case of the saint who cures ergot poisoning, we are concerned with a centuries-long expanse of human suffering which is still inscribed in the collective memory and therefore revered.

The reasons for these phenomena need not concern us here, since analysis will uncover them. It is the crude interplay of the long and the short term which serves to determine how long a cult will endure. Yet there are also curiously sudden eruptions, as is the case with the contemporary diffusion of Christian cults in the West. One instance of this is the dramatic increase in supplications to Rita, a saint concerned with hopeless causes, who was a fifteenth-century Augustinian nun from Umbria, and who has only figured on altars since the end of the nineteenth century. She has performed miracles for some Italian congregations in particular, and people have recourse to her in cases of common, day-to-day anxiety, itself so poignant a thing in the shifts and changes of our own period. The crude fact of a long-lasting cult, which is both revered and conjuratory, releases, for a given collectivity, the language of the beyond, a beyond which is not merely the other life, but which unites in one whole the transcendence of the self and the emergence of a paragon, a liberation from both physical and moral evil, in short, a plenitude of power which represents the fundamental meaning of the religious act as lived in its exalted and fructifying creative tension. The inner soul of a given human group surrenders itself to this historically hierarchised orchestration. The cult of the virgin Catherine, for the eight centuries that are properly documented, and through the countless altars or chapels and through the still widespread representation of the saint with her princely crown and her iron-spoked wheel (the image of her martyrdom), is the embodiment of feminine nubility for the collective consciousness of the Christian West, her fate encapsulated in the legend surrounding the Eastern princess whose body is miraculously preserved in the monastery at Sinai. Sometimes we may discern in the image of the virgin with a sword, which *Catherinettes* on occasion wear on their bonnets, and which suggest whether unconsciously or not, the motif of castration, the temptation to despair about sexual fulfilment and fertility. Historical demographers have not yet produced a statistical analysis of the forms of the cult of Saint Catherine. There can be no doubt, however, that it is the key to many of the secrets of feminine sexuality in the Christian West, in both the mediaeval and the modern period.

Collective illnesses or panics may likewise be discerned in the repeated emergence of the cults of famous curers, of plague saints or of other thaumaturges. These may be represented either as belonging to the learned culture, as was the case with the two doctors, Gervase and Protaius, or as elected by the people, in which case the large monasteries, seeking material support, often played a significant part.

Informative though it may be to give some impression of the enduring nature of sacralities, it is not sufficient. For within the broad sweep of continuity there are variations, if not leaps, substitutions and more or less obvious transpositions. An anthropology of the sacred would be deficient if it did not present a history of lived sacralities, for it is only through such a history that the impulses of a collective existence that is both passive and traditional, frenetic and careworn, may be apprehended. It would be quite erroneous to treat the cultic universe as if it had been in place for centuries. Major shifts or alterations occur gradually, but there are many minor episodes to be noted.

Evidence for such changes may be identified at at least three different levels. First, one may consider specific, isolated cases. For example, in the case of cults, it is necessary to identify, to the extent that the documents enable one to do so, successive diachronic levels within the range of titulars. Where an obviously ancient cult is concerned, that of an apostle or an Eastern saint, and one that the contemporary Ordos record as still having the same title, it would seem quite reasonable to assume an almost timeless fixity. In the diocese of Chartres, in particular, denser sections in documents suggest that throughout the nineteenth century, the ostensibly immovable titular was repeatedly displaced in the believers' affections by a secondary figure, whose memory has now faded and who was usually a therapeutic saint. Were it not for this information this impulse would have been buried, and we thus discover that the people in their fervour had their own saint rather than one imposed by higher canonic or cultic authorities. For want of this historical perspective, these 'obscure' cultic observances would have been hidden for ever.

Second, we are concerned with the creation of myths. By which I should stress that I mean the creation or awareness of them, and not the life of myths, for where existence in time is concerned, the historical approach is the sole legitimate one. Creation is an act that stems from an anthropological impulse, as analysis of the example of the crusade serves to show. This is true at any rate of the 'crusade' as a word or as a notion, if not of the 'crusade' as seen in historical terms. There is of course no comparison, historically speaking, between the episodes of the eleventh to thirteenth centuries, or indeed the subsequent ones, and today's crusades, as they are represented and celebrated. Yet, from the close of the eighteenth century, at the time of revolutionary crisis, this same term 'crusade' emerged in a mysterious manner as a support for the expression and crystallisation of confused collective impulses. Was the word simply raided, as it were, from the language or does its revival represent rather the resurgence of needs analogous to those experienced in the past?

For all its evident wastefulness, language has its rigorous side and does not revive things at random or without reference to a heritage. The fragile but tenacious link of the sign draws our attention both to the continuities in a centuries-old historical tradition, that of the crusade for Christian guardianship over the Holy Land, prolonged by the Turkish war up until the beginning of the modern period, and to the progressive revival of a cause, almost at the very moment at which the historical fact had itself reached its final point of historical exhaustion. Without in any way wishing to posit artificial continuities, it is sufficient (now that the entire history lies behind us) to note the synchronies and transpositions that do occur, even if only at the level of the sign. Thus, analysis of the psychosocial content of this sign in its contemporary usage, as when the need for a crusade is suddenly announced, is instructive in two ways. First, we are able to intuit that previously latent forces are coming to fruition, and we thereby gain access to a life of the depths which is otherwise opaque to us. Second, we are able to draw conclusions about acts in the distant past from our understanding of the content of contemporary ones, and we are also able to use our analytic understanding of the ancient phenomenon to shed light upon what today is not expressed or is not conscious.

It would be rash to draw any hard and fast conclusions about these data, but it seems fair to assert that the diachronic unfolding of these signs, for all their fragility, is an anthropological operation which expresses a collective need for the creation of a 'supersociety', a collective sublimation which explodes patterns of servitude, habits and humdrum modes of existence, and which expresses a completion of power opening out the human condition into a domain lying beyond itself, such that the other world is finally conquered.

A crusade thus entails a dynamic of 'passage', which is both a mastery of the energy of the elements involved, an appropriation of the keys between the two worlds, and a therapy for collective panic. The solar imprint of the cross is a feature both of the call to a crusade and of the actual act. It is the case that the vernacular languages of the furthest fringes of the West, of France, England and the United States of America, have as yet found no other sign to express the best, the greatest and the most sublime of collective acts than that used, relatively late in history, to describe the journey to Jerusalem, whose initial enthusiasm was informed by a nigh irresistible promise of salvation. Only a diachronic study enables us to recover the vicissitudes of such a sign, its changes, and the manner in which its content has shifted from the eleventh to the twentieth century. We are thereby able to discern both the silent and exalted appeals of the modern period and the mystery of these tumultuous migrations within ancient Christendom. It is thus the task of history to shed light on the process whereby the depths emerge from within a collective act of transgression of the world, an act which, in human terms, is redolent of the omnipotence of the sacral.

We then have to give some account of a third and possibly even more profound level. After the mythical creation of a collective omnipotence, with all its pomp and works, we have to confront the fact of lived time. I ought properly to have referred to 'times' rather than to 'time', for it is multiple rather than single. Interwoven with the, as it were, linear time of historical continuities, and thereby forming a kind of arabesque, is the emotional and sacral time of expectation, which may be prophetic or, more solemnly still, may refer to the ἐσχάτη. This eschatological time is apparently more homogeneous, but it contains rhythms and periodisations, as for instance when we arrive at a new century or approach a millennium. There may be other phenomena of this sort too, which have as yet been little explored.

What sorts of interval are there between the announcement and the revival of a prophecy? Upon what traditional motivations, hidden anxieties, fears, anguishes, wishes for revenge or weakening of the will to live is it founded?

A straightforward and objective listing of prophecies and eschatological events gives one some insight into the nature of eschatological time, which in general is absorbed or obscured by processes of historical levelling. At the level of pure duration, in all its poignancy, there are no watches or calendars but rather a tension, which may sometimes stretch to breaking-point, and through which there surges up, again by transcending itself, a human drive towards completion. An enactment of what was promised or a fulfilment of what was announced demonstrates both the truth of the announcement and the capacity of human beings to master the future, and is therefore one more instance of the unleashing or of the exercise of power. Historiographic description alone enables one to measure the extent of these frenzied contractions of collective existence in time, and it does so by identifying turning-points or underlying rhythms, the different sorts of delay which occur, and thereby analyses the struggle for immortality, which is in some sense soteriological, in terms of the exercise of power. This wish to conquer time is in fact another fundamental aspect of the human quest for omnipotence.

The desire for time to end involves the dimension of eternity, and in satisfying, or simply aspiring to this condition, we are engaged in the creation of the sacral. We are too much inclined to live through a trade in sacred objects which are external to us, and which appear to have been deposited in the midst of the human groups who place their trust in them by a hand extended from the beyond. If, however, we apprehend acts as instrinsically dynamic, the tension of sacral creation must be taken into account. As far as the human condition is concerned, there is certainly no loftier aspiration than the mastery over time which immortality, through its imperious subjugation of it, represents. In apprehending this dynamic quality, we are undoubtedly historicising the anthropological, but ridding it of its ostensible timelessness serves to incarnate it the better, i.e. to give fuller expression to certain human needs which are usually silenced.

Identification of those moments at which men grow weary of themselves and strive desperately to find a way out of history, living out the panic-stricken madness intrinsic to power, enables one to assess their deeper energies and their capacity to tolerate or to live within duration and therefore to accept it as such. At this level of struggle between man and his history, how can this latter be anything but crucial? How can this struggle do anything but enable us to arrive at a better understanding of man's existential reality, inasmuch as it provides, for each human group, a picture of its ability to exist? At the heart of such an insight there is the crucial choice between event and advent. The former is the actual woof of history; the latter represents the looming up of the 'other', and precedes the moment at which one steps outside history. The advent is an illumination or a transcendence, but does its power inform all human groups or societies equally? Or is there rather a distinction between those who reiterate the *in illo tempore* of the primordial cosmogonies and those who are free, or so they believe, of any memory of beginnings (an obvious link with Eden), who live in the expectation of a return and who are more disposed to announce than to reiterate?

I would advise against using this question as the basis for a classification, since all classifications are intrinsically reductive, as much for the object as for the actor. It serves, however, to suggest a new mode of analysis, involving a descriptive comparison of historical materials. Description isolates the materials by means of which one can assess proportions, variations or transpositions, and the different parts played in these latter by memory and progress or, to put it theologically, between lived faith and hope. The results may be significant in futurological terms, but not simply in these terms, for all knowledge regarding collective behaviour is, anthropologically speaking, of inestimable value. It is particularly valuable for an anthropology of the sacred, in which the meaning of sacral time, the actual process of sacralisation, along with the unexpected reversals, all shed light on the sacral creativity of *homo religiosus*.

I want now to situate the above observations regarding historical description more precisely, since they represent the third contribution, in the way of evidence, that history may make to anthropology. Indeed, through the overlapping of documents, history enables us to discern both continuity and change. In other words, it brings to the front of the stage the work that is done in the very depths of collective creation, and is therefore to a large extent an expression of it, employing its language. The relation between this language and meaning, i.e. creative motivation, has been very little investigated. All we are able to do at present is to pose the question and thus to remain aware of its pertinence to every analysis we undertake. This is why history serves as a kind of go-between in establishing this language as only roughly coherent and sometimes as actually discontinuous.

A few examples will demonstrate the usefulness of this language for constructing an anthropology of the sacred. Consider, for instance, the cult of the Virgin Mary, a cult which in modern times has been kept alive by apparitions, especially those of Mary on her own. There has clearly been a mutation, as far as the sacral is concerned, over the last eight centuries, if we compare the present cult of the image at Lourdes with the Black Virgins of the *sedes sapientiae* type, who were a feature of the blossoming of the Roman Church. In the former case, there is a lady glowing with purity and proclaiming her immaculate conception, a solitary figure whose ovum is crossed by rays and lit by a radiant light as if she clung to the mandorla. In the latter, we find a mother who rules, who is shrouded in as much mystery as the chthonic depths are, and who serves as an iconic support for manifestations of the divine, requiring a silent and sublimatory cult. Present-day Virgins are empowered to engage in dialogue, as is borne out by the recent proliferation in our churches of statues of Bernadette on her knees, a little apart from the 'Lady' of Lourdes. Whereas, in the case of the Roman statues, there is simply an exchange of an idolatrous sort, which is both more distant and more close, certainly more extrovert, and therefore more liberating. What is the link between these two forms, divided as they are by the centuries? In order to define it exactly, we would need to carry out an exhaustive survey, across whole areas of culture, of all the imagery associated with the Marian cult, but less ambitious studies suggest that the mother–child couple has very gradually been sundered, to be replaced by a luminously virginal figure. The solitary Mother of Sorrow, an Addolorata that the Mediterranean peoples, because of their animal fervour and matriarchal affectivity, also represent as a Virgin of the Sorrows transfixed by seven blades, stands midway between the above two forms, and is undoubtedly an expression of the tearing apart of the mother and child. Yet the Addolorata bears a trace of the laceration of the dead child. Whilst the couple has apparently been destroyed, it lives on in the mother's expression of grief.

Nowadays, the Virgins who are seen in apparitions deliver their messages on their own, and they are invariably in words rather than in pictures. These features, alongside many others, involve the abandonment of a previously silent travail, inasmuch as they mould the cultic image in such a way as to render it more obviously conjuratory. They also represent a language of the collective soul that would otherwise be inaudible. It is only by reconstituting historical sequences, through the objective reordering of extremely mutilated series, that we are able to discern in the Lady of Intercession the depths of an exchange involving a liberation through womanhood, either by accepting the mortal test of the incarnation or by attempting to represent a possible sublimation of the sin of the flesh. The various episodes in the combat between the two natures, the carnal and the spiritual, are represented by these images and their gradual transformation. Through them we are able to discern the range of different emphases that may occur, whether it is the reign of a chthonic mother, enjoying an almost impersonal sovereignty, or a drama concerning the mortality of the flesh, or an 'existential' genetics which is basically informed by a notion of the feminine and by a possible rejection of the human condition and of its strictly biological limitations, and therefore of what is undoubtedly the reality behind original sin. One cannot help but feel that behind (and also in) these episodes, these data of human experience (which are more anthropological than any brief survey is able to suggest), one may discern the large-scale images of those cosmogonies or mythologies which may be said to be, to a greater or lesser extent, original. It is as if we have had to arrive at these levels of language for silence, at last, to speak.

Because we are plunged by them into silence, plastic images of sacrality are inexhaustible. They allow a privileged access to inner voices; they are representations of the mysteries. This is the case with the Trinity, or with that aspect of the Incarnation which we term the Annunciation. Nowadays the mystery is primarily an intellectual or theological one; the image of three persons bound together or joined by the curious signifying link of the Spirit in the form of a dove, is now defunct or buried. Only historical description will enable us to establish how it is that it has become either impossible or pointless or irrelevant to represent this divine key to the life of the universe, not least because a famous event occurred to this effect, namely, what was effectively a prohibition on representations of the mystery on the part of the Council of Trent. A secret of the soul lies buried within this long drawn-out rejection of symbolic correspondence.

Only through a proper sequence of historically rooted materials can we shed any light on what would either appear to be less and less experienced as a need, or represents a fear of treating objects as the repositories of the unfamiliar, or is an actual refusal to do so. A quality of strangeness still dominates a description presented by Santiago de Compostela, in his *Codex Calixtinus*, a work of the mid-twelfth century, of a ciborium of the altar of the Apostle, a triangular ridge-tile monument placed at the top of a building. The Father faces west, the Son faces south and east, and the Holy Ghost, north. The manuscript does not state whether this was random or deliberate, but this rigorous placing reveals an order of correspondences which ought not to be lost sight of, i.e. a universal rule.

Where the Annunciation is concerned, a serial ordering of the documents is sure to prove both fruitful and instructive, especially if we investigate the relative permanence of the various structures and the meanings borne by the mass of different details. These would include the constitutive elements of the locus or of the framework involved; the spatial relations between the two persons, and the stances assumed; the Virgin's attire and objects; the need (or otherwise) for the written word in the Scroll of the Annunciation; and the closed or open nature of the scene. Whether the scene is closed or open, it will serve as a backdrop for the above-mentioned features (along with many others) as they elicit an equally wide range of verbal responses in a moving attempt to hear and sometimes even to understand the mystery or, more simply still, to ensure that the image is readily received, memorised and therefore at all times recognised. The sacred tale, through which sacral images are transmitted down the centuries, discloses the other concern intrinsic to the human condition, namely, the question of the reception of, or communication of, the mystery. It therefore provides access to Vulcan's workshop, to the shadowy areas of the human soul where, through the energy supplied by impulses which are both immediate and confused, a vocabulary of extroversion, whose effect is therapeutic and stabilising, is forged.

A historical perspective is still more vital for the study of the development of liturgical language, and for the study of the liturgy. Liturgy is actually the core of sacral ceremony. Language and rites provide the basic conditions for the sacral. Indeed, it would seem that no language adheres so closely to acts, objects or to conjuration as liturgical prayer does. Every word is crucial, because it bears the weight of the whole endeavour. The centuries must surely have worked with great delicacy on material of this sort. Along with questions of language, vocabulary and the rhythm of modulated or sung phrases, we must consider the ordering of the various stages and actions within the ceremonial.

In the Catholic world of the ancient monastic orders, up until the late eighteenth century the canonic hours represent a book of life. Indeed, the spread of the book of hours into religiously committed lay circles testifies to the existence of a profound sense of obedience to this ordering of existence, which also represents the imposition of a sanctifying rule over the day, and therefore over time. It thus provides a new approach to the anthropological analysis of man's fight with time, or of therapeutic (or indeed, conjuratory) forms, as defined by monastic experience, the cardinal experience of a single-sex community.

The monasteries educated the West, and were a creative source of so total a kind that historical researchers are still far from having accounted for their effect upon the formation of the *lectio divina*, the relationship holding between prayer and the reading of the Psalms, the illumination of the antiphons, the subtle and varied orchestration of psalms of pity and those of hope and of glory, and the purifying and soothing experience of compline, which, at the end of the day, through the shadowy *Salve Regina*, provided a refuge for the faithful in the protective bosom of the Mother. These features all emerged gradually, and in the constitution of this sacral process one may discern an ordering of relations between the human and the divine which is both a system of sacral exchanges and a source of sacral energy, i.e. a way of acting so as to acquire the power or the peace of God. It represents a dramatic staging of the play of elements within the sacral, through which the human condition is transcended. By highlighting, or simply by uncovering the motivations informing the history of a particular society's liturgy, we are able to define man in terms of his noblest ambitions, or to demonstrate the mantic secrets by means of which he establishes an equilibrium. In the same way, a festival may be regarded as a heightened expression of the impulse to continue to exist *et nunc et semper*, a nostalgia for, or an expectation of, completion and, in the depths, a return to the sources, even if only for a physical regeneration of energy. The various phases of the festival, its unfolding in space, the composition of the masses or groups involved, the integration (or otherwise) of the individual into the festival, its disciplined nature or its purifying panic, the orchestration of its representations, all serve in different ways to bind together the means with which human ensembles or societies celebrate, i.e. define themselves and rediscover themselves as creators of glory, of joy, and doubtless at their height, of peace.

In these complex domains, which in the last analysis concern discourse on eternity and entail no problem of communication (both liturgical languages and festivals are unmediated acts between persons), it is the mutations which enable us to discern the underlying processes involved. I refer here to such events as, in the West in early modern times, the Reformation and the Counter-Reformation and, most dramatically in the case of Central Europe, the successive waves of Ecclesiasticism, or again, in a different but equally illuminating perspective, the elaboration of revolutionary festivals. A historical account of these crucial ventures, of these crude syncretisms, refusals, experiences of powerlessness and simple renunciations will provide us with an appropriately dramatic impression of the sacrality of lived time in a given society, of the dynamism intrinsic to the elaboration of a festival, and of the values, images or rites belonging to it which are likely to remain either indispensable or trapped in a subsoil of habit. A proper history of ceremonies or of festivals has yet to be written, and nothing could be more crucial for uncovering that part of the collective life of the West which is buried in silence and which nevertheless represents, in the form of cathartic inventions and therapeutic empiricism, a wide span of human experience.

Let us now return to the question of liturgy, for the treatment of liturgical texts involves not only the history of collective behaviour but also the provision of 'models'. Those verses of the psalter which make an impression and leave a trace in the collective soul are primarily based upon scriptural models. I cannot conceive of a better way to cast light upon the basic associations and impulses of religious life in the Christian West than by giving a statistical analysis, epoch by epoch, of those verses of the Scriptures, and of the Psalms in particular, which were preserved in various sorts of writings intended for collective meditation. In short, it would provide a kind of grid through which to analyse the workings of the Spirit. This would allow us to identify those words, images or representations in which hitherto silent needs or expectations found expression, whilst of course making allowances for periods of habit, inertia or sclerosis, which are passively repetitive and which coexist with the sacral, especially when it is dispersed through the *longue durée*. Yet it would be a huge task to construct such a grid, since it would involve the effects of scripture over a millennium and a half on our notions of the religious path. If such a project were ever to be completed, it could not help but disclose previously unimagined mechanisms of the collective soul, providing sustenance and energy for the sacral.

Beyond words, there are anthropomorphic images. I have already noted how the type of saint that is chosen tells us much about the collective imagery of power, for a saint must be interpreted in terms of his power rather than in terms of ethical example. We can study canonisations, collective acts whose changing emphasis and mode of occurrence tell us something about the reality or otherwise of the saint concerned, as well as liturgical calendars and breviaries, which also provide us with a substantial amount of completely historical material. In more recent times, revision of calendars and breviaries has proceeded apace. Saints whose existence has been placed in question, or who have simply been deemed undesirable, have been purged, and defined as too ancient or too alien, sometimes even as too Ultramontanist. The third lessons of the breviary have been hardest hit by this passion for the truth. As much in the actual wording of the lesson as in its mental structure, a predetermined conception of a 'model' comes to be imposed, involving modes of presentation which are both general and specific. The content adds further emphasis to the vision and one can, epoch by epoch, identify a struggle between a historical rationalising spirit and an excessively traditional legendary, and thereby observe the gradual defeat of the truth of the saints by a history which rejects a large part of their irrationality. We must therefore produce both a history and an analysis of these revisions, which may be seen both as the consequence of an intellectual trajectory through which history becomes the servant of reason, the latter being of course a desacralising agency, and a gallery of 'models', in which there is a meeting, a mutual recognition and a flowering of circumstances and souls, in their unstated assurance that sanctity is possible.

Here too, then, we aim to produce an interpretation of the depths in terms of the simple unfolding of historical sequences. History, given the limits of its invariably fragmentary material, discloses our 'doing' of things and the accidents thereby occasioned. Thus, behind the sign, there is the act and the elements which constitute the act. A concern with diachrony thus brings us up against the profound and hitherto mysterious workings of the collective soul.

Episodes, constitution of vocabularies or 'discourses' in whatever form, gradual mutations and abortive impulses, all serve as communicational mediators between the historicised fixity of 'signs' and a silent gestation. By specifying the choices and the labour involved in choosing, history allows the underlying impulse of the human group to find expression, discloses its inner working, and displays the labour involved in the collective's assertion that it exists, along with an ordering of the world which gives it both its certainty, and, since certainties keep to prescribed limits, its faith in the possibility of transcending them. There should be no need to add that a group lives out one of the highest of all its tensions in relation to the sacred, whether it approaches or rejects it. In human assertion, the sacred is the power of the 'other', a thing of which one must at least have some expectation. Whether in emulation or in rivalry, it is at any rate a Promethean ambition in which man reveals his true stature. There can therefore be no better domain in which to develop a physics and a metaphysics of his greatness. In its representations of gods or saints, in its organisation, through faith, doctrine or image, of the supernatural and of the accessible or stabilising 'beyonds', human society demonstrates the irrepressible wellsprings of its quest for immortality, of its animal and spiritual will to attain to being. In using the products of history to gain access to its workshop, one is undoubtedly illuminating originating moments, hidden impulses and silences, in short, all those aspects of anthropological data which remain unsaid.

Finally, there is an obvious sense in which history is indispensable for an anthropology of the sacred, namely, with regard to consciousness (*conscience*) and our treatment of the singular. History is, after all, exclusively concerned with singularity; this is the other sense in which it may be termed a science of the relative. Indeed, in the historical domain, we are obliged, on account of unities, unique facts, individual works or creations, or the lives of particular men, to attend as much to singularity as to the quantitative and the mass. We should not, however, conclude from this that singularity is equivalent to quality. It would be a distortion to treat such a parallelism as if it were the whole truth. A single thing is simply single, and that is sufficient. We confront it in this guise, and as an object. The reverence that a historian must necessarily feel when he recognises an object has some analogy with the encounter with a sacred object; the two actions may even be linked, or spring from a common source. At any rate, both express an individual process of participation. In this perspective, by no means a negligible one, history is educative: in schooling us through the object it sheds light upon our interpretation of the sacral experience and may possibly nourish the interpretive richness off which this latter lives. Even if history only achieves this by revealing, within the object, the implicit sacralisations characteristic of the density of duration.

As a knowledge of what is singular, history enables us to render panic intelligible, without in the least altering it or rationalising it. As a science of what has been, it opens out into the full presence of what is. It is a mental therapy of crucial importance for any attempt to investigate the powers of the human condition – which is anthropology itself. In the sacral encounter, which is by its very nature immanent in the eternal, history, precisely because it is excluded (as it apparently is) from the life of the moment (that other form that the eternal assumes in living human history), is implicitly but necessarily present. As far as the individual is concerned, it does not seem possible for there to be a sacred without its efficacy being dispersed through time, i.e. without there being a real history.

To which one should add, at the risk of seeming to utter a truism, that history only examines singularities in order to go beyond them and find their origin. This at any rate involves stemming the flow of duration, a simple act which turns a 'why' into a 'how' and may also discover an answer to the former in the contents of the latter.

Finally, and more obviously still, the peculiarity of a sacral history is to be woven with events or facts which may be said to know no tomorrow. They are therefore both eminently singular and yet entail an infinite number of consequences. They may be perpetuated through being memorised and collectively transmitted in the form of cosmogonic narratives whose explanation of the nature of existence disrupts all creative duration. On the other hand, they may be inserted into, and received by life in time. This is the case with Christ's Incarnation, which involves both the historical Christ and the Gospel account of him a good century later. There is, in addition, the elaboration of the mystery, interpretation of which must involve an acceptance of the presence of the extra-temporal within the temporal. It has thus been argued that the remarkable genius of Christianity consists in there being both a divine acknowledgement of the validity of human time and a human-and-divine dramatisation of this time. The fulfilment of the mystery occurs through events, through historical singularities, and thereby through a greater power or virtue accruing to the mystery through its capacity to be manifested in an event. The more unique an event is, the more of a mystery it seems and therefore carries in itself the possibility of putting some mark on time. To give examples would require far deeper analyses than I am able to provide here. I shall simply observe that the Annunciation is an event in time, otherwise human Incarnation would not be feasible; and that the singular event transcends time and commands it. Where the mystery is concerned, we are therefore in the presence of a dramatisation of relations between time and eternity. This would in the end seem to be the unique virtue of every singular event, particularly to the extent that it becomes sacralising. Escape outside of time is often achieved by a unique event, whether it announces grace or promises a return. Where an anthropology of the sacred is concerned, it seemed impossible to avoid a reference to its incommensurable power, which is still insufficiently measured. The unique is also, in the domain of human knowledge, the chosen prey of history, on condition that the latter submits to the spiritual deprivation indispensable for identifying, placing and analysing it. For the unique has no counterpart, and one cannot approach its secret except by discovering it each time afresh.

Why should the last item under the heading of history not involve the poet's intuition? At the close of the second reminiscence which serves to introduce his *Itinéraire de Paris à Jérusalem*, and whose purpose is clearly a scholarly one, Chateaubriand, in emphasising the persistence of local traditions of holy Christian history in the Holy Land, and in no way wishing to be critical, meditated as follows: 'It is clear that religious memories are not as easily lost as purely historical ones are. The latter are in general only entrusted to the memory of a small number of educated men who may forget the truth or disguise it according to their own whim; the former are in the care of a whole people, which passes it on mechanically to its sons. So long as religious principles are stern, as is the case with Christianity, so long as the slightest deviation from a fact or an idea becomes a heresy, it is probable that everything religious will be strictly preserved down the ages.' This is admittedly a broad generalisation, which requires refining, if not modifying. It does, however, state the need for an intellectual combat between, on the one hand, that which is merely temporal, biased, singular and existential and, on the other, that which involves collective mixing, social mechanisms of self-control and forms of memory so receptive that even fables and wanderings are recorded. So it is, that what is distinct, and must remain so, is able to merge organically, 'in spirit and in truth', in such a way as to define one of the human sciences most indispensable to man, namely, that science, Promethean in quality, which concerns his living with his gods.

7. Ideologies in social history

GEORGES DUBY

It goes without saying that social history must be grounded in an analysis of material structures. History must concern itself with properly social features such as the organisation of groups, of family and neighbourhood communities, of associations, companies and sects, as well as the nature and strength of the ties which unite them, the place of individuals within these networks of relations and complex stratified hierarchies, and the distribution of power between them. But such history must take as its starting-point a comprehensive understanding of material conditions: the space which men have occupied, organised and exploited, the different movements which have determined population development, progress in techniques of production and communication, the distribution of labour, wealth and profits and the uses to which surplus values are put. Indeed, the considerable advances made over the last thirty years in historical research in the fields of economics, demography and environment have stimulated the first flowering of social history. But further progress will necessitate developing new sets of questions, reinterpreting existing documents, exploiting new sources, and identifying and prospecting new fields of investigation.

One such field is the history of ideologies. The influence of mental phenomena on the organisation and development of human societies is just as great as that of economic and demographic factors. Men's behaviour is shaped not so much by their real condition as by their usually untruthful image of that condition, by behavioural models which are cultural productions bearing only a partial resemblance to material realities.

Social relations, and their historical transformation, thus take place within a system of values which is commonly held to be a determining factor in the history of these relations. Indeed, such a value system governs the behaviour of each individual towards the other members of the group. It is the basis of the constraints which everyone, whether he accepts or tries to transgress them, expects others to respect. It is through such systems that people perceive the community, stratum or class to which they belong, and their distance from other classes, strata or communities. Their consciousness of these things may

151

be more or less clear, may be thriving or moribund, but to ignore it would reduce the value of any analysis of social classification and the dynamics involved in it. Such a value system is responsible for making people tolerate ethical and State laws, or, alternatively, for rendering these intolerable. It is, above all, the source from which social action draws its principles, the root of any society's perception of the meaning of its own history, the place where it stores its hope for the future. It nourishes dreams and utopias, those turning back to the past, to an exemplary but illusory golden age, and those projected towards a future which is wished for and sometimes even fought for. Such a value system encourages all forms of passivity and resignation, but it also contains the seeds of every attempt at reform and every revolutionary programme, the potential for sudden mutations.

One of the major tasks confronting the human sciences today is, therefore, to determine within the indissociable totality of reciprocal actions, the respective weight of, on the one hand, economic conditions and, on the other, these sets of conventions and moral precepts with their taboos and their prescriptions. The contribution of the historians will be decisive; value systems are transmitted by various kinds of educational procedure without apparent change from one generation to another, but they do not stand still. They possess their own history, which proceeds at a different pace and in different phases from the history of population and of the modes of production. And it is precisely through such contrasts that correlations between material structures and mentalities can be most clearly defined.

The study of mental attitudes, as an essential component of social history, represents a vast new perspective for both long-term and short-term historical research. It is an area which is ill-explored and wide open to new research methods, and a necessary part of it will be the history of ideologies. This is an imprecise term. The use to which it has been put in political contexts has made it ambiguous. The historian must use it in its widest sense, and with none of the pejorative connotations which it very often bears. We shall adopt Althusser's definition: 'a system (possessing its own logic and structure) of representations (images, myths, ideas or concepts) existing and playing a historical role within a given society'.

Thus defined, ideologies have a certain number of characteristics which we must first describe.

1. They are complete systems, fulfilling, by nature, a *globalising* function: they also claim to offer an overall representation of a society, its past, present and future, integrated into a complete *Weltanschauung*. Until quite recent times, therefore, those images of society have enjoyed close links with cosmologies and theologies, thus appearing to be inseparable from systems of belief: in mediaeval Europe, for instance, any representation of social relations necessarily sought to base itself on certain key Christian texts.

2. Since the primary function of ideologies is to reassure, they also perform, by their very nature, a *deforming* function. The image of the organisation of society which they articulate is the product of an integrated set of shifts and deformations, a system of lighting and perspective which tends to highlight certain relations and obscure others, all in the service of particular interests. Thus the dualistic and clearly Manichean opposition in ninth-century ecclesiastical thought, between the 'powerful' and the 'poor', encouraged the Church and the Crown, whose interests coincided, to resist pressure from the lay aristocracy; but this image served to mask certain essential economic and social functions of the rural seigneury, hiding them from the vision of even the most recent social historians.

3. The corollary is that a given society will have several different systems of representation, quite obviously entering into competition with each other. Such oppositions are partially formal, reflecting the existence of several cultural levels. But, above all, they reflect antagonisms which are sometimes of ethnic origin but are always determined by the play of power relations. These ideologies share several common features, since their function is the representation of common lived relations, and because they are constructed within the same culture and use the same cultural languages. Habitually, however, antagonistic ideologies will appear as the inverted image of each other. In twelfth-century Christendom, for instance, courtly love with its adulterous and 'pagan' meanings appears as an almost cheeky inversion of the emotional ties of lineage and vassalage, and of new forms of devotion to the Virgin. And this reflects the fact that the ideological system of which this courtly game was an essential part serves as a cover for the attitudes of unmarried knights frustrated by family customs, impeded by the progressive sclerosis of feudal relations and whose excesses the moral code of the Church was there to moderate.

4. Globalising, deforming, competing: ideologies also perform a stabilising role. This is obviously the case with systems of representation whose function is to guard the privileges of ruling social groups: but it is also true of opposing systems which invert but nonetheless reflect the first set. The ideal social organisation to which the most revolutionary ideologies aspire is still perceived, beyond the battles fought and won in the cause, as the establishment of something permanent: no utopia preaches permanent revolution. This tendency towards stability can be explained by the fact that ideological representations share with all systems of values a heaviness, an inertia, since their framework is made up of traditions.

The rigidity of the various educational institutions, the formal continuity of the linguistic tools which ideology must use, the power of myths, the instinctive hostility to change, which is one of the deepest-rooted mechanisms of life – all these factors minimise change in ideological representations as they are passed from one generation to another. Fear of the future makes ideologies reach out to the forces of conservatism, which can be seen to predominate in most of the cultural milieux which make up the social whole. Sometimes this resistance to change is strengthened by the organisation of techniques of production. This occurs for instance in predominantly agricultural societies: their survival depends upon a stable system of tried and tested techniques whose overall balance, the fruit of long years of adaptation to natural conditions, is perceived as delicate, and indeed is so in view of the society's lack of technical sophistication. Such societies, then, live in fear of novelties which might upset this balance; they build around themselves a protective shell of customs; their foundation is respect for wisdom, which resides in the ancients.

However, the social hierarchy itself is a more solid and more common basis of conservatism. Especially when their material dominance seems assured, the ruling classes, whose interests are served by more effective ideological models than the others, generally feel free to encourage innovation in art and fashion. But, deep down, they are very attentive to any less superficial change which might threaten their power and privilege. It seems fair to say that resistance to change is nowhere more firmly entrenched than among the members of all kinds of clergy, whose power and privileges are only based upon concepts, beliefs and moral rules, which they therefore have every interest in defending.

Finally, this tendency towards conservatism is further strengthened by the pattern inherent to all societies whereby cultural models gradually filter down through the social fabric, from the top of the social hierarchy, where they take shape in response to the tastes and interests of the ruling elites, towards a progressively wider and more popular audience, on which they exert a certain fascination and which tries to appropriate them. In this process of constant popularisation, cultural models are gradually deformed; but certain attitudes nevertheless survive for extremely long periods, so that underneath the superficial air of modernity which elites cultivate in order to stand out from ordinary mortals, a bedrock of traditional reference is maintained, providing the spirit of conservatism with its strongest foundation.

5. However, in cultures which have a history, all ideological systems are based on a vision of that history: a projected future in which society will be closer to perfection is built on the memory, objective or mythical, of the past. Such ideologies are bearers of hope: their aim is to encourage action. All ideologies are 'practical', and therefore contribute to the movement of history. But by the very fact of this movement, they are themselves transformed. Three main reasons can be given for this:

a) Between social relations actually experienced and people's representation of them, there is sufficient connection for changes in the first to have some degree of repercussion on the latter.

b) Different age-groups and interest-groups are in constant struggle. When these conflicts intensify as a result of accelerating economic or demographic change, or when such change leads to political mutations, then ideologies must adapt if they are to survive or win. In their struggle with opposing ideologies, they become more or less aggressive, affirm themselves more openly, or else take refuge behind some new facade. When they are in a dominant position, they partially absorb the images or models which threatened them, taming them and turning them to their own advantage. Thus, for instance, in the thirteenth century the Church triumphant managed to extend its hegemony over what was in fact simply a less hesitant form of heretical revolt, the teachings of St Francis of Assisi. But in order to accommodate this model of perfection it had to accept significant changes to its own organisation, removing, toning down or repressing elements which were clearly incompatible with Franciscanism, and assimilating those parts of the opposing ideology which could be introduced into its own material and spiritual structure as a way of strengthening them. In the end, and not without considerable difficulty, the Church did succeed in reshaping and domesticating both the figure of St Francis and his message.

Certain social milieux play a privileged role in these processes of struggle, revolt, incorporation and integration which are the stuff of the history of ideologies. The historian must pay particular attention to the people whose profession places them at the centre of conflict and who therefore become the main agents of the forces of conservatism, resistance or conquest, and make the necessary compromises and adjustments. One thinks first and foremost of the professional educators and teachers to whom established societies delegate those tasks; but there are also all those who become the spokesmen of a particular social category which is in many cases not originally theirs. Certain frustrations may have led them to break with their own group and to attack it, so that they seek support in other naturally antagonistic social groups, bringing to the ideological positions of the latter the benefit of their experience and knowledge. Alternatively, they may simply have left their own class and, through careerism, joined the ranks of the intellectuals who are taken on as servants by the ruling classes.

c) The third principal case of change within ideological systems arises when the culture of which they are part is subjected to the influence of neighbouring foreign cultures. This cultural penetration is frequently the result of an unequal balance of power between the civilisations in question. Sometimes it is sudden and brutal, as when it accompanies political upheavals caused by colonisation or invasion. More frequently, however, it proceeds insidiously, through the distant attraction of foreign beliefs, ideas and ways of life. It can also be the result of deliberate borrowing, since ideologies will seek reinforcements from any quarter. An example here would be the courtly ethic in twelfth-century Europe, which added to its mental representations, its rituals and its modes of expression by borrowing from the cultures of ancient Rome and Spanish Islam.

It is certainly true that the processes whereby ideologies are shaken out of their natural inertia are generally very slow: changes at an economic or political level tend to be more abrupt, and ideologies adapt to these changes by gentle bending. But this does not alter the fact that the ideological systems are constantly changing. They are without a doubt a worthy object for the historian.

There can be no hiding how difficult such a history of ideology will be to constitute. The first problem concerns the collection of evidence: most of the ideological systems of the past have left only fleeting, partial or unreliable traces. This is of course the case with 'popular' ideologies, those of all social groups deprived of direct access to cultural tools which would have enabled them to translate into some durable form their world view. Such ideologies can only be guessed at if the ruling classes for some reason took notice of them, and even then what we see is vague, partial and deformed by the intervening party. The same strictures apply to all ideologies of protest and rebellion, which were attacked and often hounded until every trace of them had been erased from people's memories. These ideologies can only be glimpsed through the prism of the repressive process; we must look for clues to their features in the refutations with which they were met, in the arguments used by counter-propaganda, in instructions to inquisitors and in the reasons adduced in court sentences. Documents only cast direct light on ideologies which corresponded to the interests and aspirations of the ruling classes. This is partly because only these groups had the means to construct cultural objects sufficiently permanent for the historian today to be able to analyse what remains of them. The other reason we have hinted at: the centres of power allowed only these ideologies to express themselves openly, to spread, to infiltrate all available forms of expression and gradually to establish themselves via the systems of education and information and through the natural fascination which the attitudes of social elites exert upon dominated classes. It is an essential methodological principle not to forget this balance of power, and to be careful to correct the errors of perspective which it is likely to cause.

   Not that we should hope to have easy access to the most dominant and triumphant ideological systems. It is rare indeed for such complex structures to be given conscious expression in their totality. Even in the case of the deliberate and coherent exposition of a doctrine, we have only a partial picture: a part of the whole always remains unformulated. In order to lay this bare, we would need to be able to analyse the individual and collective behaviour of a whole society, steeped as it is in ideology. This in turn means bringing together a whole range of different indices, scattered amongst the confused and incomplete record of a society's practices. Unearthing ideological systems from the dust of the past involves identifying, linking and interpreting a mass of unrelated signs. The historian must decipher, he becomes a code-breaker. Added to which he must, as he goes about these tasks, free himself as much as is humanly possible from the ideological constraints which imprison him.

   The more accessible and instructive documentary sources obviously include

all propaganda texts, treatises on good behaviour, moral homilies, manifest-
oes, pamphlets, sermons, encomia, epitaphs, the biographies of exemplary
heroes: in short, all those texts where society gives direct expression to the
virtues it reveres and the vices it abhors, texts whose function is to defend and
propagate the ethical system upon which its own sense of righteousness is
based. But in the pursuit of such information, no text is necessarily to be
rejected. In the vocabulary of stories, dramatic works, letters, family bibles,
and, most conservative of all, that of liturgies, regulations, judicial judge-
ments, there are revealing terms to be tracked down: not only words, but turns
of phrase, metaphors, word associations. This is the unconscious expression of
a particular group's perception of itself and of others at a particular moment in
history. Non-verbal documents are likely to provide even more information,
since ideology sometimes finds more direct and richer expression through
visual signs. Emblems, costumes, ornament, insignia, gestures, the setting and
organisation of festivals and ceremonies, the arrangement of the social space:
all these testify to a certain dream of order. In this special and central area of
social history, research must be particularly attentive to all manner of figurative
objects, to the structure of monuments, to their setting, indeed to the whole
priceless documentary area of painting and sculpture. For in all civilisations
and throughout most of history, figurative representations carried a weightier
and more immediate meaning than the written word: they were particularly
effective weapons in attack and defence. The west door of the *abbatiale de
Saint-Gilles*, dating from the end of the twelfth century, is a prime example:
here, at a major crossroads in southern Gaul, an area deeply affected by the
Catharian heresy, was a *summum* of Catholic ideology buttressed by majestic
references to imperial Rome, a statement with all the permanence of stone and
all the persuasive power invested in sculpture. A little later, it was amongst the
greatest of painters that the Pontifical Church found its best allies in the fight to
rid Franciscanism of its rebellious seeds and to harness this movement of lyrical
poverty which beckoned the believer to free dialogue with Jesus, so that it
finally served an ideology of clerical authority and justification of wealth.

Once individual data have been identified, the next stage is to collate all
these traces so that the system in all its formal coherence can be reconstructed.
Here great attention must be paid to the silences. Interpreting silence as
absence represents a much greater mistake in this kind of history than in
economic history. Omissions are an essential part of ideological discourse, and
their meaning must be analysed. Then these systems of representation, recon-
stituted now as semantic systems, must be analysed in two ways. In synchronic
terms, they must be analysed sufficiently deeply for the dominant ideology to
reveal traces of competing and opposed ideologies, which can often only be
seen through the intricate play of attack and defence on the part of the
dominant ideology. Diachronically, the almost imperceptible way in which
these systems change must be closely charted. The methods of serial history can

and must be used here: the most significant elements of the different verbal, ritual and figurative languages involved can be sorted into chronological and quantifiable series. This will enable us to detect the shifts whereby one term or sign replaces another, and certain themes lose ground and disappear while others are born and become dominant. There is clearly a potential problem here, concerning the viscosity of vocabulary and the survival of formal elements masking transformations at a semantic level. But within this particular field, such discordances between form and content are relatively unimportant: ideologies are masks, systems of representation designed to reassure and justify human behaviour; observation and analysis, therefore, must concentrate, precisely, on forms, patterns and themes.

Certain critical periods of history provide particularly good material for ideological analysis. At such times, changes within material and political structures work their way through to the ideological level, intensifying conflict between different systems. In the course of these crises and rebellions, and the reforms and revolutions to which they give rise, latent structures which are usually hidden are more clearly seen. As debate within a society intensifies, those who normally either do not care to express themselves or do not have the means to do so, speak out; at the same time, the slow evolution of the dominant ideology is accelerated. Certainly, social struggles also encourage iconoclastic tendencies and there is a consequent loss of documentation. But the fact that various sections of society take up and express positions makes for a compensatory increase in documentary material. For the historian, the most revealing phase is the moment when conflict comes to an end: victory is followed by repression, and much information can be gathered from the records of investigations, interrogations and sentences which are held in judicial and police archives. Simultaneously, the victors undertake the conversion of adversaries, produce theoretical elaborations of doctrine, set about recording society: all these are rich sources for the historian of ideology. Finally, the accounts of the conflict which has just ended throw light on both the victorious and the defeated ideologies: we need to look no further than the interpretations of the French Revolution which circulated in the 1830s, or the things which were said about the Paris Commune when the centenary was variously celebrated or ignored.

So far we have been concerned with reconstructing from fragmentary evidence the ideological systems of the past, and tracing their development over time. This is in fact only the preparatory stage of a much more delicate task: the analysis of the relations between ideologies and the lived reality of social organisation. We may distinguish two stages:

a) Ideologies are the interpretations of a real situation, and tend to reflect changes in the latter. But they do this slowly and reluctantly, because they are by nature conservative. They are the locus of a process of adaptation, but this is sometimes very slow and always remains partial. Moreover, in a subtle dialectical process, the weight of ideological representations is sometimes such as to hold back the development of material and political structures; this makes measurement of the gap between ideology and lived social relations even more difficult. And yet it is the historian's responsibility to establish as precise a chronology as possible of the play between the two, since this is the basis of all further research and interpretation.

b) Such an analysis of temporal divergence between the ideological and the real necessarily leads the social historian to another task: the *critique* and demystification of the ideologies of the past. It must be shown how, at every moment in history, what we know of the material conditions of life in a particular society is subjected to a varying degree of falsification by that society's mental representations. The historian must therefore determine as precisely as possible – and the fact that in most documents the real and the ideal are freely juxtaposed makes the task extremely difficult – the relations of correspondence and difference existing at every point on a diachronic scale between three variables: on the one hand, between the objective situation of individuals and groups and the image which they have constructed for their comfort and justification; on the other, between that image and individual and collective behaviour.

It is here that Paul Veyne's critical thoughts on the methods and vicissitudes of a historian's work seem relevant. Veyne's work helps us to define the aims, limits and methods of historical research, and its general tenor is one of caution. Firstly, because he emphasises the distance in any society between men's real behaviour and the mental representations or systems of values to which they choose to refer. Social behaviour must to some extent be seen as part of rituals which are experienced as such and which should not be read as the expression of beliefs or ideas. Furthermore, men's behaviour is only very partially controlled by moral rules: morality never represents more than a 'localised sector' within a whole, operating in various ways at different cultural levels, in different societies and in different periods. Finally, we should recognise that there is always an 'enormous gap between the official title of a political or religious movement and the prevailing mood within it; this mood is experienced but not conceptualised by the participants . . . and leaves almost no written trace'.[1] For this reason it escapes observation and yet it is this mood, much more than any proclamation or declaration of principle, which influences behaviour. These remarks are a useful corrective to the temptation of exaggerating the influence of ideological systems on the course of history. Ideologies are only 'flags'. We must allow that 'the ideological mask fools no one, that it only convinces the convinced, and that *homo historicus* rarely bows to the ideological arguments of his opponent when his interests are at stake'.[2]

Veyne nonetheless recognises, and here his remarks merit particular attention, that human behaviour is more directly determined by ideological motives within that particular kind of social framework to which he gives the name 'institutions'. By this he means 'anything which is spoken about in terms of collective ideals, corporate spirit, group traditions, anything which presents a mixture of personal ambitions and collective censorship, with the result that the social group adopts and achieves more disinterested aims than its members would have pursued individually', 'a situation in which, out of motives which are not necessarily idealistic, people pursue ideal aims just as scrupulously as if they were interested in these aims for personal reasons'.[3] Such social frameworks are obviously a locus for great tensions between principles and individual interests. But they nevertheless function around an ordering principle, a set of rules whose power is immediate and persuasive, since, within the group, every member expects the others to respect them as he or she does. 'Institutions', in Veyne's sense of the word, are the first field to which the historian of ideologies must turn his/her attentions. But equal attention must be given to the great movements which spring from these institutional frameworks, breaking down institutional boundaries and setting up relations between them. For the study of these movements allows the historian sufficient critical perspective to pose in the most comprehensive terms the central problem of the relation between ideologies and what Marx calls social praxis. Veyne quite correctly chooses, amongst others, the example of the Crusades. This enterprise would never have been as successful as it was if the contradictions within the dominant strata of feudal society in the late twelfth century had been less pronounced; but it would only have drawn a 'handful of lost souls' to the Holy Land if those who organised the expedition had not conferred holy status on it. Leaving for Jerusalem, the Crusader knows full well that he is running away from a situation which offers no other solution, but at the same time he is sincere in his belief that his action will save his soul; he 'knows that the Crusade is a divine epic because he has been told so, and he expresses what he feels through what he knows, like everyone else'.[4]

I would like now to pursue and enlarge upon this example, for it is time to put some flesh on these rather abstract methodological considerations.

The main features of an ideological model of Christian society were laid down in eleventh-century Europe by those who were capable of organised thought, and able to express it in a form which stood some chance of survival: the leaders of the Church. The present state of research suggests that this model was not at the time represented through painting or sculpture. This in itself is problematical. But we do at least find it clearly expressed in a very small number of texts which should be the object of detailed study. Systematic studies should also be made of the reflection of the model in a far larger number of texts, where its mark is to be seen in the way in which certain stories are told, certain images and terms associated. This model is the reflection of the dominant social position of the people who constructed it to serve their interests. It seems legitimate to assume that it took shape under the pressure of increased social conflict within the aristocracy caused by the weakening of the king's powers of magistracy and conciliation. Such conflict took the particular form of religious heresy, and it was apparently in response to this that the ideological model in question was constructed.

Like all ideological representations, it is simple. Their function is, naturally, to offer a simplified image of the reality of social organisation, ignoring nuance and overlap, emphasising contrasts, antagonisms and hierarchies. In this case, men are split into three categories: specialists, respectively, in prayer, war and production. The latter, here, means the peasants. In a world which was beginning to feel the effects of accelerated demographic and economic growth, the model has no place for the 'workers' in the newly born towns engaged in the manufacture of quality goods, trading and dealing in money. On the other hand it faithfully reflects the overall structure of an agricultural society which entrusted its protection to two groups: the fighters defended it against visible aggressors, and the specialists in prayer against the dark forces of the other world. But the function of this image is to reassure. Firstly, it conceals tensions among the three social categories by insisting upon the balanced exchange of mutual services. Secondly, these services are used as the justification for real inequalities: the idleness and wealth which go with the specialised roles of the two social elites, and the obligations and exploitation which are the lot of the third social category. It also seeks to reassure in that its aim is to stabilise the structures of which it offers a representation, in the interests of the elites and more particularly of the Church. The divisions which it describes are conceived as 'orders', immutable social groupings whose boundaries are fixed and can only be crossed if an outwardly manifest conversion takes place. In this sense, the ideology denies the reality of the movements of social advancement which are beginning to be caused by increased agricultural productivity and growing circulation of wealth. It bases its resistance to change on a system of belief which sees Creation as the replica of a timeless Heavenly City; and the social classification which it attempts to fix forever is an expression of God's eternal plan. And yet it is plain even to the casual observer that this is an imperfect replica, and the Manichean vision which surrounds this ideological model insists upon the corrosive influence of the forces of evil, which must be repressed as sources of discord and disorder. At the same time as it stabilises, the model therefore calls for action: the original perfection of the heavenly model must be restored to society. The chief beneficiaries of this process of restoration will be the Church dignitaries who constructed the model.

This ideological representation enters into the collective consciousness at a time when change within the material structure of society is too slow to be perceived by contemporaries. It is nevertheless a dynamic model, essentially because of the conception of history which underlies it. History at the time plays an important part in the education of the religious elite, and is conceived as the people of God's march towards the light, aided, since the coming of Christ, by the bestowal of divine grace. It is the Church's job to guide its flock in this journey towards the end of time and the perfection of divine intention. Now, the Church has for a long time been established as a landowner, thus being entitled to the surplus production of peasant labour. The ideological model which it propagates thus allows the clergy and monks to enjoy the fruits of their land and the dues of their dependants in all good conscience. The only condition is that they present themselves as the defenders of the 'poor', in other words the working masses. That is why the model establishes a strict division between the upper echelons of ecclesiastical society and the lay aristocracy, two groups who in reality belong to the same class and to the same families. It further emphasises this division by imposing on all clergy a segregative moral code, formerly confined to the monastic orders, demanding the renunciation of individual wealth, of carnal pleasure and of the joy of battle. The same rigid separation can be seen in the notion of the truce of God: the original version of this ethic of peace placed a whole series of protective constraints on the whole category of fighters. In this way the model contributes to the constitution of this group as a homogeneous body, common attitudes gradually obscuring economic differences between its various members.

But the Church must also carry on the struggle against the forces of evil and, in order to perfect the model of the three orders, attempt to moralise the military world. For both these reasons, it tries throughout the eleventh century to make chivalry into a true 'institution' held together by its own particular ethic. The result is the gradual constitution of an ideology peculiar to the knights. The first traces we have of this ideology are contained in the diatribes in which the clergy attack it, but it is more clearly visible when literary works composed for an audience of warriors achieve permanence through the written word. Those clergy who are making their careers in the courts of princes play an important role in the construction of this model. And yet it is explicitly hostile to the Church's ideology: the glorification of valour, pillage, sensual indulgence and *joie de vivre* represents a systematic rejection of the spirit of penitence and renunciation which the Church preaches. The progressive strengthening of these chivalrous values reflects the divorce, which had begun as early as the tenth century and would continue to grow, between the lay and religious sections of the ruling class. Nevertheless, the two groups continue to share certain common interests which, together with the powerful influence of family relations, mean that considerable communication takes place between the two representations, and the lay model does become Christianised.

This process of Christianisation culminates in the Crusade. A contributory factor to the real or imagined mobilisation of the whole knightly class to free the Holy Sepulchre was certainly the financial difficulties of the lay aristocracy. This was not the result of a crisis in ground rents or manorial incomes, of which there is no evidence, but rather a consequence of population growth and a kinship structure which encouraged many younger sons of noble families to seek adventure. Changes in political structure, particularly the strengthening of the principalities which tended to expel the forces of aggression and disorder, also contributed. But such a mobilisation is an equally direct result of the gradual maturing of the ideology of three orders; it is a direct continuation of the first theorising of the clerics around 1000. Imposing morality on the order of warriors was not only a way of restraining its turbulent tendencies; the knights were also being invited to use their arms to fulfil the designs of God. In other words, to direct their military activity at a target outside the Christian community – the infidel. At which point, reference was made to the old millenarian myths and eschatological visions. The heavenly Jerusalem, mankind's goal in its long march towards grace, had its replica in this world, in Judaea. In that direction God's people must move in order to hasten the coming of the Kingdom. This was to be a collective enterprise. The clergy would show the way, and the sword-bearers, purified by the holy use of their weapons, would lead the vulnerable army of the poor. Crusade society, which around 1100 was thought to be taking shape, was nothing other than the fruition of the ideological model which Church intellectuals had constructed a century earlier.

But in the course of that century economic and demographic growth had continued to accelerate, causing imperceptible but real changes in human relations within religious communities, principalities, seigneurial domains, villages and families. These underlying currents were partially consistent with developments which the ideological model sought to encourage, based as it was on a realistic assessment of the state of certain major social relations in early eleventh-century France – the hierarchy of fortunes, the organisation of power and the distribution of functions. But divergences between real developments and those sought by the model were greater than these convergences: indeed, the original gap between reality and its mental representation was widening. Crusade society *was* a manifestation of the model, but a manifestation so delayed by the inherent slowness of the maturing process and by the obstacles to the propagation of the model, that it was already an anachronism. In fact, it never fully took shape. The whole of Christendom did not embark upon a final journey of redemption, and the bands of pilgrims journeying East did not offer an image of humanity pure, disinterested and peaceful, at last totally obedient to the moral order of the monks. The clergy who made the journey discovered in Eastern Christianity and the holy places little-known values; their reflections on the incarnation of Christ and the powers of the Holy Spirit were to be the basis for a transformation of their attitude to the world. As far as the warriors are concerned, the crosses on their banners could not hide the reality: the expedition was above all a prodigious opportunity for pillage and pleasure on a scale which these impoverished novices in search of glory, wealth and a wife had never known. As for the 'poor' who in their ramshackle way answered the call of the clergy, no one will ever know what they sought or what they found. Moreover, the Crusade took with it social groups who had no place in the society of three orders: clergy who had broken their vows; prostitutes; mercenaries who were paid to fight and who already represented the fighting elite of the army; the agents of princes, humble in origin but raised to a rank of importance by their office; finally, all the sailors, dealers and adventurers of trade and business. This last group played a considerable, perhaps crucial role in the whole affair. What the Crusaders found at the end of their journey was not the Kingdom or the Second Coming, but wealth, the pleasure of new sights, new and better clothes to adorn themselves, fatigue, fear, disillusion, or simply death. The great dream finally amounted to this: a few political formations trying to impose on conquered territory a shaky version of Western legal practice; the beginning of the takeover of the Levant by the Latin nations; above all, the military religious orders. These are a kind of residual institution, a miniature version of the original ideological project; here, but here alone, in the disinterested service of God, we find a fusion of monastic and military values in a rigid hierarchy separating noble knights and sergeants of base origin. Another residual element, with a long future in front of it, was a powerful myth of conquering progress and eschatological expectation, which was to nourish Western ideologies for many centuries.

I have tried in a few lines to show what we can piece together of the workings of an ideological system over a period of a century. My aim is to encourage further research in this area and clearer definition of certain problems. We need a detailed analysis of different languages (verbal, pictorial etc.), and contrastive study of their basic elements and the symbols which they employ, in order to determine their precise meaning at certain points in time: what lies behind the word *laborator*, the sign of the cross or the formulae used for blessing the sword? We need to understand all the subtle workings of a dialectic involving custom and innovation, a representation of society and a whole system of beliefs. We need to assess the degree of resistance which this ecclesiastical and probably more precisely episcopal model encountered in the first stirrings of chivalry and the inertia of the peasant masses. We also need to look outside the culture of Latin Christendom and, both backwards and forwards, beyond the eleventh century, in order to see more clearly the slow process of change through which the model based on three orders, itself perhaps a survival of the tri-functional forms which, as Georges Dumézil has shown, were deeply embedded in the Indo-European cultures, came to supplant two other models: that of a warrior–king sacred in person and liturgical in function, the source of all fertility; and the Church model of the scales of moral perfection. Finally, we must trace the survival of this ideological system through successive adaptations and examine its influence on the overall development of social relations. It is this model which serves to justify the final eclipse of ancient slavery; welds together the greatest of princes and the poorest of local lords in a common system of values; limits the artistocracy's participation in the more profitable economic activities, so encouraging the steady growth of antagonistic social groups; and, lastly, through the notion of generosity and charity which it implies, leads to redistribution of wealth on a decisive scale.

To confront these problems, and analogous ones concerning other models, would without doubt be a step towards a more sophisticated understanding of the speed with which change takes place within the specific time-scale of the history of ideologies. It would help us situate the points of contact between this historical level and overall social change, between ideological representations and the objective situation and behaviour of individuals and groups. We might, in this way, begin to glimpse something which the social sciences have not yet even begun to elucidate: the part played by human imagination in the evolution of human societies.

NOTES

1 Paul Veyne, *Comment on écrit l'histoire* (Paris, Le Seuil, 1971), p. 230.
2 *Ibid.*, p. 223, n. 11.
3 *Ibid.*, pp. 242, 244.
4 *Ibid.*, p. 227.

8. Mentalities: a history of ambiguities

JACQUES LE GOFF

> Mentalité me plaît. Il y a comme cela des mots nouveaux qu'on lance.
>
> Marcel Proust, *A la recherche du temps perdu*, vol. II, Gallimard,
> Bibliothèque de la Pléiade, 1954, pp. 236–7.

For the historian today, the term 'mentality' is still a novelty and already devalued by excessive use. There is much talk of the history of mentalities, but convincing examples of such history are rare. It represents a new area of research, a trail to be blazed, and yet at the same time doubts are raised as to its scientific, conceptual and epistemological validity. Fashion has seized upon it, and yet it seems already to have gone out of fashion. Should we revive or bury the history of mentalities?

I At the crossroads of history

The primary attraction of the history of mentalities lies in its vagueness: it can be used to refer to the left-overs, the indefinable residue of historical analysis.

After 1095 something stirs in Western Christendom, and individuals and masses alike throw themselves into the great adventure of the Crusades. In attempting to analyse this momentous period, we may refer to demographic growth and nascent overpopulation, the commercial ambitions of Italian city-states, the Papacy's desire to reunite a fragmented Christendom by taking on the Infidel. But none of these factors is sufficient to explain everything, or indeed, perhaps, to explain what is most important. For this, we need to understand the pull of Jerusalem, the earthly equivalent of the Celestial City, and its central position within a certain collective imagery. What are the Crusades without a certain religious mentality?[1]

What is feudalism? A set of institutions, a mode of production, a social system, a particular type of military organisation? Georges Duby maintains that we must go further, 'extend economic history into the history of mentalities', and analyse 'the feudal concept of service'. Feudalism must be seen as a 'mediaeval mentality'.[2]

166

The period since the sixteenth century has seen the birth of a new kind of society in the West: capitalist society. Is it the result of a new mode of production, of an economy based on money, a construction of the bourgeoisie? It is all those things, but it is also the product of new attitudes towards work and money, of a mentality which, since Max Weber, has become associated with the Protestant ethic.[3]

The notion of 'mentality', then, refers to a kind of historical beyond. Its function, as a concept, is to satisfy the historian's desire to 'go further', and it leads to a point of contact with the other human sciences.

Attempting to define the 'religious mentality' of the Middle Ages, Marc Bloch sees within it 'a whole series of beliefs and practices . . . some of them passed down from age-old forms of thaumaturgy, others, of relatively recent origin, produced within a civilisation still endowed with a great myth-making capacity'.[4] In this respect, the historian of mentalities will tend to move towards the ethnologist: both seek to discover the stablest, most immobile level of a society's existence. As Ernest Labrousse put it: 'the social changes more slowly than the economic, and the mental more slowly than the social'.[5] Keith Thomas, in his work on the religious mentality of the Middle Ages and Renaissance, explicitly employs ethnological methods, principally inspired by Evans-Pritchard.[6] Through the study of ritual and ceremony, the ethnologist tries to reconstruct beliefs and value-systems. Mediaeval historians like Percy Ernst Schramm, Ernst Kantorowicz, and Bernard Guinée, following the lead of Marc Bloch, have enriched the political history of the Middle Ages with their description of a political mentality, a mystical conception of monarchy, based on analysis of coronations, miraculous healings, the insignia of authority and the receptions accorded to kings by towns (*entrées royales*).[7] Formerly, the hagiographer was interested in the saint, but interest now focuses on saintliness: its basis in the mind of the believer, the psychology of credulity, the mentality of the ancient hagiographer.[8] The anthropology of religion has radically altered the perspective of religious history.[9]

The historian of mentalities must also assimilate some of the techniques of the sociologist, for the object of both is by definition collective. The mentality of any one historical individual, however important, is precisely what that individual shares with other men of his time. Take the example of Charles V of France. He is unanimously praised by historians for his thrift, his administrative ability, his statesmanship. He is the wise king, the reader of Aristotle who rebuilds the kingdom's finances, keeps strict accounts, and wages on the English a war of attrition which does not stretch the public purse. Now, in 1380, on his death-bed, Charles V abolishes the hearth-tax – and historians have busily sought to explain this unexpected gesture either as some obscure political strategy or as the aberration of a man no longer in control of his faculties. But why not adopt an explanation consistent with fourteenth-century attitudes: the king who is afraid of death and does not wish to face the Last

Judgement burdened with the hatred of his subjects? The king who, in his dying moments, allows his mentality to outweigh his political judgement, the commonly shared beliefs of his time to override his personal political ideology?

There are particularly close links between the historian of mentalities and the social psychologist. For both, the notions of behaviour and attitude are crucial. What is more, the increasing tendency of social psychologists like C. Kluckhohn[10] to emphasise the role of cultural control in biological behaviour represents a bridge between social psychology and ethnology and therefore a link with history as well. The reciprocal attraction between social psychology and the history of mentalities is particularly clear in two areas: the study of crime, marginality and deviance in the past, and the parallel growth of the contemporary opinion poll and of historical analysis of electoral behaviour.

Here, historical psychology has a great opportunity to develop links with another central area of contemporary historiography: quantitative history. The history of mentalities, whose object would appear to be characterised by nuance and constant flux, can in fact, if it is prepared to accept certain modifications, use the quantitative methods developed by social psychology. As Abraham A. Moles has indicated,[11] the attitude-scales method takes as its starting-point 'a mass of fact, opinions and verbal statements, initially totally incoherent', but in the end produces a 'scale of measurement' commensurate with the facts being treated; this in turn allows the facts in question to be defined. Thus, the ambiguous term 'mentality' may perhaps be defined satisfactorily, in a manner reminiscent of Binet's famous phrase, 'Intelligence is what is measured by my test.'

Similarly, the link with ethnology will allow the history of mentalities to draw on structuralist methods, one of the great tools of modern human sciences. Is not mentality itself a structure?

But, over and above the links with some human sciences which the history of mentalities opens up, one of its main attractions is the new perspectives which it offers to historians who have become too dependent on economic and social history and, above all, on vulgar Marxism.

Certainly economic and social history, Marxist in inspiration or not, has established a solid basis for historical explanation by wresting historiography from the *dei ex machina* of providence and great men, and their positivist equivalents, chance and events. But for all this, the aims of history as defined by Michelet in his 1869 Preface have not been achieved: 'History... still appeared to me to be weak in two respects: neither sufficiently material... nor sufficiently spiritual, speaking of laws and political acts, but not of ideas and manners.' Within Marxism itself, historians who emphasised modes of production and the class struggle as historical mechanisms, failed to develop a convincing analysis of the relationship between infrastructure and superstructure. The economic mirror which they held up to society revealed only a pale reflection of abstract theories: there were no faces, no living people. Man does not live by bread alone, but in this history there was no bread at all, just skeletons automatically repeating the same *danse macabre*. These fleshless mechanisms needed a new dimension, and that new dimension was provided by mentalities.

The history of mentalities, then, represents a link with other disciplines within the human sciences, and the emergence of an area which traditional historiography refused to consider. But it is also a meeting point for opposing forces which are being brought into contact by the dynamics of contemporary historical research: the individual and the collective, the long-term and the everyday, the unconscious and the intentional, the structural and the conjunctural, the marginal and the general.

The history of mentalities operates at the level of the everyday automatisms of behaviour. Its object is that which escapes historical individuals because it reveals the impersonal content of their thought: that which is common to Caesar and his most junior legionary, Saint Louis and the peasant on his lands, Christopher Columbus and any one of his sailors. The history of mentalities is to the history of ideas as the history of material culture is to economic history. People of the fourteenth century see the plague as a divine punishment, and that reaction is the fruit of the assumptions present in the teachings of Christian thinkers from Saint Augustine to Thomas Aquinas; it is a reflection of the equation, disease = sin, developed by the clerics of the Early Middle Ages, but it retains only the rough form of the idea and pays no heed to logical articulations and rational subtleties. In the same way, everyday utensils and the clothing of the poor are derived from prestigious models created by superficial developments in the economy, fashion and taste. It is at that level that we may grasp the style of a period: deep in its everyday behaviour. When Huizinga calls John of Salisbury a 'pregothic mind', thus seeing him as a precursor of subsequent historical developments, his expression evokes the notion of mentality: the historical figure becomes the collective expression of a period, as when Lucien Febvre, rejecting the anachronisms of the historians of ideas, situated Rabelais in the concrete historicity which is the object of the historian of mentalities.

What men say, whatever the tone in which they say it – conviction, emotion, bombast – is more often than not simply an assemblage of ready-made ideas, commonplaces and intellectual bric-à-brac, the remnants of cultures and mentalities belonging to different times and different places. This determines the methods which the historian of mentalities must use. Two stages may be noted: first, the identification of different strata and fragments of what, following André Varagnac's term 'archaeocivilisation', we may call 'archaeopsychology'; and, secondly, since these remnants are nevertheless ordered according to certain criteria of mental, if not logical, coherence, the historian must determine these psychic systems of organisation, comparable to the principles of *bricolage intellectuel*[12] which Lévi-Strauss sees as the distinguishing feature of primitive thought.

In the fourth book of his *Dialogues*, written between 590 and 600, Pope Gregory the Great tells the story of one of the monks in the Roman monastery of which he had been the abbot. On his death-bed, the monk tells one of his brothers that he has hidden three gold coins, which is strictly contrary to the rule whereby the monks must share all their possessions. When told of this, Gregory gives orders for the dying man to be left to die alone, without any consoling presence; his fear will cause him to purge himself of his sin, and his anguished death will be an example to the other monks. Why did the abbot, as cultured and educated as any other of his time, not go to the dying sinner's bedside in order to help him on his way to heaven by confession and contrition? Gregory was convinced that the monk must atone for this sin by external signs: an ignominious death and burial (the body is thrown onto the dung-heap). The barbarian custom of physical punishment (brought by the Goths, or a throw-back to some psychic depths?) proves stronger than the monastic rule. Mentality vanquishes doctrine.

Automatic gestures, spontaneous words, which seem to lack any origins and to be the fruits of improvisation and reflex, in fact possess deep roots in the long reverberation of systems of thought.

The historian of mentalities must pay particular attention to certain essential factors. In tracing the origins (where? who? when?) of a particular mental habit, expression or gesture, one must be aware of continuities, but also of disappearances and discontinuities. Tradition, which is a society's way of reproducing itself mentally, must be analysed, as must the historical lag produced by the slow adaptation of mental structures to change, and by the different speeds at which different areas of history evolve. The history of mentalities is in fact a particularly good school in which to learn the inadequacies of a linear conception of history. Inertia is a crucially important historical force, and it belongs less to matter than to human minds, which often evolve more slowly. While they use the machines they have invented, men keep the mentality of earlier days. Motorists use the vocabulary of horse-riders, and nineteenth-century factory workers had the mentality of their peasant forebears. Mentalities change slower than anything else: and their history is a lesson in the slow march of history.

II The history of mentalities: towards a history of the idea

What is the origin of the history of mentalities?[13] The adjective *mental*, from the Latin *mens* (mind), is clearly the origin of the word. The Latin adjectival form, *mentalis*, is unknown in classical Latin, and belongs in fact to the vocabulary of mediaeval scholasticism; but the fact that *mentalité* (mid nineteenth century) appears five centuries later than *mental* (mid fourteenth century) indicates that the noun arises in response to different needs and in a different historical context to the adjective.

The French *mentalité* is borrowed from the English 'mentality', which dates back to the seventeenth century and is a product of seventeenth-century English philosophy, referring to the collective psychology, the ways of thinking and feeling which are peculiar to 'a people, a given group of people, etc.'. But, whereas in English the term remains restricted to the specialist language of philosophy,[14] in French it quickly enters general usage. The notion which eventually develops into the concept and word *mentalité* seems to appear in eighteenth-century scientific discourse, and more particularly in a new conception of history. It lies behind Voltaire's *Essai sur les mœurs et l'esprit des nations* (1754), where the English 'mind' seems to be present in an already slightly extended form. When the word finally appears, in 1842 according to Robert's dictionary, its meaning is close to that of 'mentality', 'the quality of that which is mental'. But Littré, in 1877, illustrates the word by a sentence taken from the positivist philosopher H. Stupuy, where the word has the broader, although still 'erudite' meaning of 'a form of mind': it is perhaps not coincidental that the reference is to the Enlightenment and the 'changed mentality brought about by the Encyclopaedists'. Then, around 1900, the word takes on its broadest, popular meaning, the novelty of which strikes Proust as being relevant to his psychological preoccupations. It is the popular successor to the German *Weltanschauung*, the world vision of all members of a society, a mental universe which is both stereotyped and chaotic.

It refers above all to a depraved vision of the world, a kind of surrender to the worst psychic instincts. It has a pejorative connotation of inevitability, which is emphasised directly, or ironically, by an accompanying epithet: *une vilaine mentalité, une belle mentalité!* There is also an absolute use, as in *quelle mentalité!* English has retained this sense in the adjective: 'mental' often implies a notion of deficiency.

Two scientific disciplines have developed, or been influenced by, this connotation. The first is ethnology. Around the turn of the century, *mentalité* is used to refer to the psychology of 'primitive' peoples, which is seen by the observer as a collective phenomenon, overriding the psychology of any one individual: individuals have practically no personality, their mental life is made up of reflexes and automatisms. Lucien Lévy-Bruhl's *La Mentalité primitive* was published in 1922.

The other scientific discipline is child psychology. Again, the corollary of ceasing to see the child as just a small version of the adult is that it is reduced to a minor in mental terms. Specialised dictionaries in French of philosophy, psychology and psychoanalysis make no reference to *mentalité*, but the most recent dictionary of *Psychopédagogie et psychiatrie de l'enfant* (1970) includes a definition of *mentalité infantile*. As early as 1928, Henri Wallon had, moreover, suggested a connection between the two fields in his article on 'La Mentalité primitive et celle de l'enfant'. This parallel was strongly condemned by Lévi-Strauss in a famous passage of *Les Structures élémentaires de la parenté* (1949).

Two points should be clarified here. Firstly, it will be observed that *mentalité* is practically unknown in the vocabulary of psychology. Philippe Besnard's work on the frequency of the term in the indices of psychology bibliographies shows that it is rare in *Psychological Abstracts* from 1927 to 1943,[15] and practically extinct in contemporary psychology.[16] How can psychological history, or rather the history of collective psychology, usefully use a term when the notion has been rejected by psychology itself?

But the history of science is full of examples of the transference of notions and concepts. A word or concept arises in a particular field but soon loses its power, only to be taken up in a neighbouring area where it proceeds to flourish. Why, then, should *mentalité* not succeed in the historical field where it has failed in psychology? And, since Gestalt theory has been rejuvenated by the influence of linguistics and structuralism, who is to say that psychology will not finally realise the usefulness of the notion of *mentalité*? In any case, it is clear that, as far as scientific usage is concerned, *l'histoire des mentalités* has saved the word, reintroduced it into English and introduced it to German, Spanish and Italian (*Mentalität, mentalidad, mentalità*). It is remarkable how the success of the word, and with it of a concept and a whole type of historical research, has been assured by the prestige of the new French history: the three 'theoreticians' of the history of mentalities are Lucien Febvre (1938), Georges Duby (1961) and Robert Mandrou (1968).

The second point concerns the possible reflection onto the history of mentalities of the pejorative connotation attached to the word. Lévy-Bruhl stated that there was no qualitative difference between primitive mentality and the mentality of individuals in advanced societies; but he himself had already given mentalities a bad reputation by publishing *Les Fonctions mentales dans les sociétés inférieures* (1910). It is certainly time for the historian of mentalities to pursue his quarry through the murky waters of marginality, abnormality and social pathology (but hopefully not as far as the purgatory of 'collective memory'). Mentalities seem to be most clearly revealed in irrational and abnormal behaviour. Hence the proliferation of research – some of it outstanding – on witchcraft, heresy and millenarianism, and the fact that historians of mentalities who do work on common social feelings and socially integrated groups nevertheless often choose themes at the margins of everyday existence, such as attitudes to miracles or to death, or social groups at an early and fragile stage of development, such as the merchants in feudal society. Similarly, a social psychologist such as Ralph H. Turner, whose interest lies in the study of crowd behaviour, has based his work on the observation of panic occasioned by disasters, using data from a 'Disaster Research Group'.[17]

III The history of mentalities: practices and pitfalls

History is first and foremost a trade, relying on materials. So what materials does the historian of mentalities use?

The specificity of the history of mentalities lies rather in the approach than in the material, and any source can be useful. Take, for instance, an administrative, fiscal document such as a thirteenth- or fourteenth-century register of the king's revenues: the organisation of the document will reflect a particular vision of authority and administration, and a particular approach to statistics. Or the objects found in a seventh-century tomb: finery such as a bodkin, a ring, a buckle; silver coins, one of which may have been placed in the dead person's mouth at burial; weapons (battle-axe, sword, lance, dagger), a set of tools (hammers, pincers, gouges, chisels, files, etc.).[18] The remnants of these funeral rites provide valuable evidence concerning beliefs, such as the pagan ritual of Charon's obol, the coin left for the ferryman of the Styx, or Merovingian society's attribution of an almost sacred status to the craftsman who forges and decorates the sword but also wields it as a warrior.

The interpretation of material along these lines must pay particular attention to the traditional, as it were automatic, aspects of texts and monuments: in ancient deeds and titles, it is the preamble and the formulae used which express the real or alleged motivations of the text, and these *topoi* are the framework of mentalities. Ernst Robert Curtius sensed the importance of this substructure not only for literature, which was his explicit concern, but also for the mentality of a period:

And if rhetoric itself impresses modern man as a grotesque bogey, how dare one try to interest him in topics, a subject which even the literary specialist hardly knows by name because he deliberately shuns the cellars – and foundations! – of European literature?[19]

It is indeed to be regretted that this brilliant student of superstructure did not go on to adopt a quantitative approach, which would have been so fruitful from the point of view of the history of mentalities. The mechanical discourse of the past, which seems to speak without saying anything, invoking indiscriminately and according to the period, God and the devil, rain and shine, is the voice of mentalities, the unitary expression of the spirit of past societies; and it is a precious source for any history concerned more with the *basso continuo* than with the arias of the music of the past.

Certain sources do, however, stand out as particularly important for an understanding of the collective psychology of societies, and one of the first tasks of the history of mentalities must be to list these sources.

First of all, we should mention sources which reveal those marginal or paroxysmal aspects of a society's attitudes and behaviour from which we can, indirectly, learn much about the common, central mentality of a period. Here, I shall confine my remarks to the Middle Ages. Hagiography tells us much about the mental infrastructure of the period: the interpenetration between the tangible and the supernatural world, the common nature of the corporeal and the psychic, are the conditions which make miracles and related phenomena possible. If the saint, by his marginality, sheds light on common belief, so does the marginal status of the diabolical categories – the possessed, heretics, criminals. Hence the importance of documents such as the confessions of heretics, the records of inquisitory trials, letters of remission granted to criminals in which their misdeeds are recounted, together with judicial documents and other evidence of the repressive process.

Literary and artistic sources are equally important for the history of mentalities, since the latter is concerned not so much with 'objective' phenomena as with the representation of these phenomena. Huizinga, in his famous *Waning of the Middle Ages*, showed the contribution which literary texts can make to our understanding of a period's mentality and sensibility. That is the strength, but also the weakness of his work, for the forms and themes which are articulated in literature and art are not necessarily those of the collective consciousness. We should be wary of the claims of traditional historians of ideas and forms, who see these as self-generating and pay little attention to their non-literary or non-artistic context: literature and art operate according to codes which are more or less independent of their historical environment. Painting of the quattrocento seems to reflect a new conception of space, of architecture, of man's place in the universe: it seems to have something to do with a 'precapitalist' mentality. But Pierre Francastel rightly sees the representational system of the quattrocento as part of a larger whole, and points out the 'specificity of painting, a mode of expression and communication which cannot be reduced to any other'.[20]

The analysis of mentalities should never be separated from a study of where and by what means such mentalities were produced. The great precursor of the history of mentalities, Lucien Febvre, set us an example in his inventory of what he called 'mental equipment', made up of vocabulary, syntax, commonplaces, conceptions of space and time, logical systems. Philologists have observed that in the early Middle Ages when classical Latin was in decline, there occurred surprising changes in the structure of coordinating conjunctions. This should be seen as a sign that the logical articulations of spoken and written discourse are undergoing radical change. *Autem*, *ergo*, *igitur*, etc., are taking their place within a new structure of thought.

Certain local systems are particularly important in the structure and evolution of mentalities. Such 'models' serve for extended periods as poles of attraction around which mentalities coalesce. In the early Middle Ages a monastic model gradually evolves, centred around notions of solitude and asceticism; this is followed by aristocratic models, but this time the modal points are concepts of generosity, courage, beauty and loyalty. One of these travels down the centuries to our own time: courtesy. However ancient their origins, these mentalities are not to be explained as springing from the Dark Ages or from the collective psyche. Their birth and growth can be studied through an analysis of the social *locus* where they are created and popularised, and the groups and professions which act as intermediaries in their diffusion through society. Throughout the Middle Ages, the palace, the monastery, the castle, schools and courts are centres for the production of mentalities, which are taken up and sometimes elaborated at a popular level at the mill, the forge or the tavern, real centres for the reworking of mentalities. The mass media are the primary vehicles for the expression and ordering of mentalities: before the printing press, the sermon and the painted or sculpted image lie at the heart of emerging mentalities.

Mentalities cannot be separated, either, from social structures, however complex the relations between the two may be. Does each society, each period which history distinguishes as it evolves, possess one dominant mentality, or several? Mediaeval or Renaissance 'man' was denounced by Lucien Febvre as an abstraction with no historical reality; but the history of mentalities is in its infancy and must grasp at abstractions (which are hardly more solid) concerning cultural traditions, social stratification and periodisation. Still concentrating on the Middle Ages, notions such as a barbarian, courtly, Romanesque, Gothic or scholastic mentality may be adopted as working hypotheses, and suggestive sets of associations may develop around these labels. Erwin Panofsky has linked together Gothic art and scholasticism as participants in the same set of mental structures, and Robert Marchal has added the script of the period to this set: 'Gothic script can be considered the Gothic expression of a particular dialectic. There are certainly analogies between it and the architecture of the period but these are not, or are only fortuitously, visual: they are intellectual, the result of the same method of reasoning being applied to writing as to all other mental productions.'[21] The simultaneous coexistence of several mentalities in one period and indeed within one mind is a difficult question, but one which must be faced. Louis XI, whose political mentality is modern, 'Machiavellian', has a profoundly traditional, superstitious mentality when it comes to religion.

Pointing precisely to the points where mentalities undergo change is an equally delicate task. When does one disappear and another replace it? The new is hard to track down in this world of permanence and resistance, and here the study of *topoi* can be of decisive importance. When do such commonplaces appear and disappear and, more difficult but no less crucial, when has a *topos* ceased to be more than a vestige, a ghost of itself? The parroting effect of mentalities must be studied closely if we are to understand when a commonplace loses a hold on the real, becoming thereby inoperative. Are words ever empty air?

The history of mentalities was to a large extent born of a reaction against the imperialism of economic history. But it must not be the pretext for a return to outmoded spiritualism, hiding perhaps within the vague definitions of a notion of the collective psyche. Neither should it be used to shore up vulgar Marxism, seeking easy definitions for superstructures still mechanically derived from a socio-economic base. Mentality does not mean reflection.

The history of mentalities must also be distinguished from the history of ideas, out of opposition to which it also grew. It was not the ideas of Thomas Aquinas or Saint Bonaventura which, from the thirteenth century on, governed people's minds, but mental *nebulae* in which such ideas only played a part as deformed echoes, devalued fragments and words taken out of context. But this identification of bastardised ideas within mentalities *must* be linked to the history of the systems of culture, belief and values, the intellectual equipment through which mentalities appear and evolve. It is precisely in such an area, moreover, that ethnology has lessons for the historian.

This crucial attention to the history of culture should allow the history of mentalities to avoid certain other epistemological traps.

The history of mentalities is indeed close to psychology through its concern with gesture, behaviour and attitudes,[22] and collaboration between the two disciplines must eventually take place. But it must not allow itself to be swallowed up by behaviourism and reduced to a set of automatisms unrelated to systems of thought, for to do so would be to discard one of the most important problems it raises: the power of human consciousness and understanding to influence the course of history. As an eminently collective phenomenon, mentality seems to be somehow set apart from the vicissitudes of social struggle. But it would be a clumsy error to separate it from social structure and dynamics. It is indeed a vital part of social tensions and struggles. Social history is full of myths which reveal the power of mentalities to affect history in its constant process of struggle and change: the white-collar worker, the two hundred families who rule France, etc. Class mentalities exist side by side with unifying mentalities, and their workings have yet to be studied.

Finally, although the history of mentalities is concerned with the inertia of history, it is also a history of change, to the understanding of which it has a crucial contribution to make. The West, in the period from the eleventh to the thirteenth century, is shaken by one phenomenon: the growth of towns. A new society emerges from this transformation, and with it a new mentality favouring security, exchange, economy, and based on new forms of sociability and solidarity: the restricted family, the guild, the professional association, the neighbourhood (*quartier*). What part did mentalities play within the total history of these transformations?

Despite, or rather because of, its lack of clear definition, the history of mentalities is establishing its position within the current problematic of history. As long as it is not turned into a catch-all alibi for epistemological laziness, and if its tools and methods are developed, the history of mentalities has its part to play in a new kind of history which, in its search for explanations, dares to look behind the looking-glass.

NOTES

1 See the book by Alphandéry and Dupront, and the article by Dupront, in the bibliography.
2 G. Duby, 'La féodalité, une mentalité médiévale', *Annales ESC*, pp. 765–71.
3 The classic works are: Max Weber, *The Protestant Ethic and the Spirit of Capitalism*, 1904–5, English translation 1930; R. H. Tawney, *Religion and the Rise of Capitalism*, 1926; H. Lüthy, *La Banque protestante en France de la révocation de l'édit de Nantes à la Révolution*, 2 vols., Paris, 1959–60; see also J. Delumeau, *Naissance et affirmation de la Réforme*, 2nd edition, Paris, 1968, *Capitalisme et mentalité capitaliste*, pp. 302ff.
4 M. Bloch, *La Société féodale*, new edition, Paris, 1968, p. 129.
5 E. Labrousse, preface to G. Dupeux, *Aspects de l'histoire sociale et politique du Loir-et-Cher, 1848–1914*, Paris, 1962, p. xi.
6 K. Thomas, *Religion and the Decline of Magic*, London, 1971; E. E. Evans-Pritchard, *Anthropology and History*, Cambridge, 1961.
7 P. E. Schramm, *Herrschaftszeichen und Staatssymbolik*, 3 vols., Stuttgart, 1954; E. Kantorowicz, *The King's Two Bodies: A Study in Mediaeval Political Thought*, Princeton, 1957; B. Guinée and F. Lehoux, *Les Entrées royales françaises de 1328 à 1515*, Paris 1968.
8 H. Delehaye, *Sanctus: essai sur le culte des saints dans l'Antiquité*, Bruxelles, 1927; B. de Gaiffier, 'Mentalité de l'hagiographe médiéval d'après quelques travaux récents', *Analecta Bollandiana*, 1968, pp. 391–9; A. Vauchez, 'Sainteté laïque au 13e siècle: la vie du bienheureux Facio de Crémone, 1196–1271', in *Mélanges de l'école française de Rome*, 1972, pp. 13–53.
9 D. Julia, 'La Religion – Histoire religieuse', *Faire de l'histoire*, vol. 2, 'Nouvelles approches', Paris, 1974, pp. 137–67; D. Julia, in *Recherches de science religieuse*, vol. LVIII, 1970, pp. 575ff.; A. Dupront, 'Anthropologie religieuse', *Faire de l'histoire*, vol. 2, 'Nouvelles approches', Paris, 1974, pp. 105–136 (translated in this collection, pp. 123–50), and 'Vie et création dans la France moderne (XIVe–XVIIIe siècles)', *La France et les Français*, ed. M. François, 'Encyclopédie de la Pléiade', Paris, Gallimard, 1972, pp. 491–577.
10 C. Kluckhohn, 'Culture and behaviour', in G. Lindzey (ed.), *Handbook of Social Psychology*, Cambridge, Mass., 1954.
11 Preface to V. Alexandre, *Les Echelles d'attitude*, Paris, 1971.
12 Translator's note: *bricolage* = 'do-it-yourself'. This expression evokes the constitution of mental frameworks by the assembling of available elements of disparate systems.
13 I wish to thank M. Jean Viet, director of the 'Service d'Echange d'Informations Scientifiques' at the Maison des Sciences de l'Homme, Paris, and M. Philippe Besnard, who, at his suggestion, has collected a file of information on 'le mot et le concept de mentalité', which I have used extensively.
14 Compared with *mentalité*, 'mentality' has a much more cognitive and intellectual connotation. An extreme case of this is the English title of W. Köhler's: *Intelligenzprüfungen an Menschenaffen* (1921): *The Mentality of Apes* (1925). On the other hand, affective connotations are to the fore in the French word. This is shown in a somewhat paradoxical way in E. Rignano's article, 'Les diverses mentalités logiques', *Scientia*, 1917, pp. 95–125, which studies 'the fundamental predominance of affective over intellectual elements' in the two major categories of mentalities distinguished by the author: the synthetic and the analytic.
15 The more or less pejorative connotations noted by Besnard include: Arab mentality,

Hindu mentality, the mentality of the Danish criminal, the mentality of the prisoner, German mentality in 1943. An interesting expression is 'levels of mentality'.
16 The word is scarcely more common in recent anthropological bibliographies (*mentalité primitive* and *mentalité indigène* are rare). The same is true of sociological bibliographies: out of seven references in the *Bibliographie internationale de sociologie* between 1963 and 1969, four are to a series of articles in Spanish by R. Lenoir in the *Revista mexicana de sociologia* between 1956 and 1961, concerning various primitive and civilised *mentalidades*.
17 'Collective behaviour', in R. L. Faris, *Handbook of Modern Sociology*, Chicago, 1964.
18 J. Decaens, 'Un nouveau cimetière du haut moyen âge en Normandie, Hérouvillette (Calvados)', *Archéologie médiévale*, vol. I, 1971, pp. 83ff.
19 *European Literature and the Latin Middle Ages*, London, 1953, p. 79.
20 *La Figure et le lieu: l'ordre visuel du quattrocento*, Paris, Gallimard, 1967, p. 172.
21 'L'écriture latine et la civilisation occidentale du Ier au XVIe siècle', *L'Ecriture et la psychologie des peuples*, vol. XXII, Paris, 1963, p. 243; E. Panofsky, *Architecture gothique et pensée scolastique*, Paris, 1967.
22 See especially M. Jahoda and N. Warren (eds.), *Attitudes*, Harmondsworth, 1966.

BIBLIOGRAPHY

Bouthoul, G., *Les Mentalités*, Paris, PUF (coll. 'Que sais-je?'), 1952 (5th edition, 1971).
Bursztyn, *Schizophrénie et mentalité primitive*, Paris, Jouve, 1935 (thesis for the Doctorate of Medicine).
Carnets de Lucien Lévy-Bruhl, Paris, PUF, 1949.
Cazeneuve, J., *La Mentalité archaïque*, Paris, Colin, 1961.
Duby, G., 'L'histoire des mentalités', in *L'Histoire et ses méthodes*, Paris, 'Encyclopédie de la Pléiade', Gallimard, 1961, pp. 937–66.
  'Histoire sociale et histoire de mentalités' (conversation with A. Casanova), *Nouvelle Critique*, 34, May 1970, pp. 11–19.
Dumas, G., 'Mentalité paranoïde et mentalité primitive', *Annales médico-psychologiques*, May 1934.
Dupront, A., 'Problèmes et méthodes d'une histoire de la psychologie collective', *Annales*, 16 (1), January–February 1961, pp. 3–11.
Dufrenne, M., *La Personnalité de base: un concept sociologique*, Paris, PUF, 1966 (1st edition, 1953).
Faberman, H. A., 'Manheim, Cooley and Mead: toward a social theory of mentality', *Sociological Quarterly*, 11 (1), winter 1970, pp. 3–13.
Febvre, L., 'Histoire et psychologie', *Encyclopédie française*, VIII, 1938, reprinted in *Combats pour l'histoire*, Paris, 1953, pp. 207–20.
  'Comment reconstituer la vie affective d'autrefois? La sensibilité et l'histoire', *Annales d'histoire sociale*, III, 1941, reprinted in *Combats pour l'histoire*, pp. 221–31.
  'Sorcellerie, sottise ou révolution mentale?', *Annales ESC*, 1948, pp. 9–15.
  'Histoire des sentiments. La terreur', *Annales ESC*, 1951, pp. 520–3.
  'Pour l'histoire d'un sentiment: le besoin de sécurité', *Annales ESC*, 1956, pp. 244–7.
Geremek, B., 'Umysłowość i psychologia zbiorowa w historii' (Collective mentality

and psychology in history), in *Przeglad Historyczny*, LIII, 1962, pp. 629–43, and note in *Annales ESC*, 1963, pp. 1221–2.

Herzlich, C., 'La représentation sociale', in Moscovici, S.: *Introduction à la psychologie sociale*, I, Paris, Larousse, 1972, pp. 303–25.

Lévy-Bruhl, L., *L'âme primitive*, Paris, Alcan, 1927.

La Mentalité primitive, Paris, Alcan, 1922.

Le Surnaturel et la nature dans la mentalité primitive, Paris, Alcan, 1931.

Les Fonctions mentales dans les sociétés inférieures, Paris, Alcan, 1910.

Mandrou, R., 'L'histoire des mentalités', in article 'Histoire', 5, *Encyclopaedia universalis*, VIII, 1968, pp. 436–8.

Piaget, J., *La Représentation du monde chez l'enfant*, Paris, Alcan, 1926 (English translation: *The Child's Conception of the World*, London, 1929).

Ruschemeyer, D., 'Mentalität und Ideologie', in *Soziologie*, ed. R. König, 1967 (French version in *Sociologie*, 1972).

Sorokin, P. A., *Social and Cultural Dynamics*, New York, Bedminster Press, 4 vols., 1937–41.

Sprandel, R., *Mentalitäten und Systeme: Neue Zugänge zur mittelalterlichen Geschichte*, Stuttgart, 1972.

Trénard, Louis, 'Histoire des mentalités collectives: les livres, bilans et perspectives', *Revue d'histoire moderne et contemporaine*, 1968, pp. 691–703.

Violet-Conil, M., and Canivet, N., *L'Exploration de la mentalité infantile*, Paris, PUF, 1946.

Wallon, H., 'La mentalité primitive et celle de l'enfant', *Revue philosophique*, July–December 1928.

'La mentalité primitive et la raison', *Revue philosophique*, 4, October–December 1957, pp. 461–7 (on Lévy-Bruhl).

Les Origines de la pensée chez l'enfant, Paris, PUF, 1945.

EXAMPLES OF THE HISTORY OF MENTALITIES

Alphandéry, P., and Dupront, A., *La Chrétienté et l'idée de croisade*, 2 vols., Paris, 1954–9.

Bayet, J., 'Le suicide mutuel dans la mentalité des Romains', *L'Année sociologique*, third series (1951), 1953, pp. 35–89.

Bloch, M., *Les Rois thaumaturges: étude sur le caractère surnaturel attribué à la puissance royale*, Strasbourg, 1924, reprinted 1960 (English translation: *The Royal Touch: Sacred Monarchy and Scrofula in England and France*, London, 1973).

La Société féodale, Paris, 1939, reprinted 1968 (Part I, Book II: *Les Conditions de vie et l'atmosphère mentale*).

Brandt, W. J., *The Shape of Medieval History: Studies in Modes of Perception*, New Haven and London, 1966.

Dhondt, J., 'Une mentalité du douzième siècle: Galbert de Bruges', *Revue du Nord*, 1957, W 101–9.

Febvre, L., *Le Problème de l'incroyance au XVIᵉ siècle: la religion de Rabelais*, Paris, 1952, reprinted 1968.

Houghton, W. E., *The Victorian Frame of Mind*, New Haven, 1957, 7th edition 1968.

Huizinga, J., *The Waning of the Middle Ages*, Harmondsworth, 1955.

Lefebvre, G., *La Grande Peur de 1789*, Paris, 1932.

Mandrou, R., *Introduction à la France moderne: essai de psychologie historique, 1500–1640*, Paris, 1961.

Magistrats et sorciers en France au XVIIe siècle: une analyse de psychologie historique, Paris, 1968.

'Le baroque européen: mentalité pathétique et révolution sociale', *Annales ESC*, 1960, pp. 898–914.

Morgan, J. S., 'Le temps et l'intemporel dans le décor de deux églises romanes: facteurs de coordination entre la mentalité religieuse romane et les œuvres sculptées et peintes à Saint-Paul-lès-Dax et à Saint-Chef en Dauphiné', *Mélanges René Crozet*, I, Poitiers, 1966, pp. 531–48.

Pastor de Togneri, R., 'Diego Gelmirez: une mentalité à la page. A propos du rôle de certaines élites de pouvoir', *Mélanges René Crozet*, I, pp. 597–608.

Rousset, P., 'La croyance en la justice immanente à l'époque féodale', *Le Moyen Age*, LIV, 1948, pp. 225–48.

Tenenti, A., *Il senso della morte e l'amore della vita nel Rinascimento*, Turin, 1957.

9. The festival in the French Revolution

MONA OZOUF

No performance today is complete without festival, and every vision of the future includes some kind of celebration. The festival has invaded the vocabulary of the political essay, theatre criticism, and literary commentary. This sometimes reflects a nostalgic desire to restore the past: the society which speaks of festivals is one in which rejoicing is a private affair, and the collective memory which folklore is supposed to preserve and celebrate is a false one. The intention may also be a prophetic one: since May 1968, so often interpreted as an act of revenge on the festive poverty of modern society, we have been looking forward to some future festival. We are promised it by political and theological thought alike: the latter is currently engaged in rehabilitating festive gratuity as against the values of patience and tension implicit in the work ethic,[1] while political thought expects the revolution to merge with the eternal present of the festival, and deliver happiness, not at some distant future date, but now.[2]

History was for a long time more concerned with the work and effort of men than with those activities which are variously called entertainment or distraction. The festival and feast have now become legitimate objects of historical interest,[3] and this is due to the dual influence of folklore and ethnology. They have taught the historian to look at the ways in which human existence is given a structure by ritualisation, even if this is anonymous and lacking in explicit organisation and conscious cohesion. Psychoanalysis, at the same time, has taught the historian to attach importance to the apparently meaningless.

The annexation of this new area by historiography is not, however, without its problems. First of all, it is far from certain that the festival itself will accept this annexation without putting up a silent resistance, partly because of the immense problems still involved in cultural history, but also because of the festival's particular relationship with time. The present of the festival opens out onto the past and the future, and thus appears to speak a familiar language to the historian. Every festival involves reminiscence:[4] often an anniversary, it seeks to re-enact the past, and it is tempting for the historian to accept its testimony. At the same time, the festival heralds the future, is a kind of approximation of it; it simulates a future which the historian is fortunate enough to be able to compare with what will really happen.

But two dangers may be involved here. The first temptation is to see the repetition which is indeed an element of the festival as a self-conscious repetition, the past which is celebrated being held at arm's length and analysed. Such scholarly precision is not the festival's concern, and the Freudian analysis of repetition is more pertinent: an irrational attempt to deal with a traumatic event without situating or dating it, without wresting it from the unbearable present and controlling it. Repetition is the ceremonial resort of someone who cannot become the historian of his/her own life, the futile circlings of a mind which is a slave to reality. The repetitive festival, like neurosis, is not so much a pedagogy of time,[5] as a strategy of archaism in the face of fear. This attachment to the past is clearly an object of great interest to the historian, but it is clear that the history of the festival will be the history of a phenomenon which is itself blind to history.

The second temptation is the opposite of the first, but no less dangerous: it involves taking at face value the rehearsal of the future which parallels the repetition of the past. Firstly, the beginning which the festival enacts is often an illusory one, a repeated exemplary gesture meant to articulate hope; and, secondly, rather than enacting an indeterminate future which is open to multiple possibilities and for that very reason a source of fear, the festival is a kind of conjuring trick quite incompatible with notions of prediction and work, enacting in the immediate present a scene of immortality and indestructibility. How then can its prophecies be taken as a real anticipation of the future? They belong to the realm of the imagination, and are a projection of desire rather than an anticipation of reality. Here again, the historian is disarmed: we cannot expect the festival to shed light on the future which it envisages, since the time which it heralds is not historical time.

But is this true of all festivals? Surely, some at least enjoy some connection with history, reflecting the contingent reality of the exceptional circumstances from which they sprang? This is certainly one of the reasons for the attention which has been paid to the festivals of the French Revolution. We can date the first wave of such monographs and general studies very precisely: the period in the Third Republic leading up to the separation of Church and State in 1905.[6] Historians at this time take up the theme of the replacement of religious enthusiasm by civic festivals, and do so in terms very similar to those used by the men of the Revolution, and this must be seen as a response to the hidden anxieties caused by the separation of Church and State. Today, a second wave of work on the Revolutionary festivals is under way, led by North American historians who are interested in the relationship between politics and propaganda.[7] Three reasons justify continued interest in the subject, in my view. Firstly, the coherent and systematic nature of the Revolutionary festival, which develops over a period of scarcely ten years. Secondly, the mass of archival material which exists, breaking the silence which usually surrounds festivals and feasts, and which is part of the timeless dimension of folklore.[8] Thirdly, the Revolutionary festival's place in the history of an extraordinary period: such a rich and complex set of rituals, appearing at a time when another set enters into eclipse, must bear traces of the exceptional circumstances which are both the cause and the object of the festival's celebration.

But the revolutionary festival must be studied for the right reasons. It is incorrect, for instance, to start from the principle (which has been given new life by the events of 1968) that a relation of similarity or even identity exists between the festival and revolution. It is not sufficient to justify this view by pointing to the obvious need which revolutions have felt for festivals, the urgency with which they have instituted them, or even the well-documented plethora of festivals in revolutionary situations – the extraordinary festive explosion following the October Revolution, for instance. None of this proves that the two are consubstantial. The vision of a festival expanded by revolutionary liberation to encompass the whole of life is based not on observed fact, but on the hope, or illusion, of a non-repressive society in which the distinction between festival and everyday life ceases to exist.

The historian must also be cautious about the received notion that revolution sharpens and strengthens historical consciousness. The corollary of this view is an expectation that the misoneism which is the mark of the festival in ordinary times – its reluctance to alter its ritual framework – will fall away in revolutionary times. But the time which is celebrated in festivals is one which can be regenerated, and the virtue of revolutionary ferment is that it gives added conviction to this process of renovation. The joy which festivals promote – whether they celebrate the revolutions of the earth or the revolutions of history – is the expression of time's ability to bring forth the new from the death of the old. And we should ask ourselves whether this dimension of time made new in which the festival operates – which explains, for instance, the magical qualities of the Festival of the Federation for contemporaries who were present and historians who have written about it[9] – is the same as historical time. Is the revolutionary festival a means of affirming history, or an escape route from it?

The organisers of the Revolutionary festivals, however, have no such doubts. From the very start, their expressed ambition was to embrace history. For M.-J. Chénier, they will represent an annual commemorative history of the Revolution. For Jean Debry, they will establish links between the distant past and the present. There is a general expectation that festivals should bring the Revolution to those who have no direct knowledge of it. The festival-makers are so obsessed with commemoration that their projects extend it to private life, in the form of homely family ceremonies. Leclerc wants every family to have a book, brought out and consulted on important family festivals, so that nothing should be lost. Such loss is the great fear: there must be no forgetting the 'big occasions', but neither must the memory of tyranny, the indispensable counterpoint, be lost. Even the modest details of everyday life will be solemnised in written form. When, in 1797 and 1798, the Institute offers prizes for answers to the question: 'What are the appropriate institutions for founding the memory of a people?', the projects sent in reflect the same desire to preserve: newspapers publishing the acts of worthy citizens; columns placed in public squares for the names of criminals to be inscribed; village festivals overflowing with opprobrium and praise. The written and spoken word will let nothing escape.

The Revolutionary festival is perfectly adapted to these commemorative ends, in that it is spoken, rather than shown or played. These festivals are an endless source of discourse, paradoxically, since one of the values they seek to celebrate is a healthy laconicism. Interminable speeches are made, defining the historical significance of the event. They always seek to limit the uncertain drift of interpretation by providing placards and banners identifying the meaning of the different groups as they file past. They use maxims to underline the meaning of the most universal gestures: throwing into the flames before the assembled villagers the crowns and 'baubles' of royalty, the president of the municipality sees fit to enumerate the emotions which this spectacle should arouse in the hearts of those present.[10] Even the setting shows little faith in its own pedagogical capacities, and needs words to demonstrate its appropriateness to the ceremony. We feel that these festivals are less concerned with renewing emotion than with setting out a story.

Finally, they seem inseparable from Revolutionary history in that each one appears to reflect a specific 'phase' of the Revolution and illustrates a particular historical intention: they thus become the mirror through which the entire history of the Revolution can be read. The Festival of the Federation? Its joyfulness tells of a Revolution which is still open and bubbling over with hopes. The Festival of the Supreme Being? Its 'creaking' stiffness heralds the 'freezing' of the Revolution. The festival of 1 Vendémiaire Year VII? Its gymnastic competitions and exhibitions of work and talent at the Champ-de-Mars are a foretaste of the nineteenth century. These festivals seem locked into the events of the Revolution, enjoying little autonomy.

Albert Duruy[11] is a typical representative of the historiography of the festival when he says that they have no autonomy at all: they proceed from the new political institutions, and are part of a system which accounts for every aspect of them. If this is true, then every element of the festival is history: their birth and death, since they spring from the exceptional and disappear with it; their content, since their task is to bring about the triumph of a particular historical system of meaning over rival systems. If we accept this view, we must also accept that nothing in these festivals can be used in an anthropological analysis: they must be left to history, which can purge them of all meaning.

This apparently self-evident truth goes a long way to explaining the triumph of political interpretations of the Revolutionary festivals. Aulard[12] set a model for this, which is then repeated in innumerable local monographs: the festival in the Revolution is the 'expedient' resorted to by patriotism, prospering as long as the latter lives in fear and disappearing once it feels more assured. The defeat of the Austrians signals the decline of the Cult of the Supreme Being, to which Fleurus delivers the final blow. The history of festivals is in this view totally dependent on the events of the Revolution. Circumstance decrees the festival, improvisation puts the decree into effect. No global philosophical project or collective need can be seen in it; only the panting urgency of the task of defending the nation. Even Jaurès adds his weight to this circumstantial vision of the festival:[13] the Festival of the Supreme Being is nothing less than the posthumous revenge of Hébertism. Behind it can be seen the decree of Floréal and the 'decisive political error' which this in turn represents.

The value of this political type of interpretation is that it suggests a rich typology of festivals. There are as many festivals as there are political strategies, and the specificity of each festival can be clearly demonstrated. What a variety, stretching from the Festival of the Federation to 1 Vendémiaire Year VII! The Cult of Reason is seen by one historian (Aulard) as a specific creation of Hébertism, by another (August Comte)[14] as the makeshift but prophetic invention of the 'Dantonists'. The Festival of the Supreme Being is both the ultimate expression of Robespierre's mysticism and the signal for his downfall. The festival of 9 Thermidor Year IV is the expression of the post-Thermidorean balance. But one worry persists, even if we accept these interpretations. For these differences paradoxically produce the same ceremonial, despite the conflicting intentions of the organisers. This uniformity can no doubt be related to the organisers' desire to stress homogeneity at the expense of festive variety. The similarity of the different festivals appears in this light as a common guarantee of authenticity, a brake placed in each case on the tendency to establish or encourage hierarchies, a promise of unanimity. This is the meaning of Thibaudeau's reflections on costume when the time comes to ask questions about its necessary contribution to the composition of the festival: 'I recall that costume has always been one of the pretexts of the aristocracy ... the representatives of the people do not need costume; I will say more, they must not have any.'

But this desire for uniformity is not always present. One is sometimes struck by an effort towards diversification which fails to impinge on the real festival. The Festival of Victories, on 30 Vendémiaire Year III, is probably the clearest illustration of this desire to innovate. Parliamentary debates, speeches, newspaper reports endlessly underline the elements which distinguish it from the Robespierrist ceremonial. But what do we actually see take place? Military games in the Champ de la Fédération; the President of the Convention inscribing the names of the armies of the Republic on the Pyramid of Immortality. Where are the 'new and great ideas' which the *Journal de Perlet*[15] would like to see giving the festival its particular character? A reading of a few descriptions of festivals is sufficient to know what to expect: the pyramid, the simulated redoubt, the eternalising inscription are the settings and acts common to the whole Revolutionary ceremonial. No, the truth is that ceremonies of markedly different political meaning use the same symbols and obey the same rites as ceremonies from which they correctly claim to be distinct. Let us take, for example, a Girondin festival of reparation after Thermidor, celebrated at Lons-le-Saunier in Germinal Year III and explicitly meant to extol 'the federalism of virtue', as against the 'rallying of crime'. And what do the organisers think of to distinguish it from a Montagnard festival? They simply pile the signs of Jacobinism on top of the signs of royalty on the passing tumbrels: an unimaginative detail, and probably one which the spectators could not even see.

For if today's reader, enjoying the advantage of being acquainted with the organisers' intentions and programmes, finds it hard to tell the difference between festivals claiming to serve radically different ends, what must have been the perception of contemporary spectators, obliged to interpret quickly a set of symbols as they filed past? Here is an account[16] by a Colmar locksmith, Dominique Schutz, a well-informed and keen observer, who writes in a reasoned tone. For him, all the festivals which took place from 1792 to 1794 were much alike: the same adolescent theorising, the same 'young women of both religions' with the same flowing hair, the same companies of national guards, the same arrangements of flowers and ribbons. Nothing here suggests the opposition set up by Quinet between the visual exuberance of the Festivals of Reason and the stark severity attached to celebrations of the Supreme Being. Moreover, both Guillaume and Mathiez have conclusively demolished this contrast for its excessive reliance on a political interpretation of the Revolutionary cult. Against Aulard, who had nevertheless suspected resemblances, Mathiez[17] shows that the two ceremonies are not only similar, but structurally linked. In the face of all the traditional historiography, with its unanimous vision of the Festival of Reason as some kind of unprecedented Bacchanalia, Guillaume[18] proves that this supposedly new ceremonial had gone through at least thirty performances at the Opéra; and that few people saw any difference between this famous 'Reason' which has given rise to so many admiring or indignant commentaries, and 'Liberty', a concept more familiar to those involved: even the official accounts of these festivals mix up Liberty and Reason indiscriminately. After all this, what originality remains in the Festival of Reason? The fact that it chooses the new setting of Gothic arches to perform a worn-out libretto. Even then, as Mathiez points out, similar scenes had taken place in churches before. One cannot escape the question: are all these spectacular differences between festivals not in fact the invention of partisans of the political interpretation, who needed them to back up their case?

It was predictable that these disappointing attempts to categorise the festivals of the Revolution would, one day, encourage the opposite emphasis: a search for similarities and equivalences. Could the festival not be seen as one block, with a common thread running through the different Revolutionary cults? Clearly, such a reappraisal is reinforced if they are all seen as the product of a single desire: the replacement of Catholicism by a new cult, catering in a new but equivalent way for the needs of its congregation. Mathiez took this view,[19] and there is no shortage of parallels: through the signs which it uses and the organisation of its processions, the patriotic ceremony appears as a transposition of Catholic ceremonial. A host of contemporary texts could be cited in evidence: here is one chosen for its uncomplicated self-assurance. It is 2 Pluviôse Year VII, the place is Sucy-en-Brie, and the commissar of the Directory is pointing to the Statue of Liberty:

Let us raise our eyes to this image of our liberty. I have often heard it asked by men and children who have gained no instruction in republican virtues or have been prevented from gaining it: who is that saint? Has she performed any miracles? I will reply to them in their language: this is an image through which the corrupt court of Rome, the ignorant court of Sardinia, and now, surely, the ambitious court of Naples, have been swept away. What greater miracle could you ask for?

A general reading of the official accounts of the festivals of the Revolution certainly does incline one to see more similarities than differences. But there is a weakness in Mathiez's argument: the desire to see one cult as a substitute for the other may also reflect political motivations. Seeing that as the mainspring of the Revolutionary festival does not distance Mathiez from Aulard as much as he believes. According to Mathiez, the replacement of the manifestly bankrupt Civil Constitution is a 'remedy', and, having chanced the word, he finds it very difficult to distinguish it from Aulard's 'expedient'. There is, however, one important difference: in Mathiez's view, the rational political imagination draws on a source less calculating and more authentic, and the men of the Revolution took the idea and the model for later festivals from the great mystical scenes of the Festival of the Federation, spontaneous and free from all taint of artifice. The most artificial of festivals has its roots in original spontaneity. The idea of substitution did not spring fully grown from the minds of the politicians, but from the spectacle or the memory of a substitution which had already taken shape, unconsciously. Mathiez does not deny that each festival may then take on a particular political emphasis: but it nevertheless draws its distant meaning from the great religious drama which was played out at the Revolution's dawn by men who were unaware of what they were enacting. It is at this point that Mathiez encounters Durkheim's idea of the analogous relationship between the religious and the social. For the features which for Durkheim distinguish a religion can also be seen in festivals: the existence of a congregation, unanimity, independence from individuals, the element of coercion. Plus, of course, the commemorating function. 'The Revolution established a whole system of festivals to maintain in a state of eternal youth the principles which had inspired it.' This statement from *The Elementary Forms of Religion* illustrates the idea, dear to Durkheim, that religion contains 'something eternal, which is destined to survive the particular symbols in which religious thought has successively clothed itself'.

One element is strikingly absent from these interpretations: a collective need which is clearly reflected in innumerable pamphlets and anonymous plans buried in dusty archives. The men of the Revolution thirst for festivals. Why has no one tried to analyse this desire, to delve beneath the stiff, conventional language of official accounts in order to find the deep needs which the festival satisfies? Official accounts are a rationalisation, and do discourage such analysis; but even they cannot hide this thirst. We must seek the reasons for the silence of historians on this subject, a silence broken only by Michelet, who felt the link between the festival and fear. One reason, clearly, is that this need is hard to measure; another is that the festivals of the Revolution, despite the burlesque ambivalence of their use of animal symbolism – Marie Antoinette depicted as a goat, Louis XVI as a piglet, and as many donkeys as France has enemies – are on the whole relatively lacking in compensatory features which might suggest the liberation of desire. Finally, too close identification with interpretations offered by the Revolutionaries themselves is probably another reason why this dimension has not been pursued.

For one thing is clear: the historians of the festival describe it in the same terms that are used by the organisers. All the major themes are clearly present in the contemporary pamphlets reflecting on the limits of the festival, the contradiction between order and spontaneity, and the psychological resistance to new ceremonial habits. The theme of substitution is as alive here as in the work of Mathiez. Why such credence in the evidence of contemporaries? Why do the *Mémoires* of Levasseur tell us more or less the same thing as a nineteenth-century historian? Certainly, this is because the Revolutionary festival was immediately rationalised: from the start, it was made to bear multiple rational meanings by those who sought to unite moral and political aims with the picturesque. This overloading with aims explains the fact that historiography of the Revolution rushed headlong into the problem of the festival's aims: what purpose must it serve? But the reader of these histories must wonder to what extent the notion of utility offers an understanding of the phenomenon. Is there not an element of overdetermination even in those festivals which were meant to serve the clearest of pedagogical ends, which were so closely tied to everyday reality that their authors foresaw the crowds going home afterwards 'loving and esteeming each other more'?

This scrupulous respect for the evidence of contemporaries explains the fact that historians have privileged the intended meaning of the festival at the expense of its lived meaning. Historians have conferred a strange omnipotence on the organisers' plans and commentaries. The festival is presented as a docile piece of equipment, assembled and dismantled in the twinkling of an eye to serve the cause. Aulard notes how, the day it pleased Robespierre to suggest that the Cult of the Supreme Being was a good weapon against the foreign enemy, the goddesses of Reason fell, immediately and practically everywhere, from grace. The innumerable local monographs all share this idea that the festival was an unmediated application of voluntarist rationalism. More elaborate histories suggest the same thing. Taine[20] sees the Festival of the Federation as a perfect illustration, via a 'formula laid down by the philosophers', of the abstract fiction of the eighteenth century: 'the idyll is enacted like a written programme'. Mathiez himself says that the Cult of Reason is only born 'when all the Revolutionaries agree on the need to replace the old religion with a civic cult'.

As a result, like Fabrice's war in Stendhal's novel, the festival is always somewhere else. As a doctrinal invention linked to accidental circumstances, it is invincibly allegorical, always saying something other than what it shows; it is in that direction that we should look for an explanation of historians' indifference to its literal meaning, to what it says clearly and actually enacts. This also tells us something about the totally unsystematic oscillation between two contradictory descriptions of the festival, of which A. Duruy[21] offers a good illustration. Sometimes he sees the Revolution engendering 'bizarre, heteroclite conceptions incompatible with the French genius'; the opacity of these festivals, with their drunken women and disconcerting symbolism, is such that it becomes hard to distinguish the meticulous execution of a philosophic intention: does this mean that a failure of execution – which is not adequately explained – makes for a successful festival? Then, on the other hand, Duruy sees these festivals as a monotonous series of exact replicas: in this case, are we to conclude that success in execution leads to the failure of festival? Duruy is manifestly unable to decide.

Finally, historians too often take at face value the link which the organisers seek to establish between the festival and history. None doubts that the object of the festival is the time of the Revolution, that it must reflect the latter's phases and periods. The master of ceremonies at a Festival of Victory, held at Carcassonne to celebrate the fall of Courtrai to the army of the North, even suggests that the festival should not be confined to periodic commemorations, since 'there are others which must spring from events, preserving that irregularity which is so suited to the movements of the soul'. This is an interesting text, since it sees the history of the Revolution as not yet 'frozen'; it relegates periodic festivals to an ahistorical dimension, and opens up a fundamental problem: can we at least say that the commemorative festival is one in which historical consciousness is sharpened and strengthened?

An important feature is, indeed, the way in which it offers an extraordinary review of the pre-Revolutionary past: the orators expound the crimes of the monarchy, their eloquent periodisation telling of 'eighteen centuries of slavery'. But, dramatic though they may be, the bloody scenes of the St

Bartholomew's Day massacres are evoked in speech; and in general the colourful episodes of this history are told, not depicted. The festival is more likely to show scenes from the Revolutionary past, and, even then, this reverent repetition is meant to recall an archetypal situation rather than to awaken memories. In terms of Henri Hubert's analysis,[22] the commemorative function of repetition is secondary to the function of 'making present'. However distant its origins in the long line of Revolutionary events, the event which is celebrated here is always as new as the morning. 10 August, 21 January, 1 Vendémiaire: all are contemporary with the Revolutionary dawn, and even celebrations of 9 Thermidor will try to return to this common origin. How can we fail to see that the function of repetition is to lessen the disruptive shock of new events, removing them from profane time and conferring on them the prestige of a new beginning?

We must therefore be suspicious of hasty identification between the return to the past and a conscious repetition of the past. Is Dowd[23] really correct when he suggests that the funeral festival of Lazowski, with its red flag, its tocsin, its pikes and cannon, propagates the spirit of insurrection? Does it not rather herald the fact that there will be no more insurrection? We favour the latter hypothesis, for two reasons. Firstly, because of the innumerable texts – in which visions as far apart as those of Robespierre and the Thermidoreans agree – where an explicitly conservative function is assigned to the festival: single-handed, it can prevent the radicalisation of the Revolution. Secondly, because of the internal structure of the festival, in the sense that the emblems and rituals on which it draws often represent closure. The commemoration is also an exorcism. Far from reducing the opposition between festival and history, the particular case of the festivals of the French Revolution tends to exacerbate it. The festival is a temporary world which denies its temporary nature; and, since the morrow must also be a festival, there is also an element of flight from history towards the utopia of the eternal festival. Rabaut Saint-Etienne is unambiguous: 'History is not our code.'

It is time for an example. Of all the Revolutionary festivals, the one in which the historical event is likely to play a most obsessive role, and which, like the Revolutionary *journée* of which it was a part, seems most clearly determined, is the festival of 21 January. The exact title is 'The Festival of the Just Punishment of the Last King of the French', a string of genitives pregnant with multiple meanings. To speak of 'just punishment' is doubtless to plead one's own innocence in a trial not yet over; but it also represents a euphemistic detour to avoid getting too close to images which are too painful. As for the adjective 'last', it may represent a simple statement of fact – Louis XVI is indeed the last in the neutral order of succession – but it may also represent a wish or indeed a programme: the ordinal number falls like a guillotine blade, ensuring that he really is the last.

From Pluviôse Year II onwards, the death of the king is celebrated. But these are sporadic celebrations, largely improvised, not tied to the precise date of the anniversary, and preceded here and there, before the execution, by festivals 'of the disappearance of royalty'. It is Robespierre's great speech in Floréal Year II which renders the festival official and gives it a national character. Thermidor brings it into doubt, as it does the other celebrations belonging to Robespierre's programme, but by Nivôse Year III it has taken on its definitive features, with the decree which sets the broad outline, if not the detail, for the rest of the Revolutionary period.

How much of the event to be represented will actually be depicted? The Revolutionary festival does not favour dumb-show, partly because of material limits, but also because of a Puritan hostility to the theatre; and yet it seeks to provide a place for the 'sensible objects' to which the sons of Condillac obviously wish to anchor institutions – hence the occasional simulated battle, apparitions and miracles. But in the case of the death of the king, the subject defies figuration. The only figurative element proposed by the Comité d'Instruction Publique is not particularly imaginative: Thirion's plan includes a set of bonfires, useful not simply as a source of heat during this winter festival, but also for burning the trappings of royalty and feudalism. The bonfire is indeed a common element in republican festivals. But this exhausted symbol does draw some sharp comments. Lecomte asks ironically: 'What is meant by these bonfires which are proposed in order to burn before the people the remaining signs of feudalism?' He offers the following alternative: either such signs still exist in reality, in which case there are better things to do than make-believe; or they no longer exist, and the ceremony is superfluous. This takes us to the heart of the general debate surrounding the festivals of the Revolution. Is it possible for a festival which sees itself as a manifestation of Enlightenment to portray darkness and horror? The superstitious fear of engendering that which one wishes to deny is always present in the festival, but it comes to the fore in discussion of the festival of 21 January: this explains the brevity of the official arrangements and, in the actual execution of the festival, a certain figurative poverty. On the public squares of France on 21 January, parchments and sceptres are joyfully consigned to the flames; and the processions weave their way amongst figures of Brutus, Liberty, Rousseau, Franklin and, occasionally, Royalty. And Louis XVI, last king of the French, specifically? He is present less than the others, and, even where he is, the means of representation is often such as to disguise the royal figure: 2 Pluviôse Year VII, in Bordeaux, a figure of Perjury is placed between the two doors of the 'temple'. A spectator with a good place can no doubt read on the crown which sits on the head of this allegorical figure, the words 'Louis XVI'. But the official and newspaper accounts only seem interested in the abstract value of the event: the punishment of Perjury is what they remember.

The anniversary festivities of Year II were spontaneous until the authorities took them in hand, and therefore reflect a freer invention. But even here, despite the atmosphere of joyous inversion reminiscent of a carnival, one feels a certain unease. At Conches, 20 Ventôse Year II, the hapless object of public mirth who is paraded on a cart is not Louis XVI but the former Saint Louis in his royal mantle – perhaps a statue taken from the church. This is an overdetermined image, for it also represents Louis XVI: it is 'the head of Mr Capet, Saint, representing big Veto, his grandson many times removed'. This amalgam suggests a loss of parodic force, a softening of the farcical representation of vengeance. The carnivalesque insult does certainly serve to dethrone a king firmly established on his throne: it is good to be able to shout insults at him, beat him, dethrone him for a day. But the story which the festival tells dethrones a king already dethroned: its purpose is simply to mirror an event whose tragic force and power to shock it cannot hope to equal. Indeed it does not even attempt to do so, and shows as little as possible. As for the less explicit area of audible effects, the underlying unease can be felt: at the Paris festival in January Year III – the first great official model – the funeral march performed by the Institut National de Musique was judged to be too mild, almost as though there was a desire to bemoan the death of the tyrant. Gossec tried to justify his composition: 'we simply enjoyed the sweet emotions inspired in sensitive souls by the happy event of deliverance from a tyrant'.

The event, then, is hidden from direct view by an intentionally truncated symbolism in which the image quickly gives way to discourse: either the sententious maxims borne aloft on the banners of the processions, or the speeches pronounced on the altars of the nation by municipal officers, which are obviously richer from the point of view of rhetoric and euphemistic detour. Some speakers manage to confront the event head-on, while others make no reference to it. But the most interesting and most frequent case is that of the speaker who finds a way of speaking of 21 January in such a way as to spirit it completely away. Two features are particularly striking in these speeches: the masking of the figure of the king, and, more remarkably in view of the festival's official title, the blurring of the notion of punishment. Memories are fading. Various oratorical devices are used to hide the image of the king's punishment. There are few references to Louis XVI or Capet. The speeches refer at will to the 'perjurer', 'a perfidious king', 'the last crowned tyrant', 'the plaything of an evil and lewd woman'. The expression, 'the first civil servant', probably represents the most successful attempt to hide the holy figure of the Capetian king, by transforming it into a secular institution. The arguments used also serve to blur the king's features: far less attention is paid to him than to the royalty which he represents, by chance and almost by ill-luck. His personal crimes are simply part of the stock list of royal crimes, and lose their colour and definition. For the favourite theme of these speakers is the idea that in punishing its last king, France has punished the excesses of his predecessors, who were just as guilty as him: 'the terrible example of justice finally done, in whatever age, to the usurpers of authority'. 'In whatever age': this historical indifference has a very precise function. Rather than reflecting history, the telescoping of time expresses a kind of second, deviant nature; and the idea of collective responsibility blocks out the image of too personal a punishment.

The use of euphemism, in fact, reaches a high point with the execution of the king. There is no trace of the scaffold in these speeches, and the 'national sword' is the clearest reference to the guillotine. Death is hardly spoken of: it is rather 'the price of all crimes', a 'terrible event'; or, in a euphemism which expresses a nervous desire to externalise a personal sense of guilt, 'so true, just and natural a consequence, so justly part of the order of the day'. And in the midst of this enormous movement of neutralisation and naturalisation, 21 January becomes the day on which the throne of liberty was raised: the birthday of the Republic. It might just as well be 10 August or 1 Vendémiaire: the anniversary has disappeared. In this sense, but only in this sense, this short-memoried festival is a second execution.

Who exactly has punished whom? One can listen quite attentively to these speeches and not find an answer. They say not a word about the trial, and the divisions it provoked in the Convention; the punishment of the king is associated either with Providence or with the allegorical triumph of a particular virtue – Beneficent Liberty, or Wisdom, or, if the speaker is concerned to show the originality of this period of the Revolution compared to others, Justice. The festival of 21 January presents an image of virtue as static, its only purpose seems to be an adequate expression of this: it needs no other named characters.

Images and speeches are, however, essentially ornamental, and what has already been said would be insignificant but for the fact that the historical kernel at the centre of the whole ceremonial is absent. The instructions of Nivôse Year III gave the festival the features which it was to keep up until the end: it is the festival of 'the employees of the Republic', and their declaration of hatred for royalty is to be the centrepiece. Already in Year III, this oath assures the cohesion of the event, but between then and Year VII its importance grows ever greater. It is still expedited with relative haste in Year IV, but by Year VII it has expanded and become more complex: it goes hand in hand with a compulsory invocation of the Supreme Being, as if to impress upon those taking the oath the presence of some transcendent principle, and there are more 'curses upon perjurers', which offer a fine opportunity for the teachers from the Ecoles Centrales to display their scholarly bravura in descriptions of the interminable wanderings and pangs of remorse, which are the just deserts of the perjurer. The association of ideas which the festival is meant to suggest is fairly clear. In foretelling the punishments which perjurers can expect – from the law which the takers of the oath have sworn to accept – the festival becomes a national institution of intimidation. Every year, on 2 Pluviôse, anyone can remind himself of that punishment: the example of the perjurer–king is there to underscore the lessons taught by the pedagogy of fear.

Fear would indeed be the dominant tone even without the help of sententious speeches. Every element likely to entertain such an emotion is included: the sacramental phrase inscribed in large letters on the altar of the nation; the steps up to the platform on which the oath is taken; the constitution of Year III, on which the left hand must be placed; even the heroic tension which, with the right arm raised, the swearer's body must somehow simulate. And, especially, the silent coercion exerted by the spectators' gaze. The inflexible ceremonial in which the oath of death is taken is meant to provoke terror; and this can be glimpsed through the rigid official language in which accounts of such festivals are written. Many men run away when the time comes to take the oath, or try to tone down its wording by introducing some slight modification, which the accounts correctly interpret as an annulment of the whole exercise. Many, too, are suddenly affected by a mysterious paralysis when they are about to make their declaration or sign: should we not interpret this 'sudden sickness' as a sincere simulation of hysteria?

The oath, however, only instils such fear because fear is the ground in which it is rooted. This obstinate insistence on an oath of hatred for royalty and loyalty to the Republic can only be understood as a result of the country's growing fear of a future containing the former and excluding the latter. The object of the oath is a Revolution which has reached its ultimate stage: it enacts society's unanimous agreement that there can be no going back, but above all the impossibility of a future other than one that is repetitive. To take an oath, as Sartre brilliantly demonstrates,[24] is to swear to perpetuate a sterile present. The oath denies the corrupting dimension of time. The conservative purpose of the festival is perfectly served by the pedagogy of the oath. Through the oath, everyone gains a right of life and death over everyone else; it is a collective insurance against individual weakness, and against the uncontrollable drift of history.

It will be objected that this nervous, constrained unanimity, where commemoration clearly performs a function of closure, is only the case in this particular and unrepresentative 'black' festival: all historians of the festival agree that the festival of the king's death is an inversion of the normal model. An inverted and mournful reflection of that most joyous of festivals, the Festival of the Federation, the clearest expression of the original Revolutionary notion of regeneration. There, the nation swore not hatred, but loyalty to the king. But this can be misleading, for some celebrations of the king's death are joyous occasions, and the sense of joy and freedom is reflected in the accounts. Hats are raised aloft on the end of bayonets, endless *farandoles* are danced around the Liberty Tree; the young people bring their food to the inn, play games, and drink plenty of wine, for 'if a proper requiem is to be sung to the French monarchy', one must 'have a bottle at hand'. Here, one can feel 'the honest joy of the countryside', and the crowd sometimes drops the tune 'favoured by all Frenchmen' to take up an air such as 'Tout est charmant chez

Aspasie'. Can history be the horizon of these graceful and naive festivals, which smack of an idealised Switzerland? Where the object of the festival was present, we have seen that it left no room for festive feeling; here, that feeling is free to express itself, but the object is absent. The participants no doubt see in the festival the hope of new beginnings: beyond 21 January, the festival claims to be celebrating the early days of the Revolution. But, once again, this antecedent leads nowhere. The past only serves to provide a tone and a set of norms for the present, in which the festival is totally absorbed.

At a festival for the recapture of Toulon held at la Ferté-sous-Jouarre,[25] History was represented in the procession: placed on a cart, with Painting and Victory on either side, the woman representing History rests her left hand on a golden book, 'and holding in her right hand a fine peacock feather, makes as if to catalogue the bravery of our warriors'. That is the festival's version of history: a false history which can only record one thing. If the festivals of the Revolution only want to hear that history, that clearly does not prevent any given festival from enjoying links with history. There is nothing contradictory about seeing the festival as simultaneously within time and seeking to escape to an extra-temporal dimension. But it is no longer possible to insist solely on the first part of the analysis, as so many historians have done in their impatience to reduce the enigmatic diversity of these festivals to the simplicity of a political project. We still have no clear idea of what is seen, said and done during these festivals: the routes followed by the processions, the sacramental objects which they parade, the phrases and slogans which are pronounced, the figures which appear. We know less about the ways in which meanings were perceived in all this. What the history of the festival requires is a collective lack of complacency, a climate of curiosity likely to promote research. The discipline of history must bring balance and a basis in fact to the ambitions of anthropology.

The festival invites us to a realm outside history, but the history of the festival cannot follow that road. But we must be aware that, taken collectively, the festival's ambition is to reshape and contain history in order to relive it in an acceptable form. The festival does not like change; it seeks to externalise and neutralise it through ritual, constantly attempting to correct its unpredictable indetermination. The festival is an enormous collective enterprise of rectification: the festivals of the French Revolution, at least.

NOTES

1 On this theme, see Harvey Cox, *La Fête des fous*, a theological essay on the notions of festival and fantasy (Paris, Seuil, 1971); and Jürgen Moltmann, *Die ersten Freigelassenen der Schöpfung – Versuche über die Freude an der Freiheit und das Wohlgefallen am Spiel* (Munich, Kaiser Verlag, 1971).
2 See various works taking as their starting-point the lyricism of May 1968: Jean-Marie

Domenach, 'Idéologie du mouvement', *Esprit*, 8–9 (August–September 1968); B. Charbonneau, 'L'émeute et le plan,' *La Table ronde*, 251–2 (December 1968–January 1969); R. Pascal, 'La fête de mai', *France-Forum* (October–November 1968).

3 This is shown in a wide range of collective and individual works, too numerous to be listed here. I will mention *Les Fêtes de la Renaissance*, ed. and introduced by Jean Jacquot (2 vols., Paris, CNRS, 1956, 1960); R. Alewyn and Karl Sälzle, *L'Univers du baroque*, Geneva, 1964; and James E. Oliver, *Seasonal Feasts and Festivals* (London, 1961).

4 One thinks of the totemic meal, according to Freud a re-enactment of the original criminal scene in which the sons devour the father. In this sense, humanity's first festival is already the ramblings of old age. To celebrate is, in fact, always to 'chew over', independently of the original meaning which Freud gives the term in this fantasy.

5 This is Cox's theme (*op. cit.*) According to Cox, the festival is a means of learning about certain temporal dimensions which man habitually fears or misunderstands. He learns to domesticate the past through repetition, and the future by the expression of his hopes. Paradoxically, the break in ordinary time which the festival represents allows him to become attuned to the continuity of time. Cox gives the curious name 'juxtaposition' to this therapeutic aspect of festivals. But is our awareness of historical time really increased through the festival? Cox is aware of the difficulty, and does not disguise the fact that the festival represents a brief holiday from an everyday reality which is the stuff of history.

6 Aulard's *Le Culte de la Raison et de l'Etre suprême* appeared in 1892. Mathiez's *Les Origines des cultes révolutionnaires* in 1904. Tiersot's *Les Fêtes et les chants de la Révolution française* in 1908. A host of local studies belong to the same years.

7 See, for instance, Stanley J. Idzerda, 'Iconoclasm during the French Revolution', *American Historical Review*, LX (October 1954); D. L. Dowd, 'Art as national propaganda in the French Revolution', *Public Opinion Quarterly* (Autumn 1951); Dowd, 'Jacobinism and the fine arts', *Art Quarterly*, XVI, 3 (1953); Dowd, *Pageant-Master of the Republic: Jacques-Louis David and the French Revolution* (Lincoln, Nebraska, 1948); J. A. Leith, *The Idea of Art as Propaganda in France, 1750–1790* (Toronto, University Press, 1965); J. Lindsay, 'Art and revolution', *Art and Artists* (August 1969).

8 There are immediate sources for analysing the intentions of the organisers; their justifications are too willingly offered and too self-conscious to be taken at face value. But these sources may be balanced against evidence revealing the diffusion and the reception of their plans, and the degree of resistance which they met.

9 Quinet felt, perhaps more clearly than anyone else, the astonishing novelty of this festival: 'Those who had seen the old France, bristling with obstacles at every step, were astonished to see that all the barriers were down. With old-fashioned naivety, they entered Paris as they would a holy town.' *La Révolution* (Paris, 1865).

10 Here is part of the speech at Mennetou (Archives Nationales, Loir-et-Cher, F^1 C III 7): 'At the sight of these vestiges which, together with royalty, recall all the effects of the tyranny which oppressed France for so many centuries, what emotions do you feel in your hearts and souls?'

11 Albert Duruy, *L'Instruction publique et la révolution* (Paris, 1886).

12 Aulard, *op. cit.*

13 Jaurès, *Histoire socialiste de la Révolution française*, edition revised by A. Mathiez (Paris, 1922).

14 A. Comte, *Système de politique positive* (Paris, 1851–4).

15 *Journal de Perlet* (1 Brumaire Year III).

16 *Revue d'Alsace*, III (1920).
17 Mathiez, *op. cit.*
18 Guillaume, *La Révolution française*, XXVI (January–June 1899).
19 Mathiez, *op. cit.*
20 Taine, *Les Origines de la France contemporaine* (Paris, 1878).
21 A. Duruy, *op. cit.*
22 H. Hubert, preface to *Czarnowski, le culte des héros et ses conditions sociales* (Paris, Alcan, 1919).
23 Dowd, *Pageant-Master.*
24 J.-P. Sartre, *Critique de la raison dialectique* (Paris, Gallimard, 1960).
25 *Bulletin du diocèse de Meaux*, I.

10. New approaches to the history of the book

ROGER CHARTIER and DANIEL ROCHE

Progress in the use of quantitative methods has brought new perspectives to the history of the book. Quantitative approaches have been successfully applied in two areas: the printed book as an object of exchange and profit, and as a cultural sign underpinning meanings transmitted by image or text. Historians working in this area have borrowed from the vocabulary, the conceptual equipment and the statistical methods of economic history. The evaluation of book production presupposes the development of statistical series, while book circulation can only be measured if networks and volumes of exchange can be quantified. At the same time, a broader change of perspective has occurred: traditional literary history, concerned with the great works and therefore tending to see books as the bearers of aesthetic or intellectual novelty, has given way to the extremely ambitious project of understanding the writing and reading practices of a whole society. As a result, the book must be seen not only as the favoured weapon of humanism and the Enlightenment, but also, and just as importantly, as the mirror of a society's attachment to the past. Quantitative approaches are not in themselves new: at the beginning of this century, literary criticism in the Lanson tradition looked towards statistics for a solution to the problem of influence, both that of the age on a particular writer and the writer's influence on the reading public. But counting procedures are today part of a different project: all the discourses which at a given moment find expression in book form can be assembled in a homogeneous corpus with no hierarchical structure and no arbitrary limits. The history of the book as it is now understood is a result of the collapse of the notion of the literary object, which work in semantics and cultural sociology has brought about.

Another source of new ideas has been material bibliography, which applies scientific methods to the study of those material aspects which were previously the province of the bibliophile. Refusing to study the meaning of the text and concentrating on the printer's marks, this 'new bibliography' has nonetheless much to offer the historian who seeks to situate the printed word within social history. For all its technicality, the new bibliography is not the exclusive sphere of the specialist collector, bookseller or librarian, but a source of new knowledge concerning the publication and circulation of cultural products.

Responding to these challenges has led to profound changes in a discipline which saw nothing problematical in its definition of itself: only in Germany has the old erudite science of bibliography remained intact, whereas in France, Belgium, the Netherlands and the Anglo-Saxon countries, new directions have opened up. This article will attempt to assess what has been achieved through these new developments, which are as exciting for the social historian as they are for the historian of collective mentalities. We shall concentrate principally on the seventeenth and eighteenth centuries, since this is the period which saw the book finally triumph as a cultural object.[1]

This triumph can, firstly, be defined geographically. In the early seventeenth century, the Italian book trade loses its hold on the markets of northern Europe; this is followed by the breakdown of the circuits which made Antwerp and the German towns centres of book production and exchange. Their place is taken by the Protestant publishers: Leyden and Amsterdam, building on the success of the Elzévir family, finally establish themselves in the second half of the seventeenth century.[2] In the eighteenth, the booksellers of Geneva and the Swiss typographical societies corner the Enlightenment market. The rise of the Protestant centres is contemporary with the growing importance of the civil book trade, characterised by its high rate of pirate editions and clandestine publications, and reaching its high point in the Cramer brothers who faithfully published Voltaire[3] and in the Neuchâtel Typographical Society, whose commercial network spread right across Europe. The eighteenth-century European book trade is clearly split: on the one hand, the Mediterranean world, especially the Iberian peninsula, where production is insufficient to satisfy religious and academic demand; on the other, Holland, France and Switzerland, supplying the South.[4]

Exchange continued, then, but at the same time national boundaries were becoming more important. Throughout modern Europe, vernacular languages were growing in power.[5] The triumph of French is assured by the printers of Paris in the seventeenth century: in mid-century, a quarter of books printed were in Latin, but this had dropped to one in ten by the 1660s.[6] German took longer to triumph, but did so all the same. Records of books sold at German fairs show twice as many Latin as vernacular ones at the beginning of the seventeenth century, equality between the two in the 1680s, but then a clear and growing preponderance of the national language (in 1765, 1,100 titles in German and just 200 in Latin).[7] The same is true even if we go to the limit of Christendom: in royal Hungary, Hungarian overtakes Latin in works of theology half-way through the seventeenth century.[8] Booksellers' and library records confirm this conclusion. In 1770, the Lyon bookseller Bruyset offered his customers a list of 5,000 books, 63 per cent of them printed in France;[9] in the following year, an inventory of the 3,400 volumes in the library of Dortous de

Mairan, permanent secretary of the Academy of Sciences, shows that 62 per cent were French publications.[10] The cultural space of a Parisian scientist is just as much a national one as that of a provincial bookseller. On the other hand, even in annexed territories, French meets resistance from German books: in 1786 the Treitlinger reading-room in Strasbourg had more books in German than in French.[11] The Republic of Letters did exist, but perhaps as a compensation for this fragmentation revealed in the book market.

Over France as a whole, Paris dominated the book trade. From 1660 onwards, various reasons explain the decline of provincial publishers: the movement towards centralisation, economic recession, the need to build up a cultural service to glorify the monarchy, a desire for closer control of the book trade. The growing importance of Paris is reflected both in the falling numbers of printing works and in the concentration of printing licences (*privilèges d'imprimer*). Figures revealed by surveys of 1701 and 1777 clearly underline the disappearance of printers: in Paris, the number of printing works drops from 51 to 36 (79 in 1666); in Lyon from 30 to 12, in Rouen from 28 to 10.[12] But, parallel to this movement and explaining it, the authorities' policy is to grant licences to a small number of powerful publishers in Paris. By the end of the seventeenth century the book trade was no longer a public domain, and had become a system dominated by licence-holders. Only the decree of August 1777 slightly reduced the Parisian monopoly, strengthened by the regulation of 1723 and the decree of 1744.[13] This attempt to conquer the national market[14] provoked different reactions on the part of the provinces. The grievance (*doléance*) was a reaction common to printers throughout the kingdom,[15] but some also sought more effective defences in pirate editions and simple book-dealing. The example of Lyon is a good one: at the end of the seventeenth century the Lyon book trade was active in the pirating of Paris publications,[16] in the eighteenth century it started to shift towards redistribution and exchange. The Lyonnais were not particularly interested in the opening for reprints which was created in 1777, preferring to seek a solution to their long-term decline in the distribution in southern France of books from Paris and northern Europe generally.[17]

The book, in as much as it is an object which is produced, exchanged, and sold, is naturally subject to conjunctural economic forces. The growth of publishing is a feature common to the whole of Europe, as the examples of Holland and Poland will show. The annual number of books worth one florin or more published in Dutch increases steadily over the seventeenth century, but there is a sudden leap in the following century: 150 on average after 1660, over 450 in the middle of the eighteenth century, over 800 in the 1770s.[18] The same development takes place later in Poland, but there is the same rapid expansion in the eighteenth century: after an overall tripling between 1700 and 1780, the average for the period 1781–1790 is only regained in 1840.[19]

Under the spell of economic analyses, French historians have tried to establish a cyclical analysis of national book production between the end of the sixteenth and the beginning of the nineteenth century. This is a difficult task, and the choice of a corpus is immediately problematical. Two possibilities exist: either the administrative archives, based on licence applications and copyright records of the *Librairie* (the official censorship body, Tr.), or bibliographies of those works which have survived to our day. In both cases, statistical certainty is impossible. The latter solution can only offer a distorted image of total production, since the survival of antiquarian books seems to vary, Latin folio volumes surviving better than smaller volumes in French. As for applications for a licence, they reflect the desire to publish rather than actual publications, they offer no indication of print runs and, above all, they totally ignore clandestine works and those which circulate with tacit approval.[20] Despite the incompleteness of the sources, which has particularly serious consequences for the study of one printing shop or a short period, the major features of long-term movements can nevertheless be identified.

For the seventeenth century, analysis of titles published in Paris which have survived show a long period of increasing production from 1601 to 1643, particularly marked from 1635 onwards; this is followed by a period of deep crisis, with a sharp fall in the number of titles, which is only gradually reversed in the 15 years from 1650. Production at the end of the century is higher than in the 1640s, but there is no dramatic increase, and the levelling-off of the curve points to persistent problems.[21] Within an overall framework of growth, the phases of production approximately match the conjuncture in manufacturing industry in northern France: rising production carried over from the previous century, but a conjunctural shift around the middle of the century, followed by a period of recession until the beginning of the eighteenth century.

After 1700, the conjuncture within book production seems at variance with the price conjuncture: growth until 1730, a static period to 1770, followed again by growth from 1770 to 1820.[22] This is certainly opposed to Labrousse's picture of a period of prosperity beginning in 1730 but terminated by the intercyclic recession of the 1770s; but the explanation does not necessarily lie in some necessary, long-term opposition between printing production and agricultural prices.[23] Be that as it may, a certain coming-together of the two curves occurs at the end of the *ancien régime*: the general economic crisis within France is reflected in publications.[24] The Vergennes *ordonnances* of June 1783, requiring that all consignments of books entering the country from abroad be examined solely by the Chambre Syndicale of the booksellers' and printers' guild in Paris, whatever their destination, may well have hit not only clandestine but also legal trade, with a knock-on effect on production. This example in fact shows that the book as a form of merchandise is influenced by multiple factors, including political ones; and the consequence is that the book trade may be relatively independent of economic trends in the modern period. Hence perhaps the difficulties which have confronted attempts to fit the major trends of the market into too rigid a series of ten-year cycles. Serial analysis is a legitimate ambition for the history of the book, but it must remain lucid and not lose sight of the fact that its materials only reflect a particular segment of the past, and cannot be analysed simply in terms of economic determinism.

Thematic analysis of titles enables the historian to trace the evolution of literary culture within the national framework. French research is in the forefront here, and it is already possible to draw up a profile of available reading from Henri IV to Louis XVI.[25] Religious books form the basis of this imaginary 'library' throughout the period, but the internal emphasis of this category changes in line with the progression of the Counter-Reformation. The 'mystical invasion' of the early seventeenth century is fed by a literature of prayer and spirituality, at first of Mediterranean origin and orthodox in nature, but later of French origin. After 1660 the religious book represents almost half of Paris production. These high levels at the end of the century reflect the penetration down through society of the legacy of the Council of Trent: through to the first thirty years of the eighteenth century, a wave of religious devotion provokes the massive publication of spiritual guides, and the consumers of this literature are no longer found solely among urban élites, in a country which has found its spiritual mission. The success of the small-format vernacular book introduces a new type of spiritual communication (*communication au sacré*), which is maintained in the devotional literature of the early eighteenth century, often Jansenist in inspiration. The 'crisis of European consciousness' seems to have little impact on popular Catholic literature (more than a third of French publications at the end of the 1720s); on the contrary, the long wave of the Counter-Reformation spreads over into the beginnings of the Enlightenment. Only later does the tide begin to ebb, steadily: a quarter of total production in mid-century, less than 10 per cent by 1785. This appreciable drop tallies with the chronology of dechristianisation suggested by the Provençal example. The decline of the penitent orders abandoned by their patrons, and of requests in wills for Mass to be said for the departed,[26] shed light on this falling-away of religious belief.

Moreover, analysis of book production suggests that this process may be read as one of laicisation. Perhaps we should see a kind of compensation in the expansion, in the eighteenth century, of the arts and sciences, a multiple category the unifying feature of which is a concern with the relationship between man and the natural or social world. In the previous century, the scientific revolution, with its ambitions of deciphering the world through mathematical language, had failed to have any impact on book production, which remains small and stagnant. This should make us realise that quantitative analysis cannot give us access to invention and rupture, almost always marginal, minority activities, and only tells us about innovations which have been accepted. It is in this light that the eighteenth-century curve should be seen: the growth of the arts and sciences is a sign of a society's encyclopaedic desire to classify and dominate a secularised world.

Parallel to this replacement of theology by the arts and sciences, there is, over the two centuries in question, a block of titles which remains: law, history, letters. A whole phase of the search for a national history can be reconstructed from the monarchist propaganda, Moorish philosophy and aristocratic nostalgia which thematic analysis reveals. It also confirms the triumph of the classical aesthetic, with which the novel only begins to compete thanks to the practice of tacit licensing. Such analysis does not aim to question the conclusions of historians of literature, philosophy or science, but can perhaps suggest a more refined analysis of questions of diffusion and cultural dominance. It lies at the heart of the relationship between intellectual creativity and the ways in which its fruits are popularised, and is well placed to assess resistance and date the abandonment or the penetration of cultural models.

From Colbert onwards, Paris is the centre of French publishing, and the cultural changes of which we have spoken are reflected essentially in Parisian publications. What kind of books were produced by the modest provincial publishing industry, operating through tacit local licensing (such was the case, at least, in Rouen, where the First President of the *Parlement* was an important protector of publishers) until the edicts of 1777, limiting publication rights to the lifetime of the author, gave it access to works coming into the public domain?[27]

This literature is essentially religious and local. Devotional manuals, books of hours, liturgical works for a particular diocese predominate: their share of Rouen production is consistently greater than in Paris, and, from 1778 to 1789, they represent nearly two-thirds of reprints with *permission simple*. The rest counts for little: treatises of provincial law, town almanacs and cheap novels. The provinces lag behind Paris, and their quantitative decline goes hand in hand with this concentration on archaic and local publications.

Should we turn to the other world of clandestine publishing in our search for innovative production? A distinction must be drawn between pirated and prohibited publications, even if both are subject to police seizure. Pirate editions are the fruit of provincial publishers' attempts to by-pass the monopoly of Paris, and are confined to books already licensed. The circulation of prohibited books, on the other hand, can modify the picture painted by surviving production or by the highly official registers of the *Librairie*. Here, work has only just begun and little is known for certain.[28] Clandestine publishing does appear to emerge early in the United Provinces, in the form of anti-French pamphlets, and we should note the activity of the Comtat (centred around Carpentras, in the present-day Vaucluse), although pirating is more common here than the publication of subversive literature.[29] Another element of certainty is the European status of the Swiss publishers and typographical societies. At the end of the seventeenth and up to the first thirty years of the eighteenth century, the clandestine market is dominated by religious publications of Protestant or Jansenist tendencies. Of prohibited books seized in Paris between 1678 and 1701, 62 per cent are religious works, doctrinal treatises and polemics, both Protestant and Jansenist, 18 per cent are literary works, 12 per cent pamphlets and political books, 6 per cent historical accounts.[30] Seizures in Languedoc show an identical profile, and the fairs of Beaucaire remain a centre for Protestant literature throughout the century.[31] Nationwide, a shift occurs in clandestine publications around 1750. The nature of the literature on offer changes: for example, the manuscript catalogues of the Neuchâtel Typographical Society offer its numerous French clients a category called 'philosophical books', in which both the struggles of reason and the pleasures of the imaginary are subsumed.[32] The public appears to react favourably, since records of seizures in Lorraine in the second half of the century show that erotic literature was confiscated along with Enlightenment literature.[33] Complex distribution networks took such books from the foreign printing houses to the big repositories outside Paris or Lyon and then on to the pedlar's pack, the travelling bookseller's cart or the back room of town bookshops. A whole society grows up around this illegal trade, made up of picturesque characters such as, among many hundreds of others, Réguillat, a Lyon bookseller, debarred in 1767; Jean-Baptiste Leclerc, captured in the same year at Nancy by d'Hémery and imprisoned in the Bastille for eight months; or Noël Gille, arrested in 1774 at his bookstall in Montargis. But, quite apart from anecdotal interest, this clandestine trade is of cultural importance, especially for the eighteenth century: it ceases to be realistic to equate what a whole society is reading with authorised publications. There is ample literary evidence for this, but quantitative methods have still not found a way of circumscribing clandestine production, whose scale relative to authorised production is not known. Research is indeed difficult, but it is possible at the two ends of the chain: the archives of foreign printers and booksellers, where they throw light on the quantity, theme and destination of prohibited books;[34] and the archives of the Bastille, where we can sometimes find traces of readers of clandestine literature who were caught.[35]

The analysis of titles must be complemented by a clearer understanding of the social composition of the reading public. Attentive to developments in the sociology of culture, the history of the book has attempted to define the scale of diffusion of the printed word, and to draw up a kind of intellectual typology based on different kinds of reading. It must be remembered that not every book bought is read, and that, conversely, with the development of public libraries, reading a book does not necessarily imply buying it. For 1764, a survey by Sartine gives a map of bookshops for the whole of France.[36] There is a concentration in towns with a *parlement*, a university, or college, and the mountainous and coastal regions are noticeably absent; southern France lags behind, with half the cathedral towns or towns with a presidial court having no bookshops. But the bookshop is not the only outlet for books, which are distributed to villages, small towns and manor-houses by travelling vendors. There is little justification for the frequent belief that literature sold by these pedlars is necessarily popular literature: in the case of Noël Gille, his clientele is made up of holders of civil office, lawyers, doctors, a large number of churchmen and a few nobles.[37]

But in large towns, the public library means an altogether different kind of exposure to books. In 1784, 17 towns, excluding Paris, have a public library, and the figure is probably not complete.[38] As for Paris, 4 of its 18 public libraries belong to city or university bodies (the City, the Bar, the University, the School of Medicine), 4 were founded by royal or aristocratic patronage, and 10 are religious libraries. In the provinces, this ecclesiastical predominance is even clearer: 20 of the 29 libraries are run by a chapter, college or monastery, more often than not Benedictine; 6 are connected to an academy or literary society; 2 to a faculty. Only one is purely municipal. Orléans has nearly 30,000 volumes on its library shelves, Toulouse 50,000, Nantes over 10,000. These figures make one think of the rococo ostentation of certain great collective libraries, public and private, such as the one built by F. J. Holzinger for the Bavarian monastery of Metten. The cultural role of the clergy remains a constant in Enlightenment Europe.

The books on offer in bookshops and libraries, as revealed by certain eighteenth-century provincial catalogues, correspond to developments in production, but there is a clear delay before the effect is felt. This time-lag is explained first by the relatively low showing of the arts and sciences category, which rarely exceeds a quarter of the total in Rouen or Lyon catalogues, but above all by the domination of religious books right up to the end of the century: nearly 30 per cent in the 1770 catalogue of the Lyonnais Bruyset,[39] 47.5 per cent in the 1782 catalogue of the Châlons-sur-Marne bookseller Briquet,[40] and 35 per cent in the bookshop of Jeanne and Anne Ferrand in Rouen in 1789.[41] And theology represents less than 15 per cent of public licences in the 1780s. The pressure of local demand, religious, educational and practical in emphasis, is clearly a factor explaining the presence of everyday books rather than Parisian novelties on the bookseller's shelves. As for the content of libraries, this is closely related to the manner of their constitution: a world separates the catalogues of the great religious institutions from the library of the Academy of Lyon, which reflects its founder Adamoli's predilection for natural history, history and poetry.[42]

By purchasing a book or placing it on the shelves of a private library, the man of culture clearly expresses intellectual preoccupations; but another set of motivations are at work in the possession of a book. To identify the resonances of a book as a cultural object, the iconographic role which the painter assigns to it is perhaps an avenue of research. Often it appears as a necessary adjunct, giving a historical underpinning to the lessons to be read in the great portrait, both religious (*Saint Jerome*, by Carpaccio, Uffizi Gallery, Florence) and humanist (*Erasmus*, by Quentin Metsys, National Gallery, Rome). In the portrait of a contemporary, on the other hand, a book is part of a system of signs of social superiority, whether the latter is justified by knowledge ('Jaco. Bar', *Portrait of Luca Pacioli, 1495*, Museo di Capodimonte, Naples), office (Raphael, *Portrait of Tommaso Inghirami*, the Pope's secretary and librarian, Isabella Stewart Gardner Museum, Boston) or wealth. The book in painting also allows us to recognise social categories, since the system of objects of which it is a part reflects certain socially marked practices. A symbol of power in all its forms, it can also symbolise the perversion of the Word, as in Berruguete's *Miracle of Saint Dominic* (Prado), where heretical books are seen burning while those of Saint Dominic remain unscathed, or the charms of worldly vanity. Placed next to the skull and the mirror, the book, together with the chess-set, the guitar, coins, is the object which distracts men from the thought of inescapable death (*Vanitas* by Herman van Steewijck, Lakental Museum, Leyden).

In eighteenth-century French painting, the book expresses a new set of meanings, either directly, as an object with a use, or indirectly, as part of a system of representation. Often it appears as the intimate companion, inducing Romantic reverie (*romanesque* has an echo of *roman* (novel), absent in the English, Tr.), as in P.-A. Baudoin's *La Lecture*, or alternatively strengthening the soul in adversity (Hubert Robert's painting of Camille Desmoulins in prison). The book is already part of the familiar world of childhood, a screen between innocence and the world, an object of initiation to Knowledge (Fragonard, *L'Etude*). In polite society it imposes its presence, providing a focus for *salon* life (De Troy, *La Lecture de Molière*, 1728) or a setting for amorous audacities (De Troy, *La Jarretière*, 1724). But in the eighteenth century, the book is above all a sign of power: the power of knowledge to classify and therefore dominate the world, the power of ideas to change the world, or at least reform the State (Aved, *M. le marquis de Mirabeau dans son cabinet*). Power can no longer be represented without the books which contain the laws of good government or the memory of the centuries (Mme Vigée-Lebrun's portrait of Calonne, 1784); the arms with which the world will be conquered are no longer those of Mars, but those of the *Encyclopédie*, the book of power *par excellence* (Quentin de La Tour, *Madame de Pompadour*).[43]

The contents of private libraries may, as a first step, be used as an indicator of cultural divisions within an elite. As far as the eighteenth century is concerned, a tempting hypothesis may be put forward on the basis of such analysis, establishing an opposition between the sword and the robe, conceived as two different types of individual destiny rather than two distinct societies.[44] The library of the man of law reflects a concern with the humanist values of *auctoritas* and ethics, whereas noblemen of the sword promote a more innovative set of values: modest readers at the end of the sixteenth century, they gradually become open to new literary fashions, Cartesianism, and science, acquiring small-format books as well as more traditional luxury editions. At the end of the seventeenth century, it is the aristocracy of the sword which becomes the bearer of the ideal of the urbane and well-read *honnête homme*, but this cultural model is vanquished by the circulation of books of moral science: the robe's attachment to this tradition, as shown in the libraries of members of the Paris *Parlement* in the eighteenth century,[45] represents too powerful a resistance. Drawing from each of these traditions, the Enlightenment develops a new ambition, stressing the book's privileged status as a source both of knowledge and of authority.

The book can also shed light on socio-cultural hierarchies within a town or province.[46] Three examples will suffice here: the small town, exemplified by Châlons-sur-Marne; Lyon, a provincial capital with 100,000 inhabitants; and Brittany, a whole province. In Châlons, at the end of the *ancien régime*, books appear in inventories of people's possessions made after their death in less than 10 per cent of cases, their frequency increasing as one climbs the social ladder.[47] In Lyon, 20 per cent of artisans and 75 per cent of civil officers and liberal professions possess a book or books, the latter category owning, on average, ten times as many volumes as the former. But in the case of the large city, other hypotheses may be ventured: can one identify cultural levels by reference to types of reading? The novel is an interesting case: it is found neither among the small collections of artisans, nor in the libraries of prominent academicians, but is popular with a whole class of urban readers belonging to the middle bourgeoisie. The relationship between literacy and reading is another question: nearly 70 per cent of Lyon silk-workers, both artisans and wage-earners, can sign their name, but only 20 per cent of them possess even a few books. The conclusion seems to be that the presence of books is a better criterion for defining a certain threshold of cultural attainment than literacy, which is often no more than a necessity for the worker's job.[48] Looking, finally, at Brittany overall, a hierarchy of reading can be established on the triple basis of number of volumes, manner of constitution, and contents of a library. Leaving aside the clergy, the parliamentary aristocracy comes at the top of the list: more than a hundred volumes, built up over the years and dominated by a traditional humanism but showing some interest in history. The commercial bourgeoisie occupies a roughly comparable position, followed by a class of minor aristocrats still strongly attached to religious values, and the middle bourgeoisie, which is turning to the literature of the century and whose purchasing habits are more homogeneous.[49] But, here as elsewhere, the reading public is a minority, and in the three examples mentioned, the excluded majority corresponds more or less to the lower classes. However, half the merchants in the Lyon study, and the majority of the Breton nobility, possess no books. No sociology of culture can ignore the fact that the world of reading is a limited one until late in the eighteenth century.

Does this mean that no popular reading-matter exists from which one might define the culture of the socially dominated? The exciting discovery of the *Bibliothèque bleue* and of the almanac has suggested that such an enterprise is possible, whether such popular reading took the form of reading aloud in the evening or of an elementary form of private 'reading', a deciphering of illustrations and individual words rather than a reading of the whole text.[50] Maggiolo's research on literacy rates, although insufficient in that marriage signatures are not a reliable criterion of educational attainment, nevertheless authorises such a hypothesis, since the literate areas in pre-Revolutionary France which it identifies, tally with the distribution of almanac printers. But doubts persist, to the extent that the little blue-covered books of the *Bibliothèque bleue* are not found where one would expect them: in Lyon, for instance, the few books owned by silk-workers are almost exclusively religious – lives of the saints or books of hours.[51] On the other hand the 'popular' almanac is well represented among the elites of small provincial towns, supplied in the absence of local bookshops by itinerant hawkers, who often sell their wares at the local château as well. We can therefore conclude that this literature, defined by its common form and themes, reaches a composite clientele, made up of those bourgeois who do not buy learned books, as well as the common people of town and country. Between those who are excluded by illiteracy and those whose exclusion is cultural, there is room for an intermediate reading public, vaguely defined in social terms but homogeneous in its expectations.

The sometimes unexpected thematic content of this corpus of texts is now well known: the almanac is dominated by astrological predictions concerning natural and legal matters, but to these are added, in the eighteenth century, accounts of contemporary events and advice on everyday matters. The world of the *Bibliothèque bleue* is one of miracle and mediaeval legend, a charmed world of fairy-tale, religious miracle and Carolingian epics extolling an idealised nobility. Here again, changes take place in the eighteenth century, the fantastic element often being replaced by a resolutely human wisdom. The problem here concerns the status of these themes: is 'popular' literature an adaptation of learned literature, or should we posit the occasional emergence of popular themes in the works of the educated? The question has so far remained unanswered, but it is crucial if we are to situate the book in relation to the culture of the majority. The analysis of group mentalities on the basis of reading practices is, in short, an ambitious project, and will only be fully valid when we have a clearer vision of certain areas of diffusion. It is relatively easy to find out what was read by priests or lawyers, but the readership of books such as *Pierre de Provence* or *Grisélédis* is much harder to establish. By a trick of history, the sociology of literature still benefits from the privileges of the past.

Certain elements nearer the surface of a book provide information about the uses to which books were put: title, illustrations, typography. Each of these is a valuable source, and work in these areas shows that the history of the book is not afraid to venture close to the frontiers of other disciplines. Various questions can be asked of titles. The title is generally a reliable indicator of content, particularly in the modern period where the long title is the rule: this can be the starting-point for the vast task of quantitative analysis of themes. But the primary function of the title is to sell the book – in this sense it represents a bridge between the two sides of the book, a cultural vehicle and a commodity – and it can therefore be the basis for a diachronic history of advertising stereotypes. The 'procurer' of the book, to use Furetière's term, can reveal the collective images shared by the potential reading public. Another stage is linguistic analysis. The whole corpus of titles for a given period represents a considerable stock of received vocabulary and the notions lying beneath. Absences can be equally revealing of ignorance, conceptual gaps, or the power of taboos in the case of subjects as liable to social censorship as love and sexuality.[52] Finally, the most ambitious project is a lexicographical one: titles are treated as a vast list of utterances, and words are analysed strictly according to their position in the lexical field in which they occur. Work on titles contained in licensing requests for the eighteenth century, concentrating particularly on the words *histoire* and *méthode*, has shown the contribution which semantics can make in analysing context and grammatical models.[53]

The illustration has concerned bibliophiles and historians for much longer than these innovative areas. The early seventeenth century marks the beginning of a new period in book illustration: copper-plate engraving replaces the wood-cut, which survives essentially in the almanac or the *Bibliothèque bleue*, and the copper-plate engraver, supplanting the anonymous artisan, becomes an artist in his own right, signing his works. Up until the 1650s the Counter-Reformation uses the image – print, book illustration or, in the case of its missions, painting on canvas – in its quest to impose its vision. But the end of the century sees a decline in the pictorial dimension of liturgical and spiritual books. The financial difficulties of the publishing world are one reason for this, but at a deeper level this is the consequence of the Counter-Reformation's attempts to tone down the excesses of sensibility which characterised some religious illustrations in the first half of the century. Commentaries on Scripture dispense with allegorical frontispieces, their discourse thus reproducing the Word which is the object of their commentary.[54] Eighteenth-century illustrations fulfil a documentary role in two ways. The predominance of the small-format book leads to aesthetic changes: the engraving becomes an exercise in technical skills, in which Fragonard (La Fontaine's *Fables*) and Cochin (Ovid's *Fasti*) excel. The travelogue, novel and fashion album are genres which particularly favour the vignette, both picturesque and suggestive.[55] The other development concerns what I have called books of 'power', where the technical illustration triumphs. The apogee of what has been called the 'autonomous iconography of the object' – whose many meanings go beyond purely educational aims – is seen in the *Encyclopédie*. The encyclopaedic illustration (*planche*) seeks to extol the creative power of humanity, still a friend to nature and tools. It expresses a proud faith in the universality of its **message: the** pictorial inventory of the world is not the self-centred accumulation of knowledge, but a means of transmitting it to future generations, to humanity.[56] The text, then, is far from being the only language of the book: the language of illustration can be read as a system of signs, but also as an element in ideological representations; and the language of typography and lay-out, which in the modern period moves toward a clearer organisation of the process of reading, is both the expression and a condition of the rise of a new logic.

The most recent discipline to attract the attention of social historians of the book is the 'physical bibliography' of Anglo-Saxon historians. Developed in England between the wars through the efforts of the Bibliographical Society and its journal *The Library*, this discipline set out to untangle the complexities of Elizabethan editions, and this original intention long left its mark on the discipline. Its originality is that it does not concern itself with the meaning of typographical signs, and is totally distinct from research on printing methods.[57] It attempts to study the book as a corpus of physical traces, and in that sense may be described as a kind of archaeology. It has pioneered three directions of research. Firstly, it compares different editions of a work and also different copies of the same edition, which is crucially important in the modern period, where printing constraints led to the practice of correcting a text during the print run. Physical bibliography is therefore the only reliable guide which the literary historian can use in editing classic texts.[58] Secondly, working in parallel with archive research, it may one day shed light on the circulation of pirate and clandestine editions: once the characteristic methods of composition, binding and ornamentation of a particular printing house or town have been established, these norms may be set against texts which have survived, in order to detect clandestine or pirate editions. It is a long, slow process, but work in progress is already yielding fruit,[59] and the computer can be of help here. Finally, physical bibliography sheds new light on the workings of the printing house. As long as the archives exist, close scholarly work will lead to progress on two fronts: it becomes possible to follow the printworker through the successive stages of his work, observing his skills and personal idiosyncrasies; at the same time, the economic strategy of a printer can be more clearly seen through diachronic study of the production of a given book or a synchronic picture of a printer's activities at a given moment in time.[60]

The book has always been an inexhaustible source of fascination to historians. When positivism held sway, reducing history to discourse, the text of the book, together with manuscript sources, seemed to guarantee the historian access to the facts. When the yoke of textualism was thrown off and history was opened up to social and economic analysis, the book remained a legitimate preoccupation, as a commodity produced and sold, revealing the divisions within a society. With the development of the 'human sciences', its position was reinforced since it was a rich source for the study of words and signs. From the moment of its appearance, the book has always generated discourse upon itself, and this eternal youth reflects the pleasure and astonishment which we feel when we hear the languages of the past speaking to us now from distant times and places.

NOTES

1 The classic pioneering study on the sixteenth century is L. Febvre and H.-J. Martin, *L'Apparition du livre*, Paris, 1957.

2 H.-J. Martin, *Livre, pouvoirs et société à Paris au XVIIe siècle (1598–1701)*, Geneva, 1969, pp. 303–26 and 591–3, plate 20, maps 1 and 2; I. H. Van Eeghen, *De Amsterdamse Boekhandel, 1680–1725*, Amsterdam, 1960, vol. 1 (correspondence of J.-B. Leclerc).

3 B. Gagnebin, 'La diffusion clandestine des œuvres de Voltaire par les soins des frères Cramer', *Actes du Ve Colloque de la Société française de littérature comparée*, Lyon, May 1962, Printing, commerce and literature, Paris, 1965, pp. 119–32.

4 The Paris bookseller, Antoine Boudet, notes in 1763: 'In Spain it is with books as it is with all other productions, supplies come from abroad. Latin and Spanish books, nearly all theology and law, come from Italy, Switzerland, Geneva and Lyon.' (Bibliothèque Nationale, Paris, MSS Fonds français 22130, fo. 44).

5 P. Chaunu, *La Civilisation de l'Europe des Lumières*, Paris, 1971, pp. 142–51, 279–80.

6 H.-J. Martin, *op. cit.*, plate 3.

7 F. Kapp, *Geschichte des deutschen Buchhandels*, Leipzig, 1886, vol. 1, Graph 1.

8 J. Bérenger, 'Latin et langues vernaculaires dans la Hongrie du XVIIe siècle', *Revue historique*, July–September 1969, pp. 5–28.

9 Bibliothèque Municipale, Lyon, 371371, vol. XV, catalogue of books found on the premises of Jean-Marie Bruyset, printer and bookseller in the rue Saint-Dominique, 1770.

10 D. Roche, 'Un savant et sa bibliothèque au XVIIIe siècle: les livres de Dortous de Mairan, secrétaire perpétuel de l'Académie des Sciences, membre de l'Académie de Béziers', *Dix-huitième siècle*, 1969, no. 1, pp. 47–88.

11 F. L. Ford, *Strasbourg in Transition, 1648–1789*, Cambridge, Mass., 1958, p. 197. Treitlinger's catalogue offers 514 books in German, 413 in French, 23 in English, 11 in Italian.

12 On this evolution, see H.-J. Martin, *op. cit.*, pp. 662–722; BN MSS Fonds français, Nouvelles Acquisitions, 399–400, 'The state of the book trade in France under the chancelier de Pontchartrain'; and, on this survey, C. Lanette-Claverie, 'La librairie française en 1700', *Revue française d'histoire du livre*, 1972, no. 3, pp. 3–43; BN MSS Fonds français 22832, 'The state of the printing industry in 1777'.

13 J. Brancolini and M.-T. Bouyssy, 'La vie provinciale du livre à la fin de l'Ancien Régime', *Livre et société dans la France du XVIIIe siècle'*, Paris–The Hague, 1970, vol. 2, pp. 1–37.

14 Comparison between the distribution of Jean Libet's debtors in 1636 and Frédéric Léonard's in 1706 (H.-J. Martin, *op. cit.*, maps 5 and 8) illustrates the widening influence of books from Paris.

15 Numerous examples given in L. Trenard, *Commerce et culture: le livre à Lyon au XVIIIe siècle*, Lyon, 1953, and 'Sociologie du livre en France (1750–1789)', *Actes du Ve Colloque de la Société française de littérature comparée*, pp. 145–78; J. Queniart, *L'Imprimerie et la librairie à Rouen au XVIIIe siècle* Paris, 1969, pp. 59–70.

16 G. Parguez, 'Essai sur l'origine d'éditions clandestines de la fin du XVIIe siècle, *Nouvelles études lyonnaises*, Geneva, 1969, pp. 93–130.

17 R. Chartier, 'Livre et espace: circuits commerciaux et géographie culturelle de la librairie lyonnaise au XVIIIe siècle', *Revue française d'histoire du livre*, 1971, nos. 1–2, pp. 77–108.

18 Y. Z. Dubosq, *Le Livre français et son commerce en Hollande de 1750 à 1780*, Amsterdam, 1925, pp. 41–2 (figures for Dutch vernacular production).

19 M. Czarnowska, *Ilosciowy rozwoj polskiego ruchu wydawniczego 1501–1965* (The Quantitative Development of Polish Book Production), Warsaw, 1967; T. Lepkowski, *Polska Narodziny Novoczenesgo Narodu 1764–1870* (*Poland: Birth of the Contemporary Nation*), Warsaw, 1967, p. 480; E. Rostworowski, 'La France de Louis XV et la Pologne (politique, langues, livres)', *Acta Poloniae historica*, vol. XXII, 1970, p. 84.

20 A useful critique of the sources for a quantitative history of the book may be found in J.-F. Gilmont, 'Livre, bibliographie et statistique. A propos d'une étude récente', *Revue d'histoire ecclésiastique*, vol. LXV, nos. 3–4, 1970, Louvain, pp. 797–816 (the author analyses the survival in 240 libraries of a sixteenth-century book, *Le Martyrologe de Jean Crespin*, which ran through 18 editions between 1554 and 1619); and R. Darnton, 'Reading, writing and publishing in eighteenth-century France: a case study in the sociology of literature', *Daedalus, Historical Studies Today*, Winter 1971, pp. 214–56 and especially pp. 219–21.

21 J.-J. Martin, *op. cit.*, plate 1.

22 R. Estivals, *La Statistique bibliographique de la France sous la monarchie au XVIIIe siècle*, Paris–The Hague, 1965, plates VI, VIb, XIII and XIIIb, pp. 409–12.

23 R. Estivals, 'La production des livres dans les dernières années de l'Ancien Régime', *Actes du XC^e congrès national des sociétés savantes*, Nice, 1965, Contemporary and Modern History Section, Paris, Bibliothèque Nationale, 1966, pp. 11–54, especially pp. 38–42.

24 This is Darnton's hypothesis, *art. cit.*, pp. 231–8: 'far from flourishing as a result of virtual freedom of the press, as is usually maintained, French publishing underwent a severe crisis on the eve of the Revolution' (p. 237).

25 On the thematic evolution of production, see H.-J. Martin, *op. cit.*; and F. Furet, 'La "Librairie" du royaume de France au XVIIIe siècle', *Livre et société dans la France du XVIIIe siècle*, Paris–The Hague, 1965, vol. 1, pp. 3–32.

26 M. Agulhon, *Pénitents et franc-maçons de l'ancienne Provence*, Paris, 1968, pp. 139–60; M. Vovelle, *Piété baroque et déchristianisation en Provence au XVIIIe siècle: les attitudes devant la mort d'après les clauses des testaments*, Paris, 1973.

27 On the backwardness of the provinces in publishing, see J. Queniart, *op. cit.*, pp. 107–24, 125–35; and J. Brancolini and M.-T. Bouyssy, *art. cit.*

28 The classic work is still J.-P. Belin, *Le Commerce des livres prohibés à Paris de 1750 à 1789*, Paris, 1913.

29 R. Moulinas, 'L'Imprimerie, la librairie et la presse à Avignon au XVIIIe siècle', typescript, 1971, and 'Une famille d'imprimeurs–libraires avignonnais au XVIIIe siècle: les Delorme', *Revue française d'histoire du livre*, 1972, no. 3, pp. 46–78.

30 Figures from A. Sauvy, *Livres saisis à Paris entre 1678 et 1701*, Archives Internationales d'Histoire des Idées, The Hague, 1972, a remarkable critical edition of MS 21743, Fonds français, Bibliothèque Nationale, Paris.

31 M. Ventre, *L'Imprimerie et la librairie en Languedoc au dernier siècle de l'Ancien Régime, 1700–1789*, Paris–The Hague, 1958, pp. 268–78.

32 R. Darnton, *art. cit.*, pp. 238–9. The same manuscript catalogue contains, for instance: *Vénus dans le cloître ou la religieuse en chemise*; *Système de la nature*, 2 vols.; *La Fille de joie*, illustrated; *Contrat social* by J.-J. Rousseau.

33 A. Ronsin, 'La Lorraine et le commerce international du livre au XVIIIe siècle', 'La Lorraine dans l'Europe des Lumières', *Actes* of the conference organised by the

Faculty of Letters and Human Sciences of the University of Nancy, 24–27 October 1967, in *Annales de l'Est*, no. 34, 1968, pp. 138–75, especially pp. 161–6.

34 Mention should be made of R. Darnton's current research on the archives of the Typographical Society of Neuchâtel. These exceptional archives are described by J. Rychner, 'Les Archives de la Société typographique de Neuchâtel', *Le Musée neuchâtelois*, 1969, no. 3.

35 J.-P. Belin (*op. cit.*, pp. 100–4) studies the examples of Pasdeloup and widow Stockdorff of Strasbourg.

36 F. de Dainville, 'D'aujourd'hui à hier. La géographie du livre en France de 1764 à 1945', *Le Courrier graphique*, January 1951, pp. 43–52, and March 1951, pp. 33–6. This article includes a map of the distribution of booksellers based on Sartine's survey of 1764 (BN MSS Fonds français 22184, 22185).

37 A. Sauvy, 'Noël Gille dit la Pistole "marchand forain libraire roulant par la France"', *Bulletin des bibliothèques de France*, May 1967, pp. 177–90, especially pp. 184–5. A painting of this early seventeenth-century bookseller belonging to the Louvre is exhibited at the Musée des Arts et Traditions Populaires (no. 716 in the catalogue, Bibliothèque Nationale, 1972).

38 *La France littéraire*, 1784, Slatkine Reprints, pp. 451–79.

39 R. Chartier, *art. cit.*, p. 101.

40 D. Roche, 'La diffusion des Lumières. Un exemple: l'Académie de Châlons-sur-Marne', *Annales*, 1964, pp. 887–922, especially pp. 919–22 and table 3.

41 J. Queniart, *op. cit*, pp. 138–46 and fig. 15.

42 R. Chartier, 'L'Académie de Lyon au XVIIIe siècle. Etude de sociologie culturelle', *Nouvelles études lyonnaises*, Geneva, 1969, pp. 132–250, especially pp. 228–9.

43 The catalogue of the great London exhibition of 1968, *France in the Eighteenth Century*, includes all the paintings mentioned in this paragraph, except for the portrait of Mme de Pompadour by de La Tour (nos. 312, 335, 298, 108, 106, 87, 168, 26).

44 H.-J. Martin (*op. cit.*) analyses 600 private libraries, equally spread over three periods: 1601–41, pp. 472–551; 1642–70, pp. 651–61; 1671–1700, pp. 922–58.

45 F. Bluche, *Les Magistrats du Parlement de Paris au XVIIIe siècle*, Paris, 1960, pp. 289–96.

46 On the possession of books before the invention of printing, see H. Bresc, *Livre et société en Sicile (1299–1499)*, Centro di studi filologici e linguistic siciliani, Supplementi al Bollettino, 3, Palermo, 1971; on the provincial reception of Renaissance production, see A. Labarre, *Le Livre dans la vie amiénoise du XVIe siècle, L'enseignement des inventaires après décès 1503–1576*, publications of the Faculty of Letters and Human Sciences at the Sorbonne in the series 'Recherches', vol. LXVI, Paris–Louvain, 1971.

47 D. Roche, *art. cit.*, p. 919 and fig. 8.

48 On all these points, see M. Garden, *Lyon et les Lyonnais au XVIIIe siècle*, Paris, 1970, pp. 457–68, and figs. LXX, LXXI, LXXII.

49 J. Meyer, *La Noblesse bretonne au XVIIIe siècle*, Paris, SEVPEN, 1966, pp. 1156–77.

50 R. Mandrou, *De la culture populaire aux XVIIe et XVIIIe siècles: la Bibliothèque bleue de Troyes*, Paris, 1964; G. Bollème, 'Littérature populaire et littérature de colportage au XVIIIe siècle,' *Livre et société dans la France du XVIIIe siècle*, vol. 1, pp. 61–89; G. Bollème, *Les Almanachs populaires aux XVIIe et XVIIIe siècles: essai d'histoire sociale*, Paris–The Hague, 1969.

51 M. Garden, *op. cit.*, p. 460.

52 J.-L. Flandrin, 'Sentiments et civilisation. Sondage au niveau des titres d'ouvrages', *Annales*, 1965, pp. 939–62.

53 *Livre et société dans la France du XVIIIe siècle*, vol. 1, part 2: 'Pour une sémantique historique', especially F. Furet, 'L'Ensemble *histoire*', pp. 101–20, and A. Fontana, 'L'Ensemble *méthode*', pp. 151–228.

54 On the whole process, see H.-J. Martin, *op. cit.*, pp. 162–9, 381–6, 702–4.

55 G. Janneau, *L'Epoque de Louis XV*, Le Lys d'Or, PUF, 1964.

56 *L'Univers de l'Encyclopédie*, Paris, Les libraires associés, 1964, especially R. Barthes, 'Image, raison, déraison', pp. 11–16, and R. Mauzi, 'Une éphémère souveraineté', pp. 19–22.

57 P. Gaskell, *A New Introduction to Bibliography*, Oxford, 1972.

58 R. Laufer, 'La bibliographie matérielle dans ses rapports avec la critique textuelle, l'histoire littéraire et la formalisation', *Revue d'histoire littéraire de la France*, Méthodologies, September–December 1970, pp. 776–83; 'Etude de bibliographie matérielle. Le diable boiteux de 1707', introduction to Alain-René Lesage, *Le Diable boiteux*, Paris–The Hague, 1970, pp. 9–79; and *Introduction à la textologie, vérification, établissement, édition des textes*, Paris, 1972.

59 R. A. Sayce, 'Compositional practices and the localisation of printed books, 1530–1800', *The Library*, 5th series, 1966, vol. XXI, no. 2, pp. 1–45; G. Parguez, *art. cit.*, pp. 93–100; see also the two issues of the *Australian Journal of French Studies* devoted to physical bibliography, vol. 3, no. 3, September–December 1966; and vol. 7, no. 3, September–December 1970.

60 D. F. McKenzie, *The Cambridge University Press, 1696–1712: A Bibliographical Study*, Cambridge University Press, 1966; and J. Rychner's current work at Neuchâtel.

Index